D0120117

SBL

COMMAND

AL MURRAY
COMMAND

How the Allies Learned to Win the Second World War

HEADLINE

First published in 2022 by
HEADLINE PUBLISHING GROUP

1

Please see page viii for picture credits

Cataloguing in Publication Data is available from the British Library

Hardback ISBN: 978 1 4722 8459 4
Trade paperback ISBN: 978 1 4722 8460 0

Typeset in Baskerville MT Pro 13.34/16.24pt by Jouve (UK), Milton Keynes

Printed and bound in Great Britain by Clays Ltd, Elcograf S.p.A.

Headline's policy is to use papers that are natural, renewable and recyclable
products and made from wood grown in well-managed forests and other
controlled sources. The logging and manufacturing processes are expected to
conform to the environmental regulations of the country of origin.

HEADLINE PUBLISHING GROUP
An Hachette UK Company
Carmelite House
50 Victoria Embankment
London
EC4Y 0DZ

www.headline.co.uk
www.hachette.co.uk

To the Independent Company
for keeping us company

Contents

Picture Credits

First image plate section

Page 1: Montgomery in car, Bettmann/Getty Images
Montgomery and Churchill, Fremantle/Alamy

Page 2: German *Fallshirmjäger*, ullstein bild Dtl. via Getty Images

Page 3: Freyberg © Imperial War Museum London
2-pounder anti-tank gun, Northcliffe Collection/ANL/
Shutterstock

Page 4: Tuker © National Portrait Gallery London

Page 5: Gurkahs © Imperial War Museum London
Chindits, Keystone/Getty Images

Page 6: Wingate, Pictorial Press Ltd./Alamy

Page 7: Slim, AP/Shutterstock

Page 8: Mortars, The Art Archive/Shutterstock
Bradley with Anderson, Photo 12/Alamy

Second image plate section

Page 1: Bradley, Eisenhower and Patton, PJF Military Collection/Alamy

Page 2: Patton, Popperfoto/Getty Images

Page 3: Combat fatigue, Keystone-France/Getty Images
Patton, US National Archives

Page 4: Pearson, Courtesy of the Airborne Assault Museum Duxford

Page 5: Gale © Imperial War Museum London
Gale, briefing © Imperial War Museum London

Page 6: White, diary sketch, from *With the Jocks* by Peter White, first
published in 2001. Courtesy of The History Press
52nd Lowland Division © Imperial War Museum London
Gliders © Imperial War Museum London

Page 7: White, from *With the Jocks* by Peter White, first published in
2001. Courtesy of The History Press
Sherman DD-tank © Imperial War Museum London

Page 8: Hobart © Imperial War Museum London
79th Armoured Division's insignia © Imperial War Museum
London

Introduction

'Tunis fallen?!! Ups a daisy!'
Had we ordinary layabouts defeated the formidable German army?
Spike Milligan, *Monty: His Part in My Victory*

If you want the truth, go to a comedian. Spike Milligan's
ribald memoirs of his time as a conscripted man in the
Royal Artillery make an interesting point. As part of the
First Army – which had fought a rushed action to try to stop
the Germans establishing themselves in Tunisia, and then
tried to squeeze the German armies between itself and
Eighth Army, advancing from the east – Milligan's battery
had been in action almost constantly, and when not fighting, it had been on the move. His memoirs fondly recreate
the easy humour in the battery and clearly illustrate the
men's attitudes to the war. It's quite clear that patriotism is
low down their list for fighting. From starting out without
any equipment, shouting 'Bang!' as they drilled at their
guns, Milligan and his fellow 'layabouts' went on to take
part in the climactic battles which ended the war in North
Africa, then on into Italy – for all Milligan's joking, blow-
ing raspberries and flicking Vs at the enemy, he knew that
he and his friends were part of a war-winning machine.
How had this happened? Featuring large in Milligan's
experience was Major Chater-Jack, whose care and con-
cern for his men, conscripts fighting in a war they had not

sought (certainly not Milligan, who had done everything he could to avoid turning up to his depot), was a huge factor in transforming these civilians into soldiers. To Bombardier Milligan, command mattered.

The Second World War is an endlessly peelable onion, a subject that seems to offer no boundaries, that throws up new mysteries and revelations as well as mythologies even as it glides slowly further into the past. Even knowing where or when to start is daunting. Picking a subject, finding its edges, satisfying oneself with definitions and parameters is nigh on impossible. But there is a simple question that hangs over the war: how did the Allies win? And, more importantly, given the answer that some feel is self-evident: by economic and industrial might – take on three imperiums each with a larger economy than yours and you are surely done for – how did they learn to apply those obvious advantages against foes who were far more interested in waging war, at least at the outset, than they were? With so much stuff at their disposal, was the Allies' victory not assured, regardless of how their men were led?

If it is anything at a glance, the Second World War is a war of hardware, of tanks, planes, ships and factories. A war of materiel, of resources. And a war of technology. The dazzling speed of development before and during the war of weapons technology – from the Gloster Gladiators *Faith*, *Hope* and *Charity* that were used to defend Malta in 1940 to the V-2 ballistic missiles raining down on London only four years later, as well as the unprecedented and unimagined power of the atomic bomb – goes a long way to make the case that this was a war of machines and of the economies that produced those machines. And given the effort that the Western Allies put into destroying and disrupting German industry, it's clear that this was how they saw the war: they would use their own technology and industry to deny the Germans the use of theirs. The result was that 45 per cent of German industry was given over to producing aircraft, a clear indication of the extent to which the strategic bombing campaign was effective in defeating Nazi Germany. Germany's industrial opportunities were dictated by Allied bombing and blockades. Again this is an argument about stuff, tech, materiel.

Stalin made this point clearly in his speech at the Celebration Meeting of the Moscow Soviet of Working People's Deputies and Moscow Party and Public Organizations on 6 November 1941, even when the outcome of the war, from a Soviet perspective, might have appeared to be in the balance: 'This is a war of engines. It is impossible to have too many of them, and the side having the largest number of engines is bound to win.' With American mass production – perfected in the inter-war years – the Allies possessed all the motors they needed. American industry produced 62.5 per cent of the trucks used by the Allies, some 2,382,311, dwarfing German production of 345,914 trucks (the USSR produced only 257,000). The supply of American trucks to the Soviet Union freed up tank production: the Soviets produced 105,251 tanks, more than twice the amount produced by the Germans, and equal to British and American tank production combined. In every department, the British, Americans and Soviets outproduced the Germans, Japanese and Italians; even with the head start the Germans had before the war, their arms production was soon outstripped by that of their enemies. The rifle, perhaps the simplest piece of technology on the battlefield, was produced in vast amounts, the Allies making more than 20 million.

While the rifle remained essentially unchanged from the First World War – certainly the standard bolt-action rifles used by the infantry on every battlefield during the war remained their basic easy-to-operate selves – the war was also a time of incredibly rapid technological development. These leaps are perhaps most striking in aviation, from biplanes to ballistic missiles in the space of six years. In medicine too innovations were made and then rolled out industrially, and again the Allied side possessed huge advantages. And just as well – having such material advantages was the only way that a conflict could be fought on this scale and in so many theatres, or even begin to be contemplated. But these vast production numbers tell us two things. First, if you consider that every one of those 2,382,311 trucks has a story to tell, then the Second World War is essentially a limitless, bottomless pit of experience and history. The design of the trucks, their manufacture, the trucks that broke down, the trucks that were destroyed, the four corners of the earth that the trucks were shipped to, the trucks ordered at the end of the war that never were shipped anywhere . . . all of this is the story of victory. And second, while this may be a war of hardware, a war of stuff, the software of the Second World War was the people who designed, tested, made, drove, maintained and repaired these machines, planes, ships, rifles. People who had to be brought to the fight, taught and trained how to fight, and led to victory.

This was an elusive prospect. From the start of the war, at least on land, the Allies, the British in particular, seemed hell-bent on losing. With their dominion and imperial co-combatants (known in this book as DUKE, Dominions,

United Kingdom and Empire*), the British got off to a woeful start, suffering defeats in Norway and France in 1940, Greece and Crete in 1941, and, after a decent start in 1940, an almost farcical to and fro in the North African desert in 1941–2, as well as calamitous campaigns against the Japanese in Burma and Singapore. The gap between the army's ambition and its ability seemed unbridgeable. Where things went well, it tended to be against second-class opponents. Only at the Second Battle of El Alamein, carefully orchestrated to allow the Allies to bring all of their advantages to bear, did their strategic, industrial and, finally, tactical improvements deliver a decisive victory. The man who was in command in 1942, Bernard Law Montgomery, was only in the job by the skin of his teeth – he was appointed by Chief of the Imperial General Staff Alan Brooke to replace Lieutenant-General William Gott, who had been killed shortly after being given command of Eighth Army. But even then, as outlined in the first chapter, Montgomery might never have taken command in North Africa, because going into the war there was a fundamental unseriousness at the heart of how the army was facing its new encounter with Germany.

For the Americans, the war offered different challenges. The political business of mobilizing a population who right up until the war began had shown little appetite for European entanglement was a knotty problem, not just for the Roosevelt administration, itself split on the

---

* An acronym coined with the historian James Holland on the podcast *We Have Ways of Making You Talk*. It has an acronym's benefit of tidiness and being an actual pronounceable word, unlike so many military abbreviations. And, for a change, it puts the dominions first.

question, but also for the US Army. Just as the policy of appeasement in Britain had been driven by experience of the First World War, so America's involvement in that war had soured the public's appetite for conflict. During the 1930s, America had been neither sleeping nor a giant; the vicissitudes of the Great Depression were plenty for its political classes to be dealing with. And the tiny army the US had maintained between the wars lacked the deep body of experience that the British boasted, because its involvement in the First World War had been shorter than Britain's. The staggering production numbers that American industry delivered during the Second World War were not something that anyone in the US anticipated in 1939, when war broke out in Europe; although American politics had fancied itself involved in China in its struggle against Imperial Japan, there was no serious industrial or military effort to help. Some of the men at the heart of America's military dreamed of fleets of tanks rolling up imaginary enemy flanks, but the army's day-to-day endeavours were focused closer to home, with the Civilian Conservation Corps working outdoors on federal infrastructure. How it jump-started itself in the face of political opposition, and the styles of leadership that emerged, is a fascinating and complex story.

*

For this book I have had to, for reasons of practicality, confine myself to a few necessarily incomplete case studies. I will be writing about soldiers, not because airmen and sailors are somehow less interesting but because it was the Allies' trials and tribulations on land, their struggles to grasp the difficulties of land warfare, to make sure the boots they had on the ground could be used effectively against their enemies, that most illustrate the problems of winning a war. And because this story is so vast and complex, I have had to limit my scope and tell just a fraction of the tale of how the British and Americans claimed victory. (As a Brit, I feel that I can write about the former with more ease than the latter, divided as we are by a common language and all the rest of the baggage that comes with the contrasting class systems of the UK and the US. Even at this distance, the thought of the collision of working-class West Point generals with upper-class British officers is like nails on a blackboard. While the Allies chimed along fairly well during the last four years of the war, it is a miracle, in my view, that there aren't more accounts of fallings-out and high-stakes bitchiness. The common cause perhaps put more people on their best behaviour than not.)

So it is through command that I want to look at how the Allies solved the puzzle of victory, how they got their software, their soldiers, to use the hardware they had in such abundant amounts and bring the war to a successful conclusion. For without command, mass counts for nothing; quantity does not guarantee quality. Fighting in the desert in 1940, the DUKE forces were able to overwhelm a numerically superior Italian Army – although British equipment was better than the Italians', it was leadership, the ability of the army to lead and its men to be led, that counted.

To illustrate this point, I have taken on some of the marquee names of popular military history, such as, in no particular order, Montgomery, Patton – who tend to be paired as rivals when really they do not offer a like-for-like comparison, in my view, their responsibilities and experience being quite different – Bradley, Wingate and Slim. These figures each offer contrasting styles and achievements, and episodes in their careers can tell us about the organizations that produced these individuals and their wildly contrasting outlooks on dealing with the same tasks, and how serious those organizations were about achieving victory. Several of these characters were single-minded in the pursuit of their methods, and unsympathetic to anyone else's ideas, making great play of this visionary style. Others, like Bradley and Slim, sought to convey a sense of consensus in command – these contrasting approaches, which these men were keen to advertise, have survived decades of retelling and scrutiny. Yet Montgomery and Patton were perhaps more consensual than they'd have liked us to believe, and Bradley and Slim as autocratic as any of their contemporaries. Controversy still whirs around Wingate, yet I believe it is possible to place him in a deeper continuity of British military history.

I have also chosen to write about some lesser-known leaders. Bernard Freyberg, a legend of New Zealand martial culture, sits at the heart of one of the most humiliating defeats of the Second World War, for the DUKE forces at Crete in May of 1941. His place in the Allied losing streak – his responsibility for yet another evacuation – seems almost unjust: he had the intelligence he needed to defeat the Germans, yet victory eluded him. Freyberg's fate on Crete can help us to delineate the problems that the DUKE armies and commanders faced in 1941, problems that endured for another year. These problems were dissected by Francis Tuker, who commanded the 4th Indian Infantry Division for three years, leading it to victory in Tunisia and then on to Monte Cassino. Tuker regarded himself a military thinker, a historian, a philosopher of the pattern of warfare. Although he didn't gain the prominence of some of his contemporaries, his under-the-hood view of what was going wrong for the British Army in North Africa is fascinating and infuriating in equal measure. His analysis of what was happening before things started to go right in the second half of 1942 tells us what had gone wrong and why, though perhaps not what the solutions were. Ideas are one thing, execution another.

Major General 'Windy' Gale and the brigade and battalion commanders beneath him suggest a kind of state-of-the-art British command in 1944, the year of the really big Allied victories on land. They were in the vanguard of Operation OVERLORD, the culmination of five years of fighting the Germans and trying to learn how best to win. OVERLORD was a campaign in which Allied material preponderance was significant, but men still had to fight, to be led, many of them inexperienced and fresh to battle – in 1944, an eighteen-year-old infantryman would have been only thirteen when the war began. These were men who had to be taught afresh how to fight, and the experiences of the men who led them, and their use of initiative, were as crucial to victory as 100,000 tanks. And at the very sharp end were men like Second Lieutenant Peter White, whose story ends this book, a pacifist and artist who felt he should fight because otherwise someone else would have to. White's experiences are a long way from the generals reading reports and organizing operations; he lived from hill to hill, canal to canal, ditch to ditch, doing the

fighting his commanders bade him to, with his men paying the direct price of his decisions. His experience of the
final victory is where the story ends, the story of how
Spike's 'ordinary layabouts' defeated the formidable German Army and what that victory had cost, beyond the
millions of trucks and rifles.

1

Bernard Montgomery

Before 'Monty'

Two weeks of calamity and extraordinarily bad luck and it was all over. Plans shattered, expectations overturned, the global status quo upended. What had taken four years of bitter fighting to prevent in the previous war, the fall of France, had happened in little more than a fortnight – this time the Germans had finished what they had started. The British Expeditionary Force was turfed out of France, harried, routed, out-thought, outfought, outclassed, making a skin-of-its-teeth escape without its equipment. Even with Westminster in a state of headless-chicken turmoil, the political business of spinning the humiliation and disarray into a 'miracle' began. But while Dunkirk may have been a miracle, it did not guarantee any kind of resurrection. With it came the bitter understanding that the Germans and the war would need to be taken far more seriously than they had been until now. The time for complacency was over.

The defeat in France was profound, it was existential, and British policy – warmly endorsed by the self-consciously strategy-minded First Sea Lord Winston Churchill – was on its head. British plans had relied on the French Army doing the bulk of the fighting and had simply not accounted for the possibility of French collapse – and why should it? It was the French who had defeated Prussian dash in 1914 and then held resolute for four years, overcoming the challenges of maintaining such a bloody struggle. This was the French Army of Verdun, was it not?

Nor had British strategy factored in the BEF doing its damnedest to plunge headlong into the trap of the German feint into the Low Countries. The BEF, rather than holding the Germans on the French left flank, solid on the shoulder of the Maginot Line, had had to choose between fight and flight as encirclement and destruction loomed. The grand plan had been to fight a static war along the French border that would allow the Royal Navy to blockade Germany into submission, while the RAF, Britain's offensive arm, (eventually) strategically bombed it into surrender. This was entirely rational, based on the balance of probabilities and what the Allies thought they knew about their opponent and about their own state of readiness. And something similar had worked last time round. As a result, the BEF had been reassuringly small – a reflection of the amount of land fighting the British hoped to do. But Sod's Law ruled. All these safe bets were now off. The French Army had let the Germans through at Sedan for the third time in 70 years, and because the German armoured fist had an unprecedented and unanticipated momentum of its own, the die was cast. The Germans, by applying new technology to traditional ideas of concentration of force, had labelled it Blitzkrieg and rewritten the result of the First World War. A fortnight was all it had taken to turn the world upside down.

Retreating from the positions it had advanced into in Belgium, some of them historic – the 1st Buckinghamshire Battalion, for instance, had deployed at Waterloo, where their regimental antecedents the 52nd Regiment of Foot had pressed their attack late on that fateful day in

1815 – the BEF did what it could to stay cohesive, to counter-attack where it could and to stop the German Panzers from rolling them up. Fighting an action it hadn't planned for, it did remarkably well, given its campaign had failed completely. The BEF did the thing armies aren't meant to do: retreat while engaged with the enemy. Blocking actions were fought even as the men streamed back towards the French coast, tangled in queues of countless refugees, their morale shredded by apparent German aerial dominance.

When the BEF did stand and fight, it had the effect of surprising the Germans, if nothing else. Improvised chaotic actions showed that they were quite capable of giving the Germans pause: famously the tank battle at Arras, where the British Matildas proved they were the match of any Panzer, or, less well remembered, at Cassel and Hazebrouck, where Territorial battalions held up the Germans in desperate last stands. But it is hard to see these as much more than crumbs of comfort in a calamity of this scale. The danger of being surrounded and captured wholesale was very, very real and, rather than any last-minute tactical rabbits being pulled out of hats, it was only avoided by Hitler issuing his notorious 'Halt Order' on 24 May. Hitler, gifting the British their best luck of the campaign – the order was even transmitted in plain language – paused his army's seemingly unstoppable rampage mainly to show his generals who was in charge. Barely believing its good fortune, the BEF reorganized itself even as the pocket it was trapped in shrank, the threat worsening rapidly once the Germans resumed their offensive and Britain's allies faded away, with Belgium throwing in the towel as the British prepared to depart. Operation DYNAMO followed.

Lord Gort made his only sound decision since taking command of the BEF in France and decided, in less gentlemanly terms than he might have put it, to cut and run. Once the BEF had fled France, there were mutterings in London that finally the empire could now get on with fighting the war unencumbered by the flaky French, conveniently overlooking just how complacent and unserious the British effort had been.

Plainly there was an abundance of lessons to be learned, tactical lessons in particular – British strategy, how to proceed with the war, what the war now even was, would have to be reinvented from scratch. But did the army have the people who could do that? Were there men who had the strength of character and intellect to emerge from disaster and work out how to unpick the army's problems and defeat the German Army, which, even as the first boats made it back to the English coast, seemed unbeatable?

*

Complacent and unserious were words that could not be used to describe Bernard Law Montgomery, the commanding officer of the 3rd Division. He was not yet the 'Monty' of legend, the crafted persona, with his tweaked uniform and headgear and photo opportunities, though certainly his air of what could be called priggishness, which would later grate on the great and good of the US Army, was firmly in place. But Montgomery was, at this pre-fame point in his career, someone who prided himself on his professionalism; he was confident of his talent and methods, and not altogether modest about that. He liked to train his men hard, keep them on their toes. Major generals got to set the tone and training for their commands:

you could – and Montgomery certainly did – run your division your way. This sprang from the need for the British Army to be flexible in its imperial role; officers never knew where they might end up, what tasks they might have to undertake anywhere in the empire.

Montgomery's career between the wars, after serving time on the Western Front as a subaltern and then, after he had been badly wounded, as a staff officer, exemplified this imperial destiny perfectly. Montgomery had seen what these days we might call a counter-insurgency in Ireland – where his cousin Hugh was killed by the IRA on Bloody Sunday in 1920 – mixed with teaching, training, writing the new infantry manual in 1929, battalion command and more training in India at Quetta, brigade garrison command in Portsmouth and the euphemistically termed imperial policing in Palestine (a war he was sorry to leave on his return to Europe because he had 'enjoyed' it). Plainly, one central doctrine to meet the demand of all these different jobs would not and could not have worked; command was devolved, and even with the existence of an infantry manual, the circumstances would usually dictate the action taken rather than the other way round. Often, that meant the process of figuring out what to do involved blunder and calamity. But in imperial postings where things were stable and ticking along sans emergency, Montgomery and men like him were able to find time to think about the future of soldering and the possibilities of conflict ahead.

Also central to the way the peacetime army worked was the regimental system, which retained vestigial elements from the days when regiments were personally raised by their colonels; regiments were a tangle of tradition and habit and idiosyncrasy, based on counties, cities, class and other ripe quirks of British society. The regimental system had last been reformed in the 1870s as part of the Cardwell Reforms, formalizing localized regimental structures and depots (these reforms had also professionalized the officer classes and abolished the sales of commissions, flogging and branding). It had been stretched out of recognition during the First World War by the army's gigantic expansion; in peacetime the local ties of county were re-established, and Montgomery was proud of having made his start with the Royal Warwickshire Regiment. With this devolved command and devolved identity, the army offered its officers the chance to follow, within limits, their own course.

This meant that the British Army was flexible in principle and sometimes even in practice, though this flexibility could manifest itself as a lack of focus or simple institutional inertia. A lazy officer, a poor leader, someone not much interested in soldiering, not that bright or with conservative ideas about the way war could be fought, could easily hold things up. This perhaps explains the army's historical track record of getting off to a bad start in war, making it up as it went; as long as defeat could be held off, in the end someone would work out how to deliver victory in whichever particular war was being fought. That method, of course, might or might not apply to any subsequent encounter. The First World War had fallen into this pattern, just as had the Boer Wars. As the storm clouds gathered in the 1930s, men like Montgomery did harbour a sense that the army shouldn't fall into this trap again, but while the Staff Colleges in Camberley and Quetta were places where ideas were traded, back in the regimental officers' mess talking shop was generally thought non-U.

Between the wars, the army was lower in the pecking order than the Royal Navy, and jockeying for position with the new, exciting, futuristic RAF. The RAF offered the chance to perform imperial duties at arm's length and on the cheap. With funding based on the Ten Year Rule, the notion that there wouldn't be a European war to fight for a decade (Winston Churchill's idea!), the quality of training relied on the commander's grip and the serious-ness with which he applied himself to the task. Later in his career, Montgomery – once he had become 'Monty' – fought tooth and nail against this same flexibility, trying to enforce his will and his way of doing things on whoever came under his spotlight, with varying degrees of success. But we aren't here to talk about 'Monty' the self-styled man of destiny, the publicity-conscious general with the twin badges on his beret and the reputation for preening showmanship; we're here to talk about Montgomery.

*

Born on 17 November 1887, Bernard Law Montgomery was, after a fashion, an Irishman (by way of Tasmania), the son of a bishop and a formidable mother, but, to para-phrase the contemporary Royal Navy advert, he was made in the army. Or, more accurately, in the First World War. He'd joined the army after school, where he'd not done very well, and then – though the records are lost, and he may have been embellishing to burnish his legend as a self-made genius – did badly at Sandhurst. But it was his experience of the Great War, rather than his eagerness to be a soldier, that was the making of Montgomery. Wounded badly in 1915, shot through the chest and left for dead, he managed, despite the injuries to his lung, to stay in the army and became a staff officer, working under the bonnet of the British Army in Flanders, seeing how the whole thing was pieced together and gaining an intimate under- standing of the developing system of combined operations that took the British to victory in 1918. This took him away from the battlefield and brought him into contact with the political and the strategic: there is a photograph of the young Lieutenant-Colonel Montgomery (a rank he would lose when the war ended) with the Minister for Munitions, Winston Churchill, oblivious to one another in October 1918, watching a march past of the 47th (2nd London) Division. His experiences of the First World War, his injuries, the cost in men, his understanding of how to organ- ise an offensive, all fed into his thinking. After the war, Montgomery stayed on and ground his way slowly up the ranks in an army that had returned with relief to its pre- war stasis.

In 1939, Major General Montgomery was fortunate to be in France at all, and to hold divisional command, as his smoothly ascending career had nearly been permanently halted twice, once in peacetime and then again when the war began, largely because of his singular ability to put noses out of joint entirely unnecessarily. As garrison com- mander in Portsmouth in 1938, he had attempted to refloat his brigade's welfare fund by renting out the football pitch at Southsea, War Office land, to a fair that was taking place on the August Bank Holiday weekend: army and city pulling together mutually for the community. He'd charged the promoter £1,500,* and given the mayor £500

---

* The equivalent of £112,956.99 today (according to the CPI inflation calculator). The mayor did all right out of that, I'd say.

to smooth things over. The only snag was Montgomery had no authority to do such a thing, regardless of how neat he regarded the scheme or how much money it might have generated. It was ingenious but in contravention of army regulations. In his memoirs, which are a deliciously one-sided source, the kind that historians have to handle with great care, packed with I-was-right-despite-being-surrounded-by-fools-and-had-the-last-laugh stuff, he relates the tale as an unfortunate spot of hot water. The War Office took it rather more seriously and demanded he repay the money, but it had gone into the welfare fund and the mayor had put his portion into a pet council project. As Montgomery tells it, his unnamed commanding officer told him he was finished and could forget about being ever promoted – seemingly the end for Brigadier Montgomery then and there. But then his boss's boss, the 'rather amused' – according to Montgomery – General Archie Wavell intervened, and all of sudden the issue went away. Montgomery was promoted and sent back to Palestine for his first divisional command. Feathers unruffled, card not quite marked, career suicide averted.

This spot of hot water in Portsmouth occurred in the wake of the death of Montgomery's beloved wife, Betty, of septicaemia. Betty Carver was the sister of Percy Hobart, the armoured warfare pioneer, whom we will meet later. When they met, she was a widow (her husband Oswald had been killed in 1915) with two children. They had now been married for ten years, during which time she had transformed the uptight military man: she was bohemian, artistic, she introduced him to people he would otherwise never have met – their friends delighted in the contrast between them. He would issue orders for family activities; she would insist he let his hair down. Married life offered Montgomery a world outside the army, an emotional hinterland he hadn't experienced before in his austere clerical family and in the army itself, and he was blissfully happy. Betty went with him on his postings, which softened the duty for him and involved her in his career – he wasn't the sealed-up, isolated man he would become in later life. They had lived in India, Palestine and Egypt together, and had a son, David.

But on their return to the UK, tragedy struck. Betty was bitten by an unidentified insect, contracted blood poisoning – doctors amputated her leg in effort to save her life – and died. Montgomery allowed himself two days off exercises on Salisbury Plain, and then, as his brother Brian* put it, returned to his first love, the army. Betty's sons felt that she had kept him out of trouble long enough to keep his army career on track. By the time he was posted to Portsmouth, he was emerging from the grief his wife's death had plunged him into:

> I was now alone [. . .] I had always lived a great deal by myself and had acquired the habit of concentration. This ability to concentrate, and to sort the essentials from a mass of detail, was now made easier for me than formerly because of the intense loneliness that descended on me after my wife's death. I became completely dedicated to my profession.[1]

Even though his memoirs are vainglorious, boastful, pernickety – arguably a perfect reflection of the man,

---

* Montgomery's brother Brian had an interesting war: he was intelligence staff officer in Bill Slim's HQ Burma Corps (Burcorps) and saw Slim in action close up during the battle for Yenangyaung in 1942.

making it plain why you should never give yourself a character reference, let alone one that's tens of thousands of words long – Montgomery admits he could be overbearing, or at least realized he was in danger of becoming 'too overbearing': 'maybe I was too confident, and showed it'[2]. The 'maybe' is his concession to posterity. Montgomery had burrowed down into being a professional soldier in an army which at times seemed to regard fighting as a distraction from the main business of 'proper soldiering'. This placed him in marked contrast with some of his contemporaries, but this necessarily flexible organization was able to accommodate his single-mindedness, and indeed to make the most of it.

*

Recalled from Palestine, Montgomery embarked for France in late September 1939 with his new command the 3rd 'Iron' Division, an infantry division, with a brigade of guards and two brigades of classic British county infantry battalions. He had links with two of the brigades, having commanded one and been brigade major – central organizer – of the other. The limitations of British preparations for a continental war became apparent immediately, and Montgomery set about weeding out the officers he felt weren't up to standard, or 'useless', as he put it; plenty of his officers were, like Montgomery himself, veterans of the previous war, but some of them were just too old. With winter approaching, opportunities for training were limited, and further limited by a paucity of equipment. The British Army had proud aspirations to being completely mechanized in a way the horse-reliant Wehrmacht was not; in fact, it fell far short of them. For its embarkation, the 3rd Division had had to scrounge civilian transport, and then again in France. As the days shortened, preparations for war slithered into a kind of torpor. Digging defences became a substitute activity for training. Lieutenant General Alan Brooke, Montgomery's corps commander, wrote in his diary about the BEF's total lack of readiness in a way that seems grimly prophetic: 'the Corps was quite unfit for war, practically in every aspect [. . .] To send untrained troops into modern war is courting disaster such as befell the Poles.'[3] Montgomery in his memoirs, with hindsight on his side, was direct in his judgement: 'In September 1939 the British Army was totally unfit to fight a first class war on the continent of Europe [. . .] we had only ourselves to blame for the disasters which early overtook us in the field when fighting began in 1940.'[4]

At the time, Montgomery wasn't going to let the blame land on him, and he set about getting his men fit and rehearsing for possible action. In this age of marathon fun runs and British Military Fitness classes in your local park, it seems strange that Montgomery's emphasis on fitness stuck out so much at the time and caused such consternation. His insistence that his officers do two cross-country runs a week horrified some of his staff. He also ran exercises at night, getting his division into the right frame of mind to manoeuvre en masse in the dark, vehicle lights dimmed. Such preparations served him well in the chaos of the following May; during the Dunkirk battle, the 3rd Division had to move overnight to bolster the British line, and Brooke knew that Montgomery could be trusted with such a tricky movement because of his rehearsals. He also perfected what later in the war would become one of his signature pieces of behaviour – an early night. Montgomery liked to get plenty of sleep and be fresh for whatever the next day might bring.

During that winter, 3rd Division's headquarters was subject to political visits, to view the preparations of the BEF. Prime Minister Neville Chamberlain came to lunch, and afterwards asked Montgomery a question. Ever hopeful, he said, 'I don't think the Germans have any intention of attacking us. Do you?' Montgomery put him straight, telling him the enemy would attack at a time and place of their choosing. Chamberlain's question suggests that right at the top there was still hope that the war could be resolved without having to come to blows with the Germans: an essential lack of seriousness about the task the country and its empire were facing.

Even as it was becoming clear that the Germans had found a way of war that worked for them in their conquest of Poland, the BEF carried on digging defences and trying to absorb its Territorial reserves in preparation for any German blow that might come. It regarded itself as equal to the German Army and had in place a plan for stopping Panzers – a net of anti-tank weapons, 2-pounder guns – but it didn't have this equipment in the quantities needed. Integration between the Royal Air Force and the British Army had never been worked out, and relations with the French Army – a formal alliance but one in which Britain was very much the junior partner – were varied, sometimes cordial, often a state of mutual incomprehension.

This phase of the war became known as the Bore War in Britain; we know it now as the Phoney War – the Germans called it the *Sitzkrieg*, though they were otherwise occupied in Poland. While the Germans conquered Poland

and split it in two with their Soviet partners, carving the country up and brutally dismantling the Polish state, the Allies set about preparing for the anticipated strategic long haul and did nothing. Or at least nothing much. The Saar Offensive, from 7 to 16 September, was the only offensive action undertaken by the Allies, a push into a preoccupied Germany that was called off the next month; the Germans hadn't taken the bait, largely because they were unable to. The German Army was so heavily committed to Poland that its armoured forces – with which they might be expected to counter-attack an incursion into the Reich – were unavailable. This excursion into Germany doesn't quite qualify as a great 'what if?' of the war, because to expect offensive action from the Allies at this stage is to misunderstand what the United Kingdom and France wanted to happen in their confrontation with Germany and what their armies were therefore capable of. The gigantic French Army could hardly retool itself as an offensive war machine over the winter; politically, France could only commit to fighting a defensive war. That the British and French governments had declared war on Germany towards the end of the traditional campaigning season doubtless further blunted any enthusiasm for offensive action; that would have to wait until the spring of the following year. The wait presented the Allies with an opportunity to prepare, of course, even as the Germans gained experience in Poland, experience not just of military victory but of National Socialist conquest and all that that entailed. It wasn't so much that the Allies sat on their hands, it was that they hadn't planned for anything else.

Although the British had been rearming behind the scenes during the period of appeasement, the emphasis had been on air and naval power, particularly building the Fighter Command defence system that went on to win the Battle of Britain; the British Army, because of its widely varied global commitments, had not been prepared for the coming European clash. The army was also dealing with the expansion of the Territorial Army imposed on it by the Chamberlain government in 1938. Just as in the previous war, massive and rapid expansion placed huge strain on the army's ability to organize and train. Conscription followed swiftly too, unlike during the Great War, when the British government had sidled up to the prospect unwillingly, trying to rely on volunteers for as long as it could. The army and ministers knew that they couldn't wait for volunteers this time round, but this meant incorporating yet more expansion. The BEF's professional core sought to keep its head above water as comparatively untrained Territorial troops joined them in France; when the 1st Bucks Battalion deployed in France, for instance, it had only three professional soldiers, the CO, the RSM and one of the company commanders – it needed bringing up to speed very quickly. With his cross-country runs and nighttime exercises, Bernard Montgomery was very definitely part of that professional core.

*

It was his professionalism that nearly cost Montgomery his job, because he got himself into more hot water during the Bore War, over the issue of sex. Or, more specifically, sexually transmitted infections, known at the time as VD, venereal disease. Armies have always had a problem with VD. The Royal Army Medical Corps noted that war 'removes social taboos and promiscuity increases as both (male and female) civilians and soldiers are less focussed on long-term futures'[5]. That's one way of putting it. During the Second World War, the Allied armies spent a great deal of time and money on treating and trying to prevent VD, principally syphilis and gonorrhoea. And they knew they had to, from bitter experience.

Just as the BEF looked to the First World War for lessons in how to fight the Second, so that earlier war offered plenty of experience in how to deal with the problem of men and VD. The figures are as eye-watering as the symptoms must have been: amongst British and dominion men, VD had caused 416,891 hospital cases – about 5 per cent of men enlisted during the war, dwarfing the number of men admitted for trench foot, which came in at only 74,711. Given the First World War's reputation for mud and damp and the supposed prevalence of trench foot, these numbers are staggering. The largest number of men in hospital at one time with VD was thought to be 11,000 – an infantry division, give or take.[6] VD cases were treated in separate hospitals to keep them away from those injured in combat, and these men had their pay docked while in hospital, which the army felt comfortable doing because the ailment was self-inflicted – 'hospital stoppage' for other illnesses would be plainly unfair. This wasn't the only reason a man might conceal his illness – First World War cases didn't have the benefit of antibiotics, and the treatments were painful and necessarily intrusive. While VD was a serious manpower problem for the British Army in the First World War, the solution was forever out of reach. The army could not issue condoms to its men for fear of the moral outrage it might provoke at home. Nurse and activist Ettie Rout sold packs for troops with condoms in and the disgrace followed her all the way home to New

Zealand, where it became illegal to the price of £100 to print her name.[7]

Embarrassed, the army vacillated as to what to do about brothels on the Western Front, even though half the men were catching VD in the UK. Moral panic was never far away; the likes of Christabel Pankhurst weighed in, epitomizing the tone of the time, in *The Great Scourge and How to End It* (1913): 'The sexual diseases are the great cause of physical, mental, and moral degeneracy, and of race suicide.'[8] The campaign against VD took on the characteristics of a culture war. There was moral panic and vehement disagreements about education, as well as appeals to patriotism and ideas about class. A National Council for Combating Venereal Disease was established, with soldiers, bishops, peers and doctors amongst its members, which set out to educate the general public about VD. The Council made sure lectures were delivered on the home front and to soldiers. Preventative ointments for applying after sex would carry warnings: 'REMEMBER that if you have disease, not only are you doing yourself serious harm by delaying treatment, but YOU ARE HELPING THE ENEMY by rendering our men unfit to fight.' VD clinicians were brought back to the UK from the frontline hospitals, such was the prevalence of the disease at home. The Defence of the Realm Act of 1916 prohibited prostitutes from soliciting soldiers in uniform, and in 1918 the law went further with regulation 40D: women with VD were forbidden from having sex with soldiers. All this legislation was aimed at women, rather than handing out condoms to the men. Regulation 40D also came in for pushback from moralists who claimed it suggested having sex was fine as long as it wasn't diseased sex, and it punished married women for sleeping with their husbands, if their husbands had infected them. It was quickly repealed; in any case, it had been enacted the day before the Michael Offensive began on the Western Front and the old BEF had bigger things to worry about.

In France, brothels were regulated by the government to keep a control on disease. But in the end the most effective intervention in the sex marketplace for the British soldier was his low pay – his Canadian and Australian contemporaries were much better paid and therefore had more money to spend on prostitutes: in 1915 the Canadians had a staggering 25 per cent infection rate amongst their men. After the war, chastity and abstinence were seen as the answer; after all, making sex safer for people might encourage them to do more of it. The aptly named Society for the Prevention of Venereal Disease published pamphlets in the early 1920s that made it clear that VD might cause Bolshevism.

*

In the British Army, it wasn't an offence to be infected, but concealing an infection was. You could have sex, and the army understood that you might want to, but you couldn't have VD – the question of disease was only ever paradoxical. Exercise and games were recommended as possible morale-boosting diversions for the men, but like everything in the British Army, how VD was dealt with devolved down from the top to individual commanders. And commanders who cared about their men's fitness, their morale, their effectiveness in battle, and who understood the British regimental soldier, would no doubt address the question of VD. So, come 1939, Major General Montgomery was faced with the question of what to do about his men and sex and VD. And he found that things hadn't changed much in the twenty or so years since the army had last been at war. It wasn't being taken seriously enough.

In the US, the army was to grab the issue with both hands, so to speak. The pamphlet 'Sex Hygiene and Venereal Disease', printed by the US War Department in 1941 and reissued in 1943, said quite merrily: 'Sex is one of the most important things in your life, for it makes you a man. It's something to be proud of. But, like everything else you prize, it must be well cared for.' 1943 was also the year the Surgeon General, mindful of caring for this prized thing, suggested that American soldiers no longer be punished for having VD, so that they would come forward for treatment. This was hugely controversial at the time; the British had gone through a similar convulsion the year before, with the Chief Medical Officer of the Ministry of Health, Sir Wilson Jameson, deciding that while VD was on the rise because of wartime and its associated 'loose living' it would have to be dealt with as 'just another medical and public health problem'. The *British Medical Journal* agreed.[9]

A US War Department anti-VD pamphlet complete with dynamic coloured lettering appealed to the men to consider the army's plans, as well as their own more immediate needs:

[F]irst your army's plans: venereal disease can put a man OFF THE TEAM – and that is O.K. by the ENEMY . . . THEN YOUR OWN PLANS: V.D. untreated can give you plenty of TROUBLE.

This text is accompanied by a cartoon of men wading ashore from a landing craft, one of them in red – absent, I guess – with spectral letters spelling out VD beside him. My immediate thought on seeing this design was that, given how beach landings could go, maybe a dose of the clap wasn't so bad. But men were expensive to train and motivate, and propagandists weren't much bothered about how they ensured this investment was protected from VD. Dodgy women were the focus of many posters, warning: '98% of all procurable women have Venereal Disease – Why bet against these odds?' and 'SHE MAY LOOK CLEAN – BUT PICK-UPS, "GOOD TIME" GIRLS, PROSTITUES SPREAD SYPHILIS AND GONORRHEA – You can't beat the Axis if you get VD.'

Accompanying these stern messages were pictures of tempting women smoking cigarettes and generally looking like a lot of fun – perhaps a predictive echo of the unfortunate chic that arose around anti-heroin propaganda in the 1980s and '90s. Or indeed any propaganda that takes a moral tilt and tries to create the forbidden – it only makes the forbidden more exciting. Men were also warned rather vaguely that 'VENEREAL DISEASE COVERS THE EARTH' and told 'Self-Control is Self-Preservation'; and while one poster admits that 'VD CAN BE CURED', there is of course a but: 'BUT THERE'S NO MEDICINE FOR REGRET.'

So how well did these measures work? Maybe they were effective, and without them the numbers of VD casualties would have been even higher. Certainly, even with a cure in place, one thing that these dire warnings did emphasize was how terrible syphilis and gonorrhoea were. Although they seem like diseases from an over-the-top

Victorian melodrama – for instance, Ibsen's *Ghosts*, which has everything: simmering unrequited love, loss of faith, melodramatic plotting, inter-generational feuding, communication breakdown. The play includes an actually unnameable dose of syphilis; it was banned when it was first produced. Syphilis left untreated is utterly horrifying, and both syphilis and gonorrhoea can be passed on from mother to child. So not only are you off the team, but you're also letting down your own future, the very future you are fighting for, and even risking the health of your potential kids. The anti-VD propagandists weren't exaggerating. A spectre was haunting Europe, and it wasn't communism, it was syphilis.

Syphilis, which once stalked the world, is a wily, evil bastard of a disease.* Nicknamed the 'Great Imitator', it presents in myriad ways, almost to the point of being unrecognizable at times; it mimics other conditions, disappears and reappears seemingly randomly – in the nineteenth century, a whole discipline dedicated to studying it emerged, called syphilology. It was said that 'he who knows syphilis knows medicine' – presumably by 'medicine' here they meant horrible suffering, pain, insanity and death, and desperate innovations masquerading as would-be cures. The disease first appeared in Europe in the 1500s (though it may have been around earlier, misidentified as leprosy), when an epidemic started amongst the men of Charles VIII of France as his army took Naples. Amidst the victory celebrations, it became clear that something

---

* This is one of those times I'm glad I'm not a historian and can write something like that.

was wrong: Charles's men became horribly ill and at the Battle of Forova they were too ill to fight. By the end of the year – possibly because Charles's army was made up of mercenaries from all over Western Europe – syphilis spread, reaching England and Scotland only two years later. Of course this outbreak coincided with lots of European maritime exploration and on the disease went, hitching a ride as far as China and Japan by 1520 and on to Oceania. Well done, everyone! And everyone blamed everyone else – it was the Neapolitan disease, the French disease, French pox, in Russia it was the Polish disease . . . you see how this works. Around the 1520s, the penny dropped that it was spread by sex, and given the religious world view at the time, it quickly came to be seen as a very real kind of judgement.

The disease generally runs in four stages, starting off with chancres and lesions (even the words that go with it seem old-fashioned), then progressing to rashes anywhere on your body, headaches, sore throat, fever and so on. Then it can go away. Sometimes, because syphilis is a wily, evil bastard, you can have the secondary stage without the first, or it can lie dormant. This 'latent' stage is particularly insidious: a patient might test positive for the disease but not have any symptoms – so why would you test? Tertiary syphilis, which may appear many years after the initial infection, comes in three forms, all utterly horrible: gummatous syphilis, which presents as tumour-like growths that can distort your face or body; neurosyphilis, when the disease strikes at the nervous system (obvs), leading to pain, bad balance and paralysis, as well as seizures and dementia – going mad in old age was as likely to be caused by a youthful dalliance as anything; and cardiovascular syphilis, which can cause an aneurysm. This array of symptoms and variations goes some way to show why this disease was the HIV of the Victorian era and before: long-term deadly, debilitating, incurable and a sure sign of what could be pounced on as moral decrepitude by the sort of people who like to pounce on stuff like that. Reading all this is enough to put you off the idea of doing it altogether. I am typing this with my legs crossed.

Syphilis was at one point pretty much everywhere – André Gide said of syphilis, 'It is unthinkable for a Frenchman to arrive at middle age without having syphilis and the Cross of the Legion of Honour.' In the days before antibiotics and reliable condoms it certainly made its mark on the known world. Artists, politicians, musicians, kings and emperors – it was no respecter of position or privilege. Ivan the Terrible (that might explain it then), Baudelaire, Howard Hughes, Lord Randolph Churchill, Delius, Al Capone, Manet and Beau Brummel can all be found on the roll-call of the unfortunately syphilitic. Bearing in mind that syphilis changes how it appears and comes and goes as it pleases, these lists of syphilitic celebs are surely incomplete; some may simply have died before it came back to haunt them – indeed, syphilis may have been around a lot longer than is believed because either people simply didn't live long enough or it wasn't recognized. It also seems to stand in as a potential diagnosis for anyone who acted at all erratically or dangerously: all-round fun guys Lenin and Hitler make the list of possibles.

Gonorrhoea is less serious but easily as debilitating in its early stages, and could take a man out of the front line at the crucial moment. But even knowing what these diseases can do to you, even with the threat of insanity: young men want to fuck. Especially young men who are being asked to risk their lives. And they might not be too fussy about who they fuck.

*

So, faced with something this serious, what was happening in the British Army, in the BEF, in 3rd Division in the autumn of 1939? Major General Montgomery, the arch-professional, decided he should apply himself to the problem at hand. And so on 15 November 1939 he wrote the following, and once again almost derailed his career completely:

> Subject: Prevention of Venereal Disease. Div. 179/A 15 Nov. 39. List 'A'
> I am not happy about the situation regarding venereal disease in the Division.
> Since the 18 October the number of cases admitted to Field Ambulances in the Divisional area totals 44.

So far, so sensible. Idle young men were expected to seek an outlet.

> I consider that the whole question of women, V.D., and so on is one which must be handled by the regimental officer, and in particular by the C.O. The men must be spoken to quite openly and frankly, and the more senior the officer who speaks to them the better.
> My view is that if a man wants to have a woman, let him do so by all means: but he must use his common sense and take the necessary precautions against

infection – otherwise he becomes a casualty by his own neglect, and this is helping the enemy.

Entirely conventional stuff here too. Montgomery wasn't going to make the mistake of trying to enforce abstention; he wanted to make it clear where the responsibility for his men's health lay: with their officers and with the men individually. How could the division help?

Our job is to help him by providing the necessary means: he should be able to buy French Letters in the unit shop, and E.T. [Early Treatment] rooms must be available for his use. As regards the E.T. rooms – it is no use having one room in the battalion area: there should be one room in each coy. [company] area: the man who has a woman in a beetroot field near his coy. billet will not walk a mile to the battalion E.T. room. If a man desires to buy his French Letter in a civil shop he should be instructed to go to a chemist shop and ask for a 'Capote Anglaise'.

Montgomery's characteristic blunt style, with a dash of D. H. Lawrence perhaps – 'a man who has a woman in a beetroot field' – outlines the problem, and he clearly knows perfectly well how his men might behave and suggests action accordingly. Montgomery's reputation for pithy problem-solving, for boiling a situation down to a simple, understandable précis, complete with solutions in similarly straightforward style, is upheld in this memo. He goes on:

There are in Lille a number of brothels, which are properly inspected and where the risk of infection is practically nil. These are known to the military police, and any soldier who is in need of horizontal refreshment would be well advised to ask a policeman for a suitable address.

And here is the fateful phrase: 'horizontal refreshment'. That Montgomery knew there were brothels in Lille that were relatively safe, and recognized the problems of soldiers idling over the winter of 1939–40, waiting for the war to start, meant that what MPs knew about where best for British soldiers to get laid had passed across Montgomery's desk. And being a British divisional general, with leeway to run things his way, Montgomery was formulating his own doctrine regarding sex.

> The soldier on his part must clearly understand the penalties that are attached to V.D., and the reasons.
>
> Finally, then, I wish all unit commanders to keep in touch with the V.D. problem and handle it in the way they think best.
>
> We must face up to the problem, be perfectly frank about it, and do all we can to help the soldier in this very difficult matter. (Signed) . . .[10]

Given the deep seriousness of the problem, this memo is hard to fault, even for 1939. However, Montgomery also added a poem from the divisional Royal Signals, signed 'cupid', which put the issue into sophomoric doggerel. Its robust style wouldn't have been too unfamiliar to anyone who had read the Wipers Times in the previous war.

MARS AMATORIA★

The General was worried and was very ill at ease,
He was haunted by the subject of venereal disease;

For four and forty soldiers was the tale he had to tell
Had lain among the beets and loved not wisely but too well.
It was plain that copulation was a tonic for the bored,
But the gallant British Soldier was an Innocent Abroad;
So ere he takes his pleasure with an amateur or whore,
He must learn the way from officers who've trod that path
    before.
No kind of doubt existed in the Major-General's head
That the men who really knew the game of Love from A to Z
Were his Colonels and his Adjutants and those above the ruck,
For the higher up an officer the better he can f—k.
The Colonels and the Majors were not a bit dismayed,
They gave orders for the holding of a Unit Love Parade,
And the Adjutants by numbers showed exactly how it's done,
How not to be a casualty and still have lots of fun.
The Adjutants explained that 'capote' did not mean a cup,
That refreshment horizontal must be taken standing up,
They told the troops to work at Love according to the
    rules,
And after digging in to take precautions with their tools.
Now the General is happy and perfectly at ease,
No longer is he troubled with venereal disease,
His problem solved, his soldiers clean (their badge is now
    a dove)
He has earned the cross of Venus, our General of Love.
        'cupid'
            R. Signals.[11]

Saucy, but I wouldn't open with it.

All this was too much for Lord Gort's headquarters. There was, as Montgomery later described it, 'the father-and-mother of a row. They were all after my blood at

GHQ.'[12] The feeling was that the order was inappropriate and improper, a poor reflection on the officer who drafted it and the army. The phrase 'horizontal refreshment' was the offending item, and regardless of the context, it looked as though the sky would fall in on 3rd Division's commanding officer. The chaplain at GHQ was particularly agitated – and Lord Gort took the view that Montgomery had gone too far and should withdraw his too-hot-to-handle order. It went as far as the adjutant general. The problem was that getting a major general to withdraw an order would undermine his authority with his officers. Fortunately for Montgomery, his corps commander, Lieutenant General Alan Brooke, intervened with Gort, saying that it should be left to him to handle the errant Montgomery personally.

Accounts of what happened next don't differ. Brooke's staff, through closed doors, could hear their boss's raised voice, stern and angry. Brooke's diary for 23 November tells the story:

> Started the day by having to 'tell off' Monty for having issued a circular to his troops on the prevention of venereal disease worded in such obscene language that both the C of E and *RC* senior chaplains had complained to the Adjutant General!

Well, we've seen the 'obscene language' so maybe Brooke is reflecting the breathless outrage of the chaplains rather than what he really thinks. Brooke's diaries were notionally addressed to his wife, so perhaps that is why he drew a veil over the language. Nevertheless, the complaint being booted upstairs to the adjutant general indicates the trouble Montgomery was in. Brooke goes on:

> I [. . .] pointed out to Monty that his position as the commander of a division had been seriously affected by this blunder and could certainly not withstand any further errors of this kind. I also informed him that I had a very high opinion of his military capabilities and an equally low one of his literary ones! He took it wonderfully well, and I think it ought to have done him good. It is a great pity that he spoils his very high military ability by a mad desire to talk or write nonsense.[13]

Montgomery had the good fortune of Brooke's patronage. It saved him and his career, and, in a curious way, got him further than his undoubted skills as a trainer of men and battlefield strategist alone might have – for the rest of the war, as Brooke ascended to Chief of the Imperial General Staff, he set himself up as Montgomery's – or by then Monty's – guardian.

This episode illustrates two things. Firstly, that military patronage and personal bonds of professional loyalty were as important as any other factor in the leadership of the British war effort – Brooke was able, once Montgomery got the top job in Eighth Army and British fortunes changed, to protect him from Churchill and many, many others as well as from 'Monty''s own 'mad desire to talk or write nonsense'. Brooke's approval became central to how the war was run and to officers' careers. That Brooke fell back on the people he knew and trusted can hardly be a surprise. He'd got to know them as an instructor at the

Staff College between 1923 and 1926 and they therefore understood one another – 24 of his former pupils commanded divisions in the Second World War. Monty taught there for two years too; nineteen of his pupils commanded divisions. The US Army, which had been even smaller between the wars, was a tight cadre of men who had come through together, ensuring that Marshall's guy Ike got the job, and Ike's guys got the jobs Ike wanted them to get.

But secondly what this incident also illustrates is how the BEF seemed to be sleepwalking into disaster. The professionals were having to look out for each other, while chaplains and adjutant generals got hung up on the mundane yet war-winningly essential business of talking to the men about VD in language they might understand. Montgomery's guardian angel Brooke was an exception and understood how demanding the war to come might be, and who needed protecting. It would take calamitous defeat, the political fallout from that defeat – and many others to follow – as well as the entry into the war of allies who would challenge the status quo, for the professionals to get their hands on the reins and grind victory out of the disastrous strategic situation. Brooke could not have possibly known in November of 1939 that Montgomery would become 'Monty', but he backed the right horse. After all, as Montgomery's brother points out:

> It took just under six years to move from the landing
> exercise of 1938, with its one infantry brigade, a dozen
> or so naval aircraft, and a few warships, to the million
> or more troops, over ten thousand aircraft and the

fleets of two nations, assembled for an opposed landing on the French coast. On both occasions the
commander of all the land forces was the same man,
Bernard Montgomery.[14]

*

The issue of VD didn't go away: when he came to command Eighth Army in 1942, Montgomery clamped down
on the brothels in Egypt, and yet again the army prelates
did what they could to preserve the men's moral integrity.
In general, the army struggled with VD as the war progressed. In the Middle East in 1941, for every thousand
men there were 41.3 VD cases and 35.5 battle casualties –
VD was the third most prevalent disease that the army
had to deal with. This reduced over the next two years, to
21.8 VD cases and 22.5 casualties per thousand. In Italy,
VD rates rose: in 1943, the figures stood at 31.3 VD cases
per thousand to 63.9 battle casualties, VD coming sixth in
the disease pecking order. But by 1945 these figures were
dramatically reversed: a staggering 68.8 men per thousand were recorded with VD (and it was the number-one
disease the army in Italy was dealing with), compared to
9.8 battle casualties per thousand. In North-West Europe,
battle casualties outweighed VD cases – in 1944, the rate
of VD per thousand men on ration strength (all the men in
a formation drawing rations, not just the men in the fighting parts of an army) was 5.9 to 61.3 battle casualties,
which points to the toughness of the fighting. Burma,
though, leaves the other theatres for dust. In 1943, the VD
rates were soaring – 157.9 VD cases per thousand to 13.9
battle casualties. Considering that this was the year of the
disastrous first Arakan offensive, these figures suggest a

story of their own. By 1945, the figures are almost level –
72.2 to 73.2. VD never went away, and it hospitalized more
men than combat. By 1945, Eisenhower was fuming noisily
about the numbers of men lost to VD – but Montgomery
by then was 'Monty', and so beyond the scope of this
chapter.

Montgomery complained about the high venereal disease rate in the Second New Zealand Expeditionary Force
to General Bernard Freyberg, who commanded the New
Zealand forces in the Middle East and Italy (and later
became governor general). Freyberg apparently replied, 'If
they can't fuck, they can't fight.' And if anyone knew fighting, it was Freyberg.

2

Bernard Freyberg

A question of intelligence

A born warrior. A man with an undimmable appetite for action. An athlete. A national hero, without peer. Unsackable. Lieutenant General Bernard Freyberg VC, GCMG, KCB, KBE, DSO & Three Bars: the medals tell their own story of a man whose military career is iconic in his adopted country, New Zealand. But there's a but – of course there's a but, because no one could possibly live up to this kind of build-up – when we talk about Freyberg, we have to talk about intelligence.

New Zealand had entered the war in sync with the British government – at least it had promised to and duly waited for a coded message from Whitehall to let it know that the ultimatum against Germany had expired. At the other end of the world from the 'world crisis', the Wellington government knew that its economic fortunes – despite the distance – were tied to Britain's. Trade and economic links mattered to the most distant dominion, but some things mattered more. While Neville Chamberlain called the dispute in Sudetenland 'a quarrel in a far-away country, between people of whom we know nothing', political opinion in Wellington was opposed to appeasement. The Labour government had expressed its dissatisfaction with London's attitude to the dominions on matters of defence, and at the 1937 Imperial Conference, Prime Minister Michael Joseph Savage had made it clear to British Foreign Secretary Anthony Eden how unimpressed he was with British backsliding: 'peace at any price'. Savage also had his eye on Japanese aggression in China. In this sense he was out of step with the other dominion governments, but it did mean that when war came his government could hardly not commit.

Nevertheless, for all of Savage's tough talk,* there were complications. The Great War had seen New Zealand's men deployed most notoriously to Gallipoli – and conscription was something that New Zealand's political establishment couldn't go near. A volunteer expeditionary force was put together with the expectation that it would deploy to the Middle East – after all, the British Chiefs of the Imperial General Staff were planning on mobilizing a global response to Germany's plans for expansion, and British imperial interests in Persia, Mesopotamia and Egypt needed protecting: oil, transport links, the Suez Canal. The dominion Allies weren't particularly voluntary Allies, yet they were more than simply satraps – the men they sent were all volunteers, with their own motivations for joining up. Conscription was politically impossible. While the governments were willing to send troops, they each played a delicate balancing act on their respective home fronts to make sure their armies performed well and

* There is no doubting Savage was tough – he had postponed treatment for his colon cancer in order to fight the 1938 election. He won the election, but by the following year he was mortally ill. He directed New Zealand's entry into the war from his sickbed and died in March 1940, before the calamitous British defeat in France.

their electorates thought the whole thing worthwhile. Too cosy a home front might also aggravate men enduring hardships abroad. As the war progressed and Japan entered the fray, New Zealand remained, unlike Australia, safely out of harm's way – and that distance even from the more proximate war with Japan gave the New Zealanders' home front a strange sense of detachment. How to maintain links with London and bridge the gap with a faraway New Zealand army? Enter retired British Army Major General Bernard Freyberg, a great big adventure of a man.

*

Bernard Freyberg was part of the military and political scene in the United Kingdom, essentially an exile from New Zealand. Freyberg reflects the way London was an imperial centre – he'd been born in England, moved to New Zealand when he was two but had returned to England to fight for the British Army, though not without a detour – after failing to win a commission in the New Zealand Territorials, he had gone to fight for Pancho Villa in the Mexican Revolution. Freyberg had trained as a dentist – war was preferable to pulling teeth. He was a restless man of action, a big man, six feet tall, with a high-pitched voice. A true warrior, Freyberg had a good Great War, at Gallipoli and at the Somme, and then on the Western Front until 1918, being wounded with regularity, and decorated accordingly. At 28, in April 1917, he was the youngest brigade commander on the Western Front.* Most importantly

---

* A staggering achievement, though a reminder of the sheer churn of officers in the First World War.

for his later career, Freyberg was the kind of soldier it was hard to argue with: he was a holder of the Victoria Cross. The citation tells of him rallying his battalion and being wounded four times in the course of an attack on a village on the Somme in late 1916. After the war, he returned to New Zealand while recovering from the many wounds he had acquired, but he made Britain his home in the 1920s, establishing himself in business in London and running for Parliament – as a Liberal (unsuccessfully, in Cardiff South). When politics didn't work out for him, he concentrated on the army: he went to the Staff College, so made connections with the men who would come to command the army in the 1940s. But ill health cut short Freyberg's time in the army – he had a heart problem as well as his patchwork of war wounds, and in 1937, aged 45, he was told his services were no longer required. Though he had been allowed back into the army in 1939, his prospects weren't good; like so many of the men who entered the military's top echelons, his career was saved by the advent of war. Savage's government approached him for the role of commanding the NZEF – and he jumped at the chance.

To call Freyberg brave doesn't really do him justice. A champion swimmer – he'd won a swimming competition in Los Angeles on his way back from Mexico to London to sign up in 1914 – he had volunteered for the most daring action he could at Gallipoli: swimming naked into the bay and lighting decoy flares to mislead the Turks about British landing intentions. (Needless to say, he was wounded in Gallipoli.) Freyberg had also had the good fortune to meet Winston Churchill when he was part of the abortive raiding force that Churchill had tried to seize Antwerp with in 1914 – a connection that would become crucial to his later career. Churchill called him 'the Salamander' because he was 'impervious to fire'.

Back to that, but, I promised, though. Freyberg was an outstanding subaltern, an excellent, driven battalion commander, an inspirational figure for his men, strong, brave, indomitable, a man who revelled in the physical – he had taken up mountain climbing in response to being told he had a heart problem. But – and this is where it gets tricky if we are going to try to sell this book in New Zealand – he doesn't seem to have been very bright. At least, when he really needed to be able to make sound decisions at the level of command he'd been appointed to, he was unable to. Because as mighty a hero as Freyberg definitely was, he was at the centre of one of the greatest Allied disasters of the war: the fall of Crete.

*

As DUKE forces pulled back from Greece in the spring of 1941 – having done all they could to prop up the Greek Army and hold back the Germans – they had suffered in an unequal struggle. Unequal not just in terms of equipment but in terms of experience – German Panzers were more than a match for the tanks the British had mustered, though as ever it was more about how well coordinated the Germans were than anything else. For though the DUKE forces had done well fighting the Italians in the desert the previous year, achieving stunning victories against Mussolini's men, the first two years of land fighting were characterized by the gaps between the armies and their capabilities. The elements of the British Army that had gone to the desert in 1940 were regular soldiers, well trained and properly led, and their equipment far outstripped what the Italians had brought with them. Just as there had been a gap between the British and Italian armies, so there lay a gap between the British and the German – a gap characterized by defeat. The Battle of France hung heavy over British troops, sapping their morale – a feeling that ran through all the DUKE armies, who were beginning to feel that the Germans were unbeatable. For all the talk of a miracle at Dunkirk, the army knew it had been beaten, and soundly. And while the brass might have reasoned that it was the French who had been bamboozled and broken by the Germans rather than the defeat being the fault of the BEF, the average soldier and the men flooding into the army that had quit Europe abandoning its kit might well have thought otherwise.

The German advantage was rooted in their having had a head start in preparing for war and having had the initiative; the effect of this advantage was the voodoo of their seeming invincibility. German preparations had been offensive and tactical. The British Army, serving an imperial power, with lots of theatres and battlefields to cover, hadn't done as much thinking as it could have done, and its doctrine and training tended to be devolved to the divisional level rather than standardized. After all, the desert was nothing like France, which was nothing like the jungle, which was nothing like mountainous Greece. Germany had the advantage of being centralized; British imperial efforts were necessarily decentralized, looser and collaborative. British Staff College training tended to the strategic, which makes sense with an empire to manage; German training was more tactical, with its perceived enemies right on its borders. At sea and in the air, the progress of the war was similarly characterized by pre-war preparation – for example, the Battle of Britain was a victory for the British precisely because they had prepared a fighter defence system that the Germans had never seriously planned for.

But in Crete, the British and dominion troops and Freyberg had an advantage over the Germans. They knew what was coming. The battle for Crete was to be one of the first major encounters when the British, rather than being caught on the hop by the Germans as they had been in May 1940, were aware of what the enemy was planning and had plenty of time to prepare for it. Freyberg also had the advantage in terms of numbers. But by 1 June – ten days after the Germans began Fall MERKUR (Operation Mercury) – Freyberg and his men (and the reinforcements sent to relieve him) had been routed, defeated soundly and thoroughly demoralized, in another desperate encounter with the Germans, one that laid bare everything that was rotten in the British imperial war effort. German *Fallschirmjäger* – airborne soldiers – and the mountain troops that had reinforced them had delivered yet another shattering blow to the British.

*

Fall MERKUR was a Luftwaffe operation. German paratroopers were part of the Luftwaffe, a product of empire-building in pre-war Nazi Germany. Keen to be associated with new military developments – the preparations for war and remilitarization of Germany that were so key to Nazi policy – and to make sure that the Luftwaffe could properly rival the army, Hermann Goering (one of Hitler's many number twos) had established a parachute school in 1936 and used an existing police force as the core of the new *Fallschirmjäger* (literally 'parachute hunter') formation.

Goering had been to the Soviet Union and seen Soviet demonstrations of parachute soldiers – the men would exit the aircraft by rolling down the wing. The British had also seen demonstrations of these Soviet experiments but thought they lacked potential. Photographs of the demonstrations are completely hair-raising, but the potential to land men behind enemy lines was irresistible to the Germans, who were looking for solutions to the problem of fighting a long static war. Quickly expanded to a division, these volunteer *Fallschirmjäger* were to become the standard-bearers of Blitzkrieg – novel, modern and super-mobilized. The pioneering officer figuring out what on earth to do with these novel soldiers was Kurt Student, a First World War veteran and a player in the Luftwaffe.

The *Fallschirmjäger* did their elite thing in a self-conscious style. They had their own 'Ten Commandments', a heady mix of mission statement, motivational mantras, blunt tactical warnings and a glimpse of the brutality to come:

1. You are the elite of the German Army. For you, combat shall be fulfilment. You shall seek it out and train yourself to stand any test.
2. Cultivate true comradeship, for together with your comrades you will triumph or die.
3. Be shy of speech and incorruptible. Men act, women chatter; chatter will bring you to the grave.*
4. Calm and caution, vigour and determination, valour and a fanatical offensive spirit will make you superior in attack.

* 'Careless talk costs lives' doesn't quite have the same ring, does it?

5. In facing the foe, ammunition is the most precious thing. He who shoots uselessly, merely to reassure himself, is a man without guts. He is a weakling and does not deserve the title of parachutist.
6. Never surrender. Your honour lies in Victory or Death.
7. Only with good weapons can you have success. So look after them on the principle – First my weapons, then myself.
8. You must grasp the full meaning of an operation so that, should your leader fall by the way, you can carry it out with coolness and caution.
9. Fight chivalrously against an honest foe; armed irregulars deserve no quarter.*
10. With your eyes open, keyed up to top pitch, agile as a greyhound, tough as leather, hard as Krupp steel, you will be the embodiment of a German warrior.[1]

For all this, however, they had had a markedly mixed experience in the summer campaign of 1940. Any mention of the German offensive Fall Gelb (Case Yellow) has to include the stunning victory of the glider-borne German sappers and supporting infantry at the Belgian fort of Eben-Emael near Maastricht. Landing on the roof of this vast fort on the Belgian–Netherlands border in DFS230 gliders, each holding nine men, the sappers used charges and flamethrowers to knock out the guns and then cooped

---

* As the inhabitants of Crete were to find out.

everyone up inside it while at the same time another party landed at the nearby Albert Canal. For all its reinforced concrete and multiple state-of-the-art retractable artillery systems, the fort was rendered powerless by this daring attack – plywood gliders flying silently from the east disguised by the rising sun behind them. The men involved had filed to their gliders with the 'Ride of the Valkyries' playing; airborne assault had fulfilled its potential. The raid on Eben-Emael became the gold standard for airborne operations, tactical surprise delivering strategic results, and was only really topped by the landings at Pegasus Bridge four years later. Other German airborne efforts, though, were not quite so gleaming.

In Norway a month earlier, a company of *Fallschirmjäger* had landed to secure a rail junction at Dombås near Trondheim. Eight aircraft – precious Junkers Ju52 transport planes – were lost and the company was destroyed after five days of fighting: they blocked the railway line for five days but that was it. The German campaign in Norway was a success, so this failure was written off. Airborne operations would be central to ongoing German offensives. While the Panzers surged through the Ardennes, as the Germans' concentrated punch into France, the *Fallschirmjäger* were deployed to capture The Hague. The idea was to capture airfields, seize the head of the Dutch Army and the royal family, and the Dutch would capitulate immediately in the face of such a stunning coup. The Dutch refused to oblige; for all their elite training and obvious dash, the *Fallschirmjäger* were defeated. They didn't get into The Hague. Their intelligence about the airfield they had tried to seize was faulty; the runway was damaged by the Dutch and they couldn't be reinforced by air.

Student was hit in the head by a stray round. The airborne men resorted to holding what they could, rather than achieving their objectives, and trying somewhat pointlessly to fight it out with the Dutch. In the end, the Luftwaffe, realizing the battle had been lost, carpet-bombed Rotterdam and destroyed the city, forcing the Dutch government to capitulate, five days behind schedule. The shock and awe of landing paratroopers in The Hague hadn't paid off. The German losses in both men and aircraft again were heavy: 182 aircraft, mainly Ju52s, were lost in the attempt to land and reinforce the *Fallschirmjäger*. By any reckoning, a disaster.

Despite these notable failures, *Fallschirmjäger* were suddenly and definitely militarily hip. Eben-Emael had shown what could be done, and while the assault on The Hague might have been a fiasco, the Netherlands as a whole had fallen, the campaign had been a success, so the potential difficulties of airborne insertions were quietly ignored and the Luftwaffe expanded its airborne arm. Germany's enemies reacted by deciding to invest in parachute and glider landing troops, even if the details of what the Germans had done and how were sketchy. The ensuing panic in Britain about parachutists rather overlooked the drawbacks inherent in airborne landings: their vulnerability to counter-attack and how lightly armed they were compared to regular formations. The Germans had also used disguised '*Brandenburgers*' in the assault on the Netherlands: Dutch SS men masquerading as police. The shock of the new was keenly felt: *Fallschirmjäger* panic got jumbled up with panic about fifth columnists. A great deal of thought went into how best to deal with airborne landings; tactics were examined, conclusions drawn.

Come the spring of 1941, the German airborne arm had been expanded to a *Fliegerkorps*, commanded by Student still. Denied a role in Operation BARBAROSSA, Germany's invasion of the Soviet Union, Student and his men had been twiddling their thumbs looking for a suitable operation, and the Luftwaffe was looking for some way of clawing back prestige after the disaster of the Battle of Britain. By May, with the British withdrawing in chaos yet again, this time from Greece, Crete seemed the perfect opportunity for the *Fallschirmjäger* to ride again.

*

And Freyberg knew. He knew that Student was preparing to attack Crete because it was a Luftwaffe operation, and Luftwaffe signals discipline was, compared to that of the *Heer* (army) and the Kriegsmarine (navy), really lax. The Enigma traffic that had been deciphered by the British had uncovered the Luftwaffe's intentions for Crete. The story of British codebreaking, of Bletchley Park and Alan Turing, has become in recent years a totemic part of the British version of events of the Second World War. The appeal is easy to understand: it seems somehow bloodless, it relies on smarts rather than, say, carpet-bombing anyone, it has a maverick tragic genius at its heart and it involves computers, which figure centrally in everyone's lives now. It is a source of pride to say they were a British invention, and not only that, a gay man invented them to defeat the Nazis. The Germans never knew, the sorry saps! Who could resist such a tale? You would make a film about it, Benedict Cumberbatch banging a table and yelling at Mark Strong.

By early 1941, the British had made good enough

progress in deciphering German signals, but they had other problems. If anything, the Germans were ahead of the British in terms of reading enemy signals, having captured British army codebooks in France and Royal Navy ciphers in Norway, not that the Germans relied on good luck alone for their impetus in codebreaking:

> By 1938 [. . . they] had solved most of the Auxiliary Code, which covered traffic by minor warships, and one of the Royal Navy's two main code systems, the four-year-old and five-figure Administrative Code, which was used for the movement and deployments of warships in European waters. This success taught B-Dienst how to attack the long subtractor super-encipherment system as a whole.*[2]

RAF ciphers had similarly been attacked and cracked. The Italians did well against Eighth Army too in the desert. The Germans remained familiar with Allied ciphers throughout the war; even later in the war, in Italy, the Germans were able to crack British operational codes and find out which formations were where, and who they could expect to be up against, especially before an attack. The British also had an ongoing problem with lax radio discipline.

The ebb and flow of the codebreaking war was also shaped by the development of the German systems, which had been prioritized before the war began – German systems were ingrained and structural; Enigma was the only

---

* The British resigned themselves to this: in the wake of the fall of France, British policy reflected the limitations placed upon it by calamitous circumstance.

option for coded German signal traffic. Because the British were late to the party, their equivalent of the Enigma machine – the Typex encrypter – hadn't been rolled out in full. In the period immediately following the fall of France, encryption machines were not regarded as a priority, and the Typex machine's development had been slow and troublesome. Typex wasn't unlike the Enigma – hardly surprising as it was an adaptation of the commercially available German Enigma coding machine which the British had had a good look at. The early prototype was even called the RAF Enigma with Type X attachments. At a glance it appeared the same, though it had five wheels rather than the three that the first iteration of the Enigma possessed, and it could be operated by a single user. Typex machines with modifications were used at Bletchley Park to ape the settings on Enigma machines, as part of the effort to decode German signals. Fortuitously, the delay in getting enough Typex machines manufactured and into service worked as a positive for the British – the weaknesses that they were able to uncover and then attack in Enigma could be logged and modified out of the new versions of Typex, making it even more secure. The Germans had captured a Typex machine without its rotors at Dunkirk; B-Dienst, the German codebreaking service, had then spent six weeks trying to crack it and duly gave up, reasoning that since it was like the Enigma it too was unbreakable.

Signals intelligence was a game of cat and mouse, some steps forward and plenty back. The pattern of the war in other areas seems to be reflected in the signalling war: the Allies get off to a poor start; the Germans seize the initiative and take control, almost to the point of victory; then

the Allies, through a combination of ingenuity and technological industrial might (and with a sprinkling of luck),
dominate the signals war and crush the Axis powers from
the end of 1942 onwards. Initially, things had gone very
well for the Germans, signals-wise, especially at sea.

> B-Dienst read between 30 and 50 per cent of traffic –
> including all of the important material in the
> Norwegian campaign – and sometimes up to 80 per
> cent of traffic (though only in the less important 'Cap-
> tain's Tables', never the 'Admiral's Tables'). When
> added to German penetration of codes used by the
> mercantile marine, the successors to the Auxiliary
> Code, this intelligence especially aided the U-boat
> campaign. During the war at sea between 1939 and
> 1942, Germany gained as much from cryptanalysis as
> Britain did.[3]

The deep secrecy of the work created complications for
the Government Code and Cipher School (GC&CS). It
needed to raise funds and foreign currency, requisition
buildings and materials, second and employ people, all
without explaining what it needed them for. Reorganization and competition intruded too – within the secret
services themselves and then between the GC&CS's 'clients', the British Army, Royal Navy and Royal Air Force,
as well as MI6 and the Foreign Office, all of them making
different demands and expecting different information,
each with their own intelligence services and infrastructure. There was infighting. There was the organizational
chaos that came with the rapid expansion the war effort
demanded, not unlike the chaos that similarly plagued the
services. Deciding on priorities, methods, leadership all

took time, effort and skilled management, which weren't always to hand. There was much to invent and learn, and while Bletchley had, after a great deal of agitation and lobbying, pretty much been given a blank cheque in 1941, a blank cheque didn't necessarily provide all the answers.

After the fall of France, MI5 underwent huge organizational upheaval, internal review and leadership changes – again, not unlike the army – while at the same time GC&CS grew, with great faith placed in it by Churchill. GC&CS had been a diplomatic service essentially, reading telegrams and foreign governments' communications; now it was under pressure from the services as well as Number 10 to try to gather as much information as it possibly could about German operations, strengths and intentions. Consequently there was a sudden expansion of and emphasis on the 'Y Service', listening to German radio traffic, which generated the raw material Bletchley required to crack German ciphers – there was an understanding that volume of coded traffic would create the best opportunity to divine patterns and ciphers and attack German coded signals. Mistakes were inevitably made, as GC&CS wasn't so much being expanded as reinvented during 1940 and 1941. The Chief of MI6 (also known as SIS, the Secret Intelligence Service), Sir Stewart Menzies,* found the intelligence world expanding and changing around him at pace and tried to maintain his grip over the GC&CS's output. Menzies had the bright idea to

---

* Menzies is a deeply controversial figure, whose grip on MI6 kept him in place as chief until after the war ended. The world he occupied was so murky, it's hard to know what he got right or wrong, what decisions he made and exactly who he was spying on a lot of time.

call the source of these captured secrets 'Boniface', inventing an agent who was supposedly acting as a conduit for secrets leaked from Germany. This false trail meant that now there was an agent for the Germans to look for, and if and when they didn't find the agent, they might look to making their signalling more secure. At this stage of the war, Bletchley preferred to maintain a plain mystery and to refer simply to 'Source'. How the military got hold of its Source secrets was also overcomplicated: Menzies tried to insert MI6 in between Bletchley and the military, seeking to assess the material first, hindering the services' own intelligence people's efforts to get to grips with what the enemy was about. Gradually the services took control, asserting themselves as what the spooks call 'clients', and liaised directly with Bletchley Park. MI8, the secret government listening service that had done an excellent job during the First World War, was elbowed aside by GC&CS and subsumed into MI6.

As the codebreaking effort grew, the British realized that listening to and understanding German radio traffic would not always give them all the answers about the enemy's intentions. They could get a sense of the grand scheme of things: the British knew, for instance, that Operation BARBAROSSA was ready to roll in the summer of 1941, and shared the information, though Stalin preferred not to believe it. Realizing their own ciphers had been compromised in June 1941, the British used Ultra, as it became known, to find out what the Germans knew about their own strengths and operations. This became a fine art, and by 1943 the Royal Navy was so confident of its control of the information it was fighting with that it would direct convoys with their escorts onto the German U-boats, to force a battle and destroy them. But in 1941 this kind of 360-degree information manipulation was a long, long way off. There was still internal tension at Bletchley Park, between the boffins, Oxbridge donnish types, who would sit around discussing abstract maths and algorithmic solutions to the Enigma and Lorenz (the German naval code), and the old codebreaking sweats from the inter-war years, who wanted to get on with attacking the enemy's codes. Bletchley was a lousy posting too, with its prefabs, poor billets and siloed working method. Some Bletchley Park men were presented with white feathers in the town. As the place expanded, its methods were refined and machines like the Bombe developed. When decrypting was successful, it made up for the times they had got behind on cracking codes – material could get cold or stale the longer it was examined; other times the sheer volume of stuff to look at was overwhelming and hard to prioritize. Finding a way through was going to take time and argument, and it would be led by results.

Nevertheless, some rules evolved for Bletchley Park's clients to observe:

> The two main principles to be observed are:-
>   That it is never worth risking the source for a momentary tactical advantage, and,
>   That steps must always be taken, when an endeavour is to be made to anticipate enemy action, to cover our fore-knowledge of events by aerial or other reconnaissance.[4]

The Luftwaffe's profligacy with ill-disciplined signalling – operators with a distinctive 'fist', using the same 'random' letters to set the Enigma's wheels, as well as sending repeated sets of information which offered the possibility of patterns to any codebreaker – as well as an early breakthrough with Enigma by Polish codebreakers, meant that GC&CS had broken into the Luftwaffe's communications by the summer of 1940. Come 1941, with Fall MERKUR in the pipeline, the Luftwaffe's leaky comms had told British commanders privy to Source everything they needed to know about the upcoming attack. Numbers, objectives, the lot. An analysis of German *Fallschirmjäger* operations the year before made it clear that defending airfields was critical to repulsing an airborne landing – it had paid such dividends for the Dutch at The Hague when they prevented the Germans from flying in reinforcements the previous summer. For all their elite glamour and exciting propaganda, the *Fallschirmjäger* were defeatable. Knowing where they were headed – the airfields – would surely clinch victory for Freyberg and the newly christened CREFORCE.

*

CREFORCE itself, though, was hardly in good shape to defend the island. The British had first garrisoned Crete in November 1940 because it lay like a strategic shield between Greece and North Africa, and though its infrastructure was basic – one road stretched the length of the island along the northern coast – its position meant it could not go ignored by British planners. British priorities kept changing, so the garrison there never received the armament – particularly anti-aircraft weapons – that in an ideal world it would have. Three rudimentary airfields had been built, Maleme, Heraklion and Rethymno, and only one port, on the northern coast, was vaguely suitable, though its facilities were pretty inadequate. The fishing villages on the southern coast couldn't handle modern shipping, and besides they weren't connected to roads for loading or offloading heavy equipment. Not that there was much equipment for CREFORCE when the time came. The campaign in Greece had been a disaster, another evacuation, another withdrawal with kit being abandoned Dunkirk-style – some of the contingent that arrived in Crete from 25 April 1941 were tank soldiers without any tanks; there were artillerymen without guns too. Morale was at best shaky, in some reports plain panicky. German air power in particular had the British, Australian and New Zealand soldiers spooked. British Expeditionary Forces now had the reputation for flight: 'Back Every Fortnight.' By the time the Greek campaign had ended and men started arriving on Crete the RAF's planes had gone too, either lost in Greece or buggered off to Egypt.

To start with, Freyberg was dismayed at the men gathering on Crete. He cabled Churchill saying that what he had at his disposal wasn't up to the task of repulsing the planned German landings. The formations that had arrived in Crete were incomplete, disorganized, ill-equipped and demoralized. The island lacked the infrastructure for a modern (supposedly) mechanized army to fight. There was only one brigade that was properly organized, the 14th Brigade from 6th Division, made up of regulars. The remaining men – two brigades of Kiwis and one of Aussies – had arrived with rifles and Bren guns and little else. In Alexandria, Freyberg's boss, Archie Wavell – whose military career had fallen into the bitter pattern of managing withdrawal after withdrawal – ordered him to stand and fight, to hold Crete at all costs, doubtless buoyed by the Allies' knowledge of the Luftwaffe's operational plans. Some tanks were sent from

Alexandria, to be used against airborne troops, confidently assuming that there would be no anti-tank weapons to deal with.

In the first couple of weeks of May, Wavell and Freyberg talked themselves into thinking Crete could be defended: in a communiqué to the men, Wavell told them that the withdrawal from Greece had been a 'great feat of arms'.[5] Erm . . . Freyberg's general order of 1 May had all the necessary pep, doubtless privately seasoned with knowledge of what was to come:

> If [!] he attacks us here in Crete, the enemy will be meeting our troops upon even terms [. . .] I am confident that the force at our disposal will be adequate to defeat any attack that may be delivered upon this island.[6]

Two weeks later he wrote to Wavell:

> I have completed plans for Defence of Crete . . . Everywhere all ranks are fit and moral *[sic]* is now high . . . We have 45 field guns in action with adequate ammunition dumped. Two infantry tanks are at each aerodrome . . . I do not wish to seem overconfident but I feel that at least we will give an excellent account of ourselves . . . I trust Crete will be held.[7]

Freyberg had 42,000 men at his disposal, half of them infantry, the rest all sorts. Ten thousand of CREFORCE were Greek troops. But his defences were prepared. Even if he didn't have proper radios or air superiority, he outnumbered the expected Germans two-to-one: the Salamander was ready to face the fire.

*

The first day of Fall MERKUR was a nightmare for both sides. The *Fallschirmjäger* parachute was attached at a single point on the paratrooper's back, rather than at the shoulders, and the man in the harness would dangle helplessly as he descended. German paratroopers wore elbow and knee pads in anticipation of landing sprawled in a star shape, rather than upright on their feet. They also jumped without anything more powerful than a pistol or a knife, for fear of snagging a rifle or machine gun with their rigging lines; weapons were dropped in containers and the men had to get to them once they had landed so that they could fight. The result for the doughty *Fallschirmjäger* was a bloodbath. III Battalion, the 1st Assault Regiment suffered brutally: of a company of 126, there were only fourteen survivors – by the end of the day the battalion had lost two-thirds of its strength. The massacre was likened to a pheasant shoot. Similar slaughters occurred at Heraklion and Rethymno. Gliders – so brilliantly and decisively deployed at Eben-Emael – were mortared as soon as they landed, killing the men inside them even before they had the chance to disembark. At Kastelli, a Greek force led by a Kiwi PT instructor dished out similar punishment to the invaders; this was followed up in the spirit of point 9 of the *Fallschirmjäger* 'Ten Commandments' – 'Fight chivalrously against an honest foe; armed irregulars deserve no quarter' – with the murder of the Greek combatants.

The landings, however, were accompanied by heavy aerial bombardment – the Luftwaffe having complete command of the skies over Crete in the RAF's absence more than made up for any lack of German artillery or naval gunnery. And while what anti-aircraft guns there were had great sport shooting down approaching Ju52s at

400 feet, the planes splitting apart and men tumbling to their deaths in flames, they weren't enough to resist the air attacks plaguing the landings, which knocked out the British field guns. Morale had been badly battered by German air attack in Greece and for the men on the ground it felt like more of the same, with the RAF nowhere to be seen.

It was at Maleme airfield – which Freyberg knew the Germans were determined to capture so that they could reinforce the initial landings with heavier troops and heavier kit – that the battle was lost. Freyberg had been unclear in his instructions to his officers about how vital it was that the airfields were held; it seems he was doing this to protect Source, to make sure that the secret of the secrets he was party to would be protected. Besides, Source or no Source, holding the airfields regardless was the obvious thing to do. In the confusion of the first night, the battalions holding Hill 107, which overlooked Maleme airfield, withdrew. During the day the men of the 5th Brigade, under Brigadier James Hargest, had improvised an attack using the two Matilda II tanks that were on hand. Men from an anti-aircraft battery had joined in – although ammunition was running low there were still men up for the fight and keen to dislodge the paratroopers from the RAF buildings at Maleme. Unfortunately, the tanks were unable to press the attack home – with one gun jammed, they withdrew. The battalion commander on the ground, Lieutenant Colonel Leslie Andrew VC, decided that because his men were exhausted, and their morale worn down by the air attack, he should withdraw from Hill 107. During the withdrawal he had lost contact with two of his companies, who were left behind. Freyberg's failure to insist on defensive priorities, the disjointed nature of his command and the fragile morale situation he had inherited meant they were no match for the determination of the Germans to take Crete. Hargest certainly blamed Freyberg for the blunder of letting Maleme fall into enemy hands, a mistake which smarted all the more given his access to Source.

With Maleme seized, Student directed the bulk of his efforts there, leaving the other landings at Rethymno and Heraklion to their own devices. Maleme, at the eastern end of Crete, was nearest to mainland Greece and its airfields, which made Student's task that much easier. The Germans were able to land a battalion of more the heavily armed 5th Mountain Division troops directly by plane, rather than relying on gliders or parachutes. The British continued shelling the airfield as best they could but the initiative had swung to the Germans, even after such a bloodily disastrous first day. They brought mountain howitzers with them, their own portable artillery. In the chaos, new defensive lines were thrown up and overcome by the increasingly confident Germans.

Freyberg's response was further hindered, this time by what he knew from Source. Bletchley Park had warned of an amphibious element to the German landings, and Freyberg thought he would need to defend Crete from these landings as well, even though the Germans knew they didn't really have the capability for such a landing and, beyond air cover, had no way to stop the Royal Navy from intervening. Hesitant about what to do next, at the very moment the Germans had taken control of the battle at the eastern end of the island, Freyberg's efforts to counterattack stalled. Freyberg felt that his infantry had fought well against the Germans, though his other men – sappers, cooks, clerks, tankless tank-men – had not delivered, but then, could they be expected to? It was the German command of the air, and its effect on the morale of the British, that had been decisive. A one-dimensional infantry-versus-infantry battle may have been more of an even match, but the dominance of German air power – almost regardless of the limits of its destructive power, its very presence was destructive in itself – decided the fate of CREFORCE. For all the dogged bayonet charges the Kiwis put in, the battle had slithered out of Freyberg's grasp and firmly into Student's, who, after the disasters of the first day, couldn't believe his luck. His intelligence had been all wrong: the Germans had estimated that Crete was held by only 5,000 men – had they known the true strength of CREFORCE, would Fall MERKUR even have gone ahead? Within a week of the landings, despite the arrival of 800 commandos under Colonel Bob Laycock (LAYFORCE, as satirized by Evelyn Waugh in his *Sword of Honour* trilogy*, calling the commandos HOOKFORCE), morale within Freyberg's DUKE troops wobbled and finally broke. Laycock's men had arrived just in time to join the withdrawal. Another evacuation was on. Over the spine of mountains to the southern coast Freyberg's men trekked in desperate droves, the British Empire once again defeated by German vim and decisiveness. The German aura of invincibility was further burnished.

In this pell-mell evacuation, 18,000 of Freyberg's men were rescued; 12,000 men were left behind and taken prisoner, 3,579 killed, 1,918 wounded. The Royal Navy, which

---

* Waugh's description of the chaos of the evacuation, unsentimental, disappointed, proud, is probably the best place to start when reading about Crete.

had done an excellent job of stopping what seaborne land-ings the Germans had attempted, had paid a high price, losing six destroyers and three cruisers, and 2,000 sailors. The German butcher's bill was worse: 3,774 killed or miss-ing and 2,120 wounded, these elite troops had been spent on what would quickly become a dead end. Crete became a strategic backwater for the Germans, who had neither the resources nor the inclination to turn it into an airbase to properly threaten Alexandria – Hitler had bigger fish to fry in the Soviet Union that summer. The only silver lining for the British in this evacuation was they didn't abandon their heavy kit; then again, they didn't really have any.

*

Another defeat. Another evacuation. Another intelligence failure. For all that Freyberg knew about the enemy's intentions, he couldn't really be sure of what they might do next. CREFORCE, thrown together in defeat, facing an opponent of growing confidence . . . who could have done better in these circumstances? The bloody nose that the *Fallschirmjäger* had been given by CREFORCE meant the end for airborne troops as a German strategic asset; while Göring's empire-building continued and more and more parachute formations were recruited, they were never used on such a scale again – the occasional drop went ahead but nothing like Fall MERKUR. Freyberg later consoled himself with this minuscule crumb of com-fort. Freyberg's biggest fan, Winston Churchill, placed no blame on the Salamander – instead he blamed Wavell, whom he didn't get along with anyway.

The lesson here was that it was no good knowing what the enemy might be about to do if you weren't able to counteract him. You needed heavy weapons even if the enemy lacked heavy weapons of his own, especially if you were fighting men who thought that Commandment No. 4 was the key to success: 'Calm and caution, vigour and determination, valour and a fanatical offensive spirit will make you superior in attack.' The British had to have another rethink, another bout of head-scratching, dreaming up more new ways to defeat the undefeatable. Back to the desert and the drawing board – what solutions would a soldier of a more intellectual frame of mind make of the business of beating the Germans?

3

Francis Tuker

The pattern of war

With its red eagle flash, the 4th Indian Infantry Division
fought in nine campaigns, leading the way on both sides of
the Mediterranean. It fought at Sidi Barrani, at Keren, as
part of Operation BATTLEAXE at Tobruk, as well as in
Syria, at El Alamein, in Tunisia at the Mareth Line and at
Wadi Akarit, at Monte Cassino and on through Italy to
the Gothic Line – battle honours as comprehensive as
those of any division in the Med. Formed in the hasty days
of Indian Army expansion at the very start of the war, the
4th Indian Infantry Division had been raised in Egypt from
a 'mobilization skeleton', a paper formation as part of 'R
Plan', mustered 'in the shadows of the Pyramids' and then
dispersed for training, in anticipation of whatever the
Middle Eastern theatre might bring. At the end of 1941,
the division was entrusted to a new commanding officer,
Francis Tuker. He took over from Major General Frank
Messervy, whose departing message said the division had
been given the code name of 'NONSTOP'. In that
respect, its new boss was the perfect fit. Tuker went on to
command the 4th Indian Infantry Division for three long
years of campaigning, through defeat in the desert to victory in Italy.

'Gertie' Tuker – in the way you could in the Indian

Army – shaped the 4th Indian Infantry Division into his ideal fighting unit, training his officers his way, firing anyone who didn't fit, even prepared to resign if his command was interfered with. He believed passionately in the division as the fighting unit with critical mass on the battlefield. An old Indian Army hand, he had started out commanding his beloved Gurkhas, and advocated training hard and fighting easy. It paid dividends. Major General Tuker took Von Armin's surrender in Tunisia, some 250,000 men. His division had its admirers further up the food chain too: amongst Tuker's admirers was Field Marshal Lord Wavell who rated Tuker and his division highly.

Tuker was proud to say that he knew command was his calling – as he says in his memoir of the North African campaign, *Approach to Battle*, published in 1963:

> I have tried my hand at many other things in my life – farming, commercial horticulture, authorship, training horses, painting, etching and engraving [he leaves out poetry, though he had published a volume in 1944] . . . and none have I found so testing and so difficult as the planning and conduct of a successful land battle against a worthy foe, whether against the guerrilla or the enemy who is fully equipped for war.[1]

In this book, Francis Tuker tackled his time in the desert – where he learned his trade as a divisional general par excellence – and he wrote about leadership (or rather 'command') in the book's preface. He doesn't take long over it: you get the immediate sense that Tuker wasn't a man to dwell on things or to go in for explanations of matters he already understood. Tuker's career was perhaps hindered by his lack of tolerance for those who couldn't keep up, particularly if they were his superiors, who – he felt – should have been able to follow his arguments. He could cajole, nudge and bully his peers, and his superiors if he felt he could get away with it – during the epic battles at Monte Cassino he subjected Freyberg to forthright lobbying about how best to prosecute his campaign. Freyberg found it easiest to agree with Tuker and then make his own decisions. Tuker didn't have this problem with the men he commanded as he had made sure they knew exactly what he was about and how he liked to do things. But in his memoir, he cautioned too, rather strongly, against armchair generals. He went further, suggesting that academics aren't qualified to analyse battle, and as for civilians . . .

> In war, administration is as much a matter of hard work and improvisation as of skill, whereas to fight a successful land battle against a formidable enemy is, I believe, the most difficult of all skilled achievements. What does the civilian historian really know about it?[2]

Good question.

Tuker regarded himself – amongst all his other side interests – as a historian (goodness knows what he would have made of the likes of your author). A military historian, but a historian nonetheless. He approached soldiering and command, and his experience of the men he served with, in historical terms: intellectually, almost abstractly. He saw himself as a thinker. After his career in the army ended, with his reputation as a divisional commander gleaming, after his success standing in as a corps commander in Burma when Frank Messervy (that man again) of IV Corps took a month's leave, followed by his work in handing over the Indian Army to the new Indian state, he wrote not just memoirs but several books on the history of warfare, his theory, its practice, and what he thought of the British military establishment and its approach to battle. Tuker's broad sweep took in the history of all warfare, and he offered prognostications on the future of war in the nuclear age, as well as a history of the Indian Army. In his other memoir, *While Memory Serves* (1950), he was scathing about partition, the politicians who devised it and its execution, though he remained a loyal servant of the Indian Army even as it split into two. But his theoretical book, *The Pattern of War*, published in 1948, is the product of a keen and decided mind, and boasts an encyclopaedic knowledge of the theory and history of warfare, seasoned with his personal experiences.

During the inter-war years, as a historian and a student of war, Tuker had made a name for himself as a pain in the arse. He thought that the teaching at Camberley was terrible – and said so. He submitted material to service publications under a couple of pen names, 'Auspex' and 'John Helland'. These articles had been in the Tuker style, not suffering fools and finding the current thinking insufficiently rigorous. They hadn't gone down well. When he came to write *The Pattern of War*, it clearly still bothered him that he hadn't had the reception he had hoped for. He thought the inter-war years were an 'Ice Age' of military thinking:

> when it was forbidden that one should write in the civil press about the possibilities of war and the making of war in the future: when military journals refused to accept argument which denied the rightness of

fighting a war upon a linear system: when one's files became choked with articles returned because they were so controversial that the editors and most of the readers would not agree with them.[3]

But buoyed with the prestige of his military career, Francis Tuker could lay out his intellectual stall and, for all his experience, his beliefs had not fundamentally shifted. He wrote of warfare in terms of manoeuvre, how warfare shifts from one form of manoeuvre to another, sometimes via periods when it is static. During these phases of static warfare, the single, simple problem is how to get moving again. 'Jenghiz Khan', as Tuker calls him, showed the world the full potential of the warfare of manoeuvre. Indeed, drawing on his interest in art, Tuker compared the leader of the Mongol hordes to Rembrandt and Aristotle:

> Just as Rembrandt has done almost everything that is known today of etching, just as Aristotle said two thousand years ago almost all that was then to be said of philosophy, so does it seem that Jenghiz Khan has shown us almost all that there is to be shown of land fighting.[4]

With this in mind, and rather more up to date, he condemned the policy makers behind the Maginot Line for not realizing that time was up for static warfare after four years of First World War deadlock on the Western Front. Manoeuvre was bound to return, once it was figured out how to execute manoeuvre with tanks, artillery and supply, and, lo and behold, it did. For Tuker, it all came down to three principles:

First condition. Flanks shall be tactically open or it shall be possible to create a flank by a break-in and break-through.

Secondly, the mobile arm shall be predominant (and in the mobile arm is included the mobile arm of bombardment and air landing, the air force).

Thirdly, that it shall be possible to administer the mobile arm to the point at which it will decide the battle and gain decisive victory.[5]

Being mobile, not getting stuck, not getting hung up on holding territory if it stopped you being mobile, was key to Tuker's thinking: this was what 'Auspex' and 'John Helland' had been banging on about before the Second World War began, but, given his tendency to bang on about stuff and not suffer fools, as well as making demands for an expensive way of doing things that ran against the grain, Tuker hadn't gained the traction he'd have liked. His networking wasn't what it might have been, perhaps. And besides, it was peacetime. There wasn't going to be another continental war; the Indian Army was a colonial gendarmerie and/or border force, it didn't need Gertie Tuker's ruminations on armoured warfare. But apart from this study of history, his analysis of Gustavus Adolphus in the Thirty Years' War, 'Jenghiz Kahn', of course, and Oliver Cromwell's use of horses, how had Francis Tuker come to these three immutable principles before he had to put them into practice with the 4th Indian Infantry Division?

*

Francis Ivan Simms Tuker, born in Twickenham in July 1894, educated in Brighton, had joined the army before the First World War; he'd been commissioned in 1914 into the Royal Sussex Regiment after his time at Sandhurst, but transferred to the Gurkhas later in the year.* No mud and blood for Gertie. Instead, in 1916, as acting captain with the 2nd Gurkha Rifles, he took part in the campaign in Mesopotamia (now Iraq) against the collapsing Ottoman Empire. For the first third of the year, the British fought a series of what get called inconclusive battles attempting to break out of the siege of Kut (they're defeats if what you're trying to do is win) – a long and gruelling campaign that has none of the glamour or the irresistible opportunities for ANZAC national foundation myths of the previous year's slugfest in Gallipoli, and none of the insurgent dash (perceived or otherwise) of Lawrence's exploits in Arabia. Kut was a slog and a stalemate. In April, Kut finally fell, with 13,000 British soldiers falling into Ottoman hands; that same month, 21-year-old Tuker was wounded.

Then – fully promoted to captain – in 1918, he had fought in the Kuki punitive expedition, leading a Gurkha column as part of the British effort to put down a rising, a campaign that went so badly that it was completely denied by the embarrassed Indian government. This sort of thing was the bread and butter of the Indian Army, beyond its role as the empire's Middle Eastern reserves. The campaign played out in the Assam hills, where Bill Slim would bring the Japanese to battle in 1944. The Kuki people had given the Indian Army a proper runaround; locals armed with muskets had shamed the

* Tuker loved the Gurkhas so much he wrote their history: *Gorkha: The Story of the Gurkhas of Nepal* (1957).

Indian Army's finest. The rising had been triggered by the First World War and is a sorry tale of imperial misrule and religious tensions in imperial India. Asked to supply labour rather than soldiers for the war effort, the rulers of the Indian Princely States set about levying a workforce. Manipur, in north-eastern India, offered a labour corps of 2,000 men. However, there was a catch. Hindu subjects were spared and the burden fell on Christians and animists, Naga and Kuki tribesmen, 1,200 of whom were pressed into service. If village chiefs couldn't meet the required levies, they were forced to. An uprising followed, understandably, an asymmetric struggle between an Indian Army that didn't know the land and the highly motivated Kuki villagers.

The campaign had run for two years, and the Kukis paid the price of pulling the imperial lion's tail: 140 rebel villages were destroyed, 112 villages 'submitted', while 25 were found deserted. The Indian Army quietly dished out awards – military OBEs and CBEs and Indian Distinguished Service Medals – in a way that marked it as a proper low-key disaster; men who had served in the Kuki punitive expedition were denied a clasp on their Indian General Service Medal, though they got British Victory Medals. Two men were mentioned in dispatches but that were unpublished – almost perfectly militarily oxymoronic. The Indian Army had defeated the Kukis by using modern firepower, marching into villages, confiscating livestock and demanding their submission. A village that submitted would have a political officer placed with it and its chief arrested – problem supposedly solved. Little wonder that when the Japanese invaded in 1942 plenty of Burmese were delighted to see the back of the British. Characteristically for a campaign in Burma, most of the Indian Army's casualties came from disease.

Tuker wrote about the Kuki campaign in *The Pattern of War*, how 'some half-naked savages' had taught him a lesson in the three principles of warfare. Tuker had taken the advice of old hands on how to move between villages, in a long, snake-like column with men at the front like horns covering its head. The Kuki rebels would strike from their villages at the vulnerable Gurkha columns, using their mobility against Tuker's men. The villages were stockades and Tuker would not know where the next attack would come from. He hadn't recognized it yet but the enemy was using the very principles he would shortly arrive at. Captain Tuker realized, 'after nearly being destroyed on my second day out', that the old advice, the received wisdom, was no good to him. It seems strange that the Indian Army, with its traditional role of 'watch and ward' as it was known, and with so much experience of fighting these kinds of punitive campaigns, might not really have known what it was doing. Even with its advantages in terms of weapons technology, it couldn't prosecute a counter-insurgency. Sticking to roads, relying on columns and getting outflanked all sounds very much like what would later go wrong in Burma in 1942. The problem, Tuker felt, was deep-seated: officers simply weren't serious about soldiering, hadn't given enough, if any, thought to the essentials and how they would then apply those essentials to every new campaign that came their way. Reeling from his near-disaster in the Assam hills, Tuker relied on his own counsel.

A very much bewildered young officer, the night after
the battle, I sat in the middle of my column while the

men built a stockade for the night about us and there on a piece of paper I wrote down these conditions which were working against me, and devised the manner in which I would operate in order to turn the tables upon the enemy.[6]

Captain Tuker decided the way to go was patrol, find the enemy and ambush them as they tried to move into position to attack him. It worked – though Tuker also made sure he gave credit to the superior weapons he had at his disposal.

He got back to Imphal and wrote a paper delineating his experiences and laying out his conclusions. His recommendation was to copy the Kuki people: build fortresses in the jungle as solid bases from which to patrol, locate the enemy and then proceed to attack – using the enemy's method against them, because the enemy understood the three principles of warfare better than the Indian Army did. Having superior weapons would then offer the Gurkhas the advantage that they sought, and the enemy could be driven into the jungle 'to starve'. He submitted his paper for discussion.

After a great deal of discussion this course was adopted and the campaign swiftly brought to an end.[7]

I imagine the discussion was pretty lively.

After the Kuki expedition, Tuker fought in yet another forgotten British imperial campaign. While the Great Game may have ended with the collapse of Tsarist Russia, a new game with Bolshevik rules had begun with the Soviet Union. While the Civil War raged in Russia itself, with Britain sending troops to assist the White Russians in their struggle against the Red Army, the new Soviet Union had been making friends on its southern border. This was a war of changing countries and polities, of moving borders, and rather upsets the popular perception of the First World War as static and pointless. Inside Persia/Iran (depending on your point of view at the time, which mattered greatly), a growing communist movement had been encouraged (to say the least) by the Russian Revolution. A Soviet republic in Persia was born, known as the Socialist Soviet republic of Gilan. The British garrison in the port of Anzali on the Caspian Sea had to bugger off sharpish with the arrival of the Soviet Caspian fleet in May 1920. During the last year of the Great War proper and into 1919, the British Malleson Mission had been doing what it could to keep the Germans out of neighbouring Turkestan and, while it was at it, also tangling with the Bolsheviks. With the end of the war, there were tens of thousands of German and Austrian prisoners of war fleeing Russia in the mix, as well as Cossacks trying to resist the Soviets and general indecipherable chaos. In Persia, Dunsterforce, under Major General Lionel Dunsterville, had been spinning similar political plates, trying to keep the Soviets out and the right people in, all as the end of the war and its consequences were playing out. A column with armoured cars had headed north from Baghdad towards the Caspian, and they spent their time trying to work out who was friend and foe. Operations the following year, 1920, were supposed to stabilize and protect British interests. The Soviet republic eventually collapsed; a friendly Persian government was installed. Tuker was left frustrated by how amateurish the whole thing seemed.

In the 1920s, Tuker returned to Britain, married and

attended the Staff College from 1925 to 1926. Then he headed back to India, where his army career got under way properly and he busied himself developing his training techniques. While Tuker may have been regarded as too pushy by his contemporaries, he did at the same time gain a reputation for being an excellent trainer of men: a phrase that tends to linger around generals known for being hard work, a little too keen. He laid it out clearly in *Approach to Battle* using the old axiom 'Train hard: fight easy'.

*

In many ways Tuker's career is not unlike those of plenty of his contemporaries who went on to reach high command during the Second World War (nor is it that unlike those of the duds either). But I am acutely aware as I write this, and take you through his musings on the nature of his trade, that he is one of the more obscure figures in this book. He didn't achieve fame or acclaim outside the army. Why does the man who commanded the best division in the Indian Army for three years not have a reputation as such? Why did he not attain higher office? Why is he in the who-is-this-guy file?

Two reasons spring to mind immediately, reasons that go beyond the fact that Indian Army officers always seemed to be at the back of the queue for recognition, especially if they only fought in the Mediterranean and further east. Tuker's inability to suffer fools, especially his superiors or men alongside him at corps level who, he thought, should have known better, meant that he rubbed lots of important people up the wrong way. However, this can't completely explain why he isn't remembered and why he didn't go further. After all, the story of the Second World War and Allied Command often seems stuffed with prima donnas and feuds, ill-tempered exchanges between key players, passive-aggressive sniping, men being humbled by circumstance or the enemy and taking their revenge on those around them. Montgomery, for instance, once he had become 'Monty', definitely gained an indelible reputation for appalling behaviour – quick to brand those who had failed him as 'useless', upsetting his superiors, distressing his allies with his attitude, falling out with senior officers during the last phase of the war almost to the point of losing his job.

Another simple factor working against Tuker was his health: it wasn't quite up to it. Tuker suffered from bouts of rheumatoid arthritis that would force him to his sick bed – often at moments of crucial importance (though when you are a divisional commander, most moments are of crucial importance). In the end, in February 1944, Tuker's arthritis meant he had to relinquish command of his beloved 4th Indian Infantry Division. He wasn't the only high-ranking Allied officer to suffer from an illness that hampered his ability to do his job. It was common, and given the high-stress jobs commanders were doing (though usually* away from the immediate peril of the front line), not exactly surprising. Ill health dogged even those at the

---

* Generals did get killed. For example, a fondness for being in the thick of it did for the 1st Airborne Division's Major General George Hopkinson in Italy in 1943, when he went forward to see what was going on and was killed by machine-gun fire. The memory of this tragedy may have contributed to the air of caution that surrounded Major General Roy Urquhart the following year when he went forward at Arnhem to see what was happening.

very highest level – the strain of the war killed Roosevelt and almost saw Churchill to his grave.

For all Churchill's desire to become a man of destiny and his enjoyment of the thrill of war, the workload and the strain were almost too much. By the time the Big Three met in Tehran in 1943, the war had only really being going the Allies' way for twelve months (Burma aside, where good news still remained elusive), and the reversals and collapses and evacuations of the first three years of the war had played havoc with Churchill's health (not to mention his personal diet and habits). Passenger flights were relatively novel in the 1940s and far more dangerous than they are now, and the strain of long, cold flights on a man in his seventies who was a keen smoker and drinker was enormous, regardless of the immense responsibilities he bore. On returning to Cairo after Tehran, where the Big Three had vigorously and provocatively toasted each other into the small hours in a dense fug of tobacco smoke, Churchill started to go downhill fast, and by the time he had got to his third stop in Carthage, his personal doctor, Lord Moran, decided that his patient needed an X-ray. A patch of pneumonia was discovered on his lung. Churchill was given antibiotics – in themselves novel at the time – and Moran had also made sure that he ordered heart medicine, as the patient was complaining that his heart was alarming him. Churchill's wife, Clementine, was flown to North Africa and for a couple of days Moran feared for the Prime Minister's life. (Shockingly poor health didn't deter Churchill from the pursuit of power in later life; when he returned to office in the 1950s he was entirely clapped out and suffered a series of mini-strokes.)

There was no shortage of casualties at the top. General 'Hap' Arnold, who commanded the US Army Air Force on a similarly relentless schedule, had four heart attacks, two in 1943, one in 1944 and the last in 1945. He was kept on after his first heart attack on the condition that he didn't work so hard; unable to take this medical advice, he carried on working and his health didn't improve. Montgomery's right-hand man and diplomatic shield Freddie de Guingand suffered from nervous exhaustion and depression. De Guingand's illness tended to kick in when things were going really badly for his chief (or, chicken-and-egg style, when he was sick, things went really badly for his boss). Tuker was not exceptional in this regard, he was simply unlucky.

When he took command of the 4th Indian Infantry Division, Tuker's workload was exacerbated by how dispersed the 4th Indian Infantry Division was; he had to fly all over the Levant and Egypt to stay in touch with his men. He found this greatly frustrating, believing as he did in the division as the army's key large unit, and he wanted his division to train and fight as a whole; being dispersed was an impediment to perfection. He was also, as he later recorded, dismayed with the quality of the equipment available. Tuker makes it clear, in his memoir *Approach to Battle*, that he believed you should train with what you have rather than wish for weapons that might yet arrive, but then goes on to outline the deficiencies of British weapons in the desert. The issue of equipment was to bedevil the British Army right through the war: there was a nagging sense that the supply was always slightly behind. Central to Tuker's – and everyone else fighting in the desert's – complaints were the anti-tank weapons. In 1941, while

British industry was gearing itself to building a strategic bombing fleet, the manufacture of tanks and anti-tank weapons fell behind. The 2-pounder anti-tank guns sat at the centre of British woes, and Tuker makes it clear how much he was irked by them, calling them 'pop guns'. The 2-pounder had neither the firepower nor the range to be effective in a mobile offensive role or in defence. A 2-pounder would have to be dug in in the hope German tanks would be lured into passing by with their flanks vulnerable, yet the desert was very difficult to dig into. The British faced a crisis in their equipment.

The 2-pounder, which had been an adequate defence against tanks in France the year before, was now obsolete. But, to Tuker's (and everyone else's) frustration, it had been rendered obsolete by a change in the terrain it was being used to fight in, rather than by any particular advances in German technology. The 2-pounder, on its platform, was essentially a defensive weapon, but a defensive weapon designed principally for fighting armour in North-West Europe, which was, after all, and it is perhaps ungenerous in hindsight to fault this, where the British expected to be fighting tanks.

With its 40mm shell, the anti-tank version of the 2-pounder was built by military-industrial heavyweight Vickers (it had first arrived fitted to Vickers' own Cruiser Tank Mk I in 1938), and it boasted an innovative three-legged gun carriage that folded out beneath it; the wheels would be popped off and placed either side when the gun was deployed. It was, when it was delivered, entirely state of the art, with magnification optics and a high-velocity shell that travelled at 2,600 feet per second. The BEF had 2-pounders distributed within its infantry divisions, though nowhere near as many as it thought it needed. It then left them behind at Dunkirk: the Germans took and redesignated them. Even at this point it was clear that a harder-hitting anti-tank weapon would be needed, and work on what was to subsequently become the 6-pounder quickly began. However, because of the spectre of imminent invasion by German Panzers, the decision was made to produce as many anti-tank weapons as possible – and that meant sticking with the 2-pounder rather than switching to the more powerful 6-pounder.* The army needed anti-tank weapons. Something was better than nothing, and switching to mass production of an untried type was beyond even the mighty Vickers.

British doctrine in 1940 called for anti-tank defence in depth – enemy tanks would be drawn into a grid of anti-tank artillery and destroyed. In France, in close or even open country, there was sufficient cover or ground that the gun could be dug into: guns could be concealed and used as they had been designed. Unseen, the gunners could wait for the enemy tanks to approach and strike at a range that would cause lethal damage. This country evened out the advantages that different weapons' ranges offered. The Germans had essentially the same kit in the desert in 1941, the early marks of Panzer, the simple, light tanks that had swept to victory from the Ardennes, and the notoriously powerful 88mm Flak guns, but in the desert there was no cover, the ground was difficult to dig into. A 2-pounder crew, as Tuker explains, would have to wait for the

* At this point the awesome 17-pounder, which came into service within a mere two years of the 2-pounder being everywhere and letting everyone down, was a mere twinkle in the Corps of Artillery's eye.

Germans to get close enough – the Germans with their 88s and their other artillery could safely pick off the 2-pounder crews from a distance. Fortunately, in dire straits the army's field gun, the 25-pounder, designed for an indirect role, could fire solid shot and could be used in the anti-tank role. But this meant they weren't being used elsewhere, besides if German tanks got close enough to the 25-pounder artillery batteries then things had gone badly wrong. The army's planned mode of defence, defending in depth with 2-pounders, was impossible. This disadvantage extended to tanks, unfortunately, again because of the 2-pounder.

*

British tanks were a mixed bag.* There is no doubt that by the end of the war the British had figured out what they wanted from their armour and how to build a machine to deliver it. But the path to the Centurion – which arrived in time for VE Day – was not smooth. British tank doctrine had bifurcated: cruiser tanks and infantry tanks were the order of the day in the run-up to war. Simply put, the infantry tank would support the infantry, the cruiser would then exploit the breakthrough. The infantry tank would be slower, with no real need to go faster than walking pace; the cruiser tank was designed to be quick. That meant the infantry tank had thicker armour, and the cruiser's speed and manoeuvrability made up for its light armour: a fleeting target was harder to hit. In 1941, the infantry tank supreme was the Matilda II, which had shone in France in

* Here your author sails blithely into a battlefield drenched in ink. I'll keep it brief.

the Arras counter-attack the year before, when a scratch formation of British armour had given Rommel himself a fright (though this was in 1940 and he was plain old Rommel rather than 'Rommel!' or the 'Desert Fox'). The Matilda II's thick armour had served it well against everything the Germans had, except for the dreaded 88s. In the desert, in terrain it hadn't been designed for, it was slow and Tuker was not alone in regarding it as a sitting duck. The Valentine which followed was quicker but had no protection for its suspension. By 1942, the latest cruiser tank, the Crusader, which in theory would do better in the desert purely because of its speed, had come on line. The Crusader had many of the attributes that would endure in British tank design through the rest of the war, but it was unreliable – a broken-down tank was yet another easy target for the German guns with their longer range. But the thing that united these tanks in their unsuitability for the desert – apart from the mechanical drawbacks of being designed for temperate climes – was, you guessed it, the 2-pounder gun they were armed with.

And here I've done what tends to happen in tank discussions, I've got hung up on their anti-tank capabilities rather than describe them as part of an integrated combat system. Roughly and simply: tanks, infantry and artillery were supposed to work mutually to help one another. Tanks were supposed to protect infantry and artillery, infantry were supposed to protect tanks and artillery, and artillery to provide protection for the other arms. But if tanks were vulnerable at such a distance as to render them ineffective, they couldn't offer the protection and assistance they were meant to. So, of course, tanks needed to be able to tackle other tanks, but they also needed to be able to knock out infantry strong points like bunkers and machine-gun nests, as well as engage enemy anti-tank artillery (and, if they were on a roll, artillery proper). And guns that were suited to the anti-tank gun role were not ideal for this: the anti-tank gun firing solid or hardened shot doesn't really cover the high-explosive or more artillery role that was also needed. So not having a multi-purpose weapon and being equipped only with an anti-tank weapon, the 2-pounder, that was inadequate, made the tanks doubly badly armed. It wasn't until the American Grant tank, which carried two guns, arrived in 1942 that British tanks were able to shell German targets – whatever they were – from a safer distance.

At the heart of this problem were the contradictions and restrictions around which defence policy revolved. Britain, as a maritime power, knew that any army it would put into the field had to be transportable by sea. Tanks and any other weapons systems it might need to use in any future war weren't going to be designed with deployment in Britain in mind. British warfare was always expeditionary. (Your author hopes that in saying this he isn't talking down to the reader, but the point really does need emphasizing.) Tanks and guns and everything else would have to be shipped to the continent or wherever else they might be needed, and to get it to port it would have to be transported by rail. In 1940, the BEF's logisticians had decided that it would operate at most 40 miles from the railhead. Rail loading gauge limits dictated how wide and heavy a tank could be and that meant that the turrets they were designed with could only house the 2-pounder gun. The tanks that were shipped to the desert met all the logistic and industrial demands asked of them, but as Tuker puts it:

It is self-evident that in a theatre of war which offered little cover from view and few obstacles to movement, long-range wagons borne on very mobile carriers would be the most effective. In the more enclosed spaces of Europe, the same hard-hitting weapon would be needed, while at least for a proportion of the carriers, high mobility would be very desirable. Therefore the tank acceptable for the Desert would in great part suit our forces operating elsewhere. Except in certain technical adjustments for the desert conditions, we did not require a specialized tank, as was demonstrated when the Sherman arrived for Alamein.[8]

The tail had been wagging the dog, and Eighth Army had paid the price. The British did possess an anti-aircraft gun, the 3.7-inch gun, not dissimilar to the Germans' 88, but this was kept back for air defence. After the experiences of 1940 and 1941, air defence had been prioritized. This is no surprise, given how German air power had punched a hole in British morale, but the lack of such a high-powered weapon in the anti-tank role had let the Germans punch another hole in British morale with their anti-tank weapons. When the 3.7-inch guns were deployed, they did a good enough job, but the promise of the soon-to-arrive 6-pounders and the paranoia about German air power kept the 3.7-inch gun from being widely adopted. And it was much, much heavier than the 88, which also reduced its chances of being repurposed. But Tuker places the blame for the years of failure in the desert elsewhere – for him, it was command that had let down the men of Eighth Army; men who had been drawn from the dominions, the UK and the empire.

The Battle of Gazala was the nadir of British campaigning in the desert. The German and Italian forces, led by Erwin Rommel, had recovered from the body blow that Operation CRUSADER had delivered at the end of 1941. CRUSADER had been a victory for the British, but not a decisive one. It had been a near-miss for Rommel, though the battle had provided him with enough clues about what his strengths were and what weaknesses Eighth Army offered him. In one respect, their primary weakness was mutual: the key to military success, which is, of course, supplies. It was simple – the further east Rommel got, the more his supply lines were stretched; the further west the British got, away from Alexandria, the harder it became for them to maintain their army. Every gallon of petrol delivered by lorry (and bear in mind the British Army, with its railhead mindset, was having to do everything with lorries) cost more fuel the further east that Eighth Army ventured. Overextended lines made it harder to manoeuvre in a campaign that was about manoeuvre and not much else. CRUSADER, despite being a British victory, had also shown up the problem of the British guns lacking the range to deal with the Germans. The toll taken on British armour by 88mm Flak guns had properly put the wind up Eighth Army, not just on the ground but at the top. During CRUSADER, Commander-in-Chief, Middle East, Claude Auchinleck had sacked Eighth Army's CO, Lieutenant General Alan Cunningham, for descending into a funk when his plans had come unstuck. Auchinleck had taken control of the battle and averted disaster, bringing it to a victorious conclusion and forcing Rommel into retreat. He replaced Cunningham with Lieutenant General Neil Ritchie. Tuker had a view on this:

Auchinleck was bred for the battlefield and there he should have stayed until he was worn out with fighting. Twenty other generals could have conducted the affairs of *GHQ* Middle East, but it is doubtful if we then possessed one other man who could have successfully fought the battles of manoeuvre which in any case were yet to come in North Africa. He had, in not adverse circumstances, given Rommel a hammering that capable general would never forget.[9]

Ritchie had no intention of fighting battles of manoeuvre. After Rommel's successful exploratory push forward in January 1942, in which he had clobbered the British 2nd Armoured Brigade, Ritchie decided that what he'd rather do was arrange Eighth Army on what was dubbed the Gazala Line. The battle that followed offered Tuker an opportunity to be an observer (the 4th Indian Infantry Division were still in training) – he was asked to keep an eye on things for GHQ. Rather than take part, he could watch history as it unfolded, as the weaknesses and vulnerabilities of the British way of doing things played out and the German strengths showed themselves. Needless to say, he didn't like what he saw.

Immediately, General Ritchie did something Tuker could not approve of. Ritchie broke the Eighth Army into penny packets and, on a battlefield on which the British found the defensive as difficult as the offensive, waited with their supply lines stretched out for Rommel to make his move. The Gazala Line was, in effect, a retreat; it was where the Panzerarmee had been before Operation CRUSADER. CRUSADER had been a high watermark for the British, it had been a victory, but it had come at too great a cost and represented risks that Ritchie no longer felt confident to take – he didn't think his men were up to another major encounter with Rommel. Rather than retreating to Tobruk and operating with a port and the sea to his back, Ritchie decided that what he should do was operate his forces in boxes, defensive redoubts spread out across the desert and down to the bottom of the part of the terrain that was deemed passable. Minefields between the boxes were supposed to channel Rommel and slow him down, but the problem was that the Gazala Line offered a series of flanks to be turned, units fighting in brigade-sized formations rather than at divisional scale, meaning they lacked mass and sufficient concentration, as well as being too dispersed to be able to help each other. Tuker's three principles were immediately forfeited. Ritchie offered Rommel something he could get his teeth into. Rommel didn't have the strength to defeat the Eighth Army en masse but he did have the men and means to defeat its formations piecemeal, using the techniques of manoeuvre that he had perfected. In other words, he would use 'the mobile arm to the point at which it will decide the battle and gain decisive victory' – Tuker's third principle. Ritchie had delivered Rommel the opportunity he needed to defeat Eighth Army.

The southernmost of the boxes that Ritchie had organized – and his plans were approved by Auchinleck back at GHQ, so he wasn't doing anything that hadn't been given the once-over – was Bir Hacheim, manned by Free French soldiers under Brigadier Marie-Pierre Koenig. The fighting at Bir Hacheim went on for three bitter weeks, the legionaries holding up Rommel's right hook for long enough to delay his offensive and stop him from encircling Eighth Army completely. But while Bir Hacheim provided essential delay for the British, it also highlighted the problem with boxes and dissipation of force, especially without Allied air superiority. These fortified boxes needed to be resupplied with ammunition and, critically, water. Holding out was all very well, but it couldn't be done indefinitely. Rommel could afford to cap off British positions and push on properly into the British rear; they would eventually have to surrender, or fight, perhaps pointlessly, to the last round. In Burma, two years later, General Bill Slim was able to use boxes to bring the Japanese onto his forces in a similar way and entangle them in battle, but he had the advantages of complete air superiority, which allowed him to amply resupply, and jungle terrain, which slowed everyone and everything down, as well as an enemy who once in battle couldn't resist the temptation to attack again and again. The formations in the boxes were larger, too, giving them the critical mass they needed to be able to defend themselves and counter-attack: retaining their mobility. Ritchie's penny-packet boxes did not suit the desert, but they did suit Rommel's way of doing things.

It also didn't help that Rommel was able to take advantage of bad Allied intelligence practice. From January to June 1942 he had a pretty good source on British strength, dispositions and plans which came to him from the American military attaché in Egypt, Colonel Bonner Fellers. Fellers reported regularly to Washington using the American diplomatic service's Black Code, which the Italians had cracked after stealing the codebook from the US embassy in Italy. Fellers didn't know everything – the information he had gleaned from his British contacts in Egypt was incomplete and given his interpretive spin – but it gave Rommel plenty to go on. Rommel called this his 'Good Source' or 'little fellow'. Others relied on this stuff, too; the Axis campaign against Malta also made great use of Fellers's information. Eventually, British intelligence rumbled what was going on. Fellers switched codes on 29 July 1942, and Rommel's source dried up; fortunately, Fellers had never heard of Ultra, or the Ultra story might be quite different. Fellers was very down on the British, as the British discovered from reading his words reported back through Ultra – he characterized Eighth Army as slow and plagued by poor morale. Rommel's other entirely reliable source of information was British internal radio traffic: under the command of Hauptmann Alfred Seebohm, the 621st Signals Battalion listened to British radio traffic and were able to follow what the British were planning to do, when and where, very often in real time. Rommel's reactive command style dovetailed perfectly with this source of information, and the British, whose radio practice was slack – much of it in plain language – and whose army W codebook had been successfully attacked by the Germans, blundered about on the airwaves, letting Rommel know what they were up to. Seebohm was overrun during the Battle of Gazala, his methods revealed; red-faced, the British did what they could to tidy up their signals traffic and Rommel's on-tap immediate intel source dried up.

The Gazala Line might have worked with an army in better morale, with better kit, better radio discipline and better led. Though of course this formulation possesses several chickens and more than one egg. Poor kit encourages poor morale, poor morale might lead to poor radio discipline, poor radio discipline to enemy attention, enemy attention to exposing the weakness of your kit. And leader-ship that had developed a battleplan with no proper appreciation of what its men could achieve is an even big-ger chicken-and-egg. Ritchie had devised a plan his men could not execute; failing to execute the plan broke his men's morale. The Gazala Line was founded on the shift-ing sands of British command as much as it was on the desert. Tuker's anger leaps off the pages of *Approach to Battle*, and he aims that anger at the teaching at the Staff College and the attitudes it had fostered in battle.

> One recollects that the motto for our work at the Camberley Staff College in the mid-twenties was 'Speed with Accuracy', and that was a very good motto so long as one learnt to put speed first when on the battlefield. One's own advice to one's staff and commanders was 'seventy-five per cent right and in time is better than a hundred per cent right'.[10]

As Rommel swung in around Eighth Army, confusion reigned as to what to do about him. As part of his hook around the Allied lines, Rommel had divided his forces, and this left him vulnerable to strong counter-attack. In the first phase of the battle, Tuker had been sent forward to try to command the British left flank, including the Bir Hacheim position. The string of disconnected units were, in his view, too weak to protect themselves, too static to reorganize and not powerful enough to counter-attack meaningfully. As the battle proceeded, so Tuker's impro-vised command fell away. Rommel was outnumbered in terms of tanks, running low on fuel and overstretched, and seemingly trapped in what was nicknamed The Cauldron, up against the British position called Knightsbridge. But with his feedback loop of signals intelligence and an indecisive and flaccid British response, he was able to make the most of a series of piecemeal attacks by Eighth Army, destroying each as it came, and was eventually able to break out.

On 5 June, ten days into the battle, a major counter-attack against Rommel's positions in The Cauldron went in. Tuker says:

> We had heard enough of it by midday to realize that unless there was an immediate basic change in method out there in the desert, we were in for one of the greatest disasters of the war. Some mysterious spell had woven itself about commanders and their general staffs, so enfeebling them that they were incapable of resolute, coordinated, concentrated action.[11]

The next day, Tuker had flown back to GHQ to give Auchinleck his assessment of the battle, begging his Chief of Staff – an old pal from Staff College – to get Auchinleck to take command once more of Eighth Army. He had, in effect, gone behind his CO's back, and in any event Auchinleck refused. Disaster followed. A week later, Eighth Army abandoned the Gazala Line, withdrawing in disarray to the east. All Eighth Army's problems fed into each other and the army was broken: a decisive opponent acting on its weaknesses exposed them all. Eighth Army retreated, Tobruk fell. Rommel had got himself a port, thousands of tonnes of supplies and a field marshal's baton from Hitler. The British, who had mounted a major set-piece offensive only the year before, had been humbled in the desert.

*

But, for all of Tuker's fury and I-knew-better-all-along attitude, as well as the shame that Churchill felt – 'one of the
heaviest blows that I can recall during the war' and bear in
mind he's including Dunkirk and the fall of Singapore –
the Battle of Gazala had its own peculiar echo of
CRUSADER. It was not decisive. Rommel, in pausing to
take Tobruk, it is argued, missed his chance to finish off
Eighth Army. Eighth Army's retreat was covered by the
Desert Air Force, which unlike the army had been getting
its act together and had found a way to deal with the enemy
in the skies over North Africa. New equipment was
coming – there were some precious 6-pounders on the
Gazala Line but nowhere near enough. And the further
east Eighth Army was, the easier it was to supply. Ritchie
was fired* on 25 June, Auchinleck took command of
Eighth Army himself and fought Rommel to a standstill at
the First Battle of El Alamein in July. He then moved on.
The appointment of their replacements – Harold Alexander and Montgomery – coincided with an influx of lots
and lots of better equipment.

And crucially, when it came to kit, on which everyone
unanimously agreed improvements were needed, Allied
industry had caught up with what the battlefield required,
and from then on would deliver what the Allied armies

---

* Ritchie had the good fortune to be given further command: he went
back to divisional command immediately after the desert. He was given
the 52nd Lowland Division to train in mountain warfare for Norway,
which must have been a military palate cleanser. We will meet them later.
He then went on to command the XII Corps in North-West Europe and
did an excellent job. Ritchie's second chance perhaps reflected an understanding that the situation in the desert hadn't entirely been of his making,
and showed that Brooke could be forgiving when he wanted to be.

needed. In 1942, for instance, 17,854 6-pounder anti-tank guns would be manufactured, and 16,586 in 1943. Then M4 Sherman tanks arrived in the desert, a match for anything the Germans had – the shipments diverted by Franklin D. Roosevelt to make sure they arrived in time for the Second Battle of El Alamein. Shermans would remain the standard Allied tank for the rest of the war; about 50,000 of these reliable and open-ended weapons systems were built. Better kit did its bit to break the spell of German invincibility and improve morale. With better weapons, bitter lessons learned and a new emphasis on training, Montgomery was able to turn around Allied fortunes in the desert. He also prized decisiveness, and letting his men know what was happening, as well as not asking them to do things he knew were beyond them. No more piecemeal penny-packet positions – 'colossal cracks' with reliable tanks and gunnery that could smash the Germans at a safe range would deliver a victory at El Alamein that had seemed unimaginable in the summer. Rommel's source had dried up and, tellingly, he was absent for the start of the Second Battle of El Alamein – British intelligence had bamboozled him rather than let him know what was coming. Because, after all, Tuker's assessment depended on having access to better weapons – the three principles he discovered in the Assam hills in 1920 aside, it was his superior kit that had won the day once he was fighting the Kuki people on their own terms tactically. It wasn't motion or mobility or turned flanks, it was having the weapons to do the job. Better equipment meant that men could be better led, because they had faith in the means put at their disposal to fight the enemy. That faith was then reflected in their ability to be led. For everything that Tuker observed about battle or believed about the theory of warfare, equipment was the critical component in rebuilding British fighting power in the desert. Perhaps this was why in *Approach to Battle* he prefaced his account of the desert battle with a critique of the equipment that he felt had let him and his men down. Without the right kit, ideas and concepts, no matter how profound or eternal or self-evident even to a young captain fighting in the Assam hills, could not be enforced. In modern war, technology mattered most.

Under new management by the end of the year, Eighth Army had chased Rommel all the way back and on into Tunisia. Although Tuker was no fan of Montgomery, finding him too stodgy and unimaginative, and certainly by the time he wrote *Approach to Battle* he had firmly placed himself in the anti-Monty camp, he appreciated that victories, even when they weren't carried out with the dash and the élan that he was sure he would have brought to them, were now the rule rather than the exception. Tuker grumbled throughout the Tunisia campaign, even unto victory. Where Francis Tuker took General von Armin's surrender:

> We were leaving now so I told Armin to give me his revolver and any other personal weapons he possessed. He threw his revolver on the table with a clatter, followed by a penknife. I put the revolver in my blouse and threw the knife across to my staff officer [. . .] throughout the conversation in Armin's caravan, he was emphatic that on no account should we hand him and his men over to the French African troops because he feared what they might do to him [. . .] I said that he and his men would be handed over to my division

and their guards would be British, Indian or Gurkhas, and there was no choice. [. . .] I myself was cold and brusque at this meeting. As a plain soldier and no diplomat, I could not in those circumstances have brought myself to be a whit more cordial to the German commanders [. . .] but the war was not won yet [. . .] that night Naik Sidiman Gurung, the Divisional Commander's batman, boiled up a hot bath and set out a clean suit of pyjamas for this dirty general. All over Tunisia, all other batmen were taking action for those who still had their pyjamas.[12]

The desert campaign had been won, and the Indian Army had been central to that victory. How would victory be delivered in the jungles of the Assam hills where Tuker had first been schooled in the principles of warfare? One man thought he knew: Orde Wingate.

4

Orde Wingate

Barking up the wrong jungle?

The first year of the British effort in Burma is probably best described as a shitshow, but it is hard to overemphasize how far wrong things went in the far-flung British colony. In Europe, in the deserts of North Africa and now in the jungles and plains and cities of its possessions in the Far East, the British were being trounced. Defeat upon defeat, humiliations piled high; international standing, imperial credibility all shattered. Out of sight and out of mind in Londoncentric imperial terms, the Japanese ran rings around the thrown-together forces that the British Empire had mustered and then drove them out of the country, earning themselves a reputation as unbeatable. Indeed, the Japanese underwent quite the sudden racial and, needless to say, racist transformation: from oriental midgets to unbeatable supermen in only a matter of months.

The Japanese attacked west from Thailand on 22 December 1941 – into a country that hadn't been on anyone's list of enemy objectives. Given the oil resources in Burma, as well as the strategic importance of the Burma Road supply line into China – from Rangoon to Yunnan, American supplies for Chiang Kai Shek's Kuomintang nationalist efforts to fight the Japanese ran up the Burma Road, subject to looting and delay, but a lifeline nevertheless – it seems perhaps naive at best that British strategic thinkers hadn't realized Burma might be one of the Japanese priorities. Then again, things were changing so fast in the Far East and the Western Allies were hard-pressed enough in the West that perhaps these realities slipped everyone's attention. It was certainly a mark of how low on everyone's agenda the war in China had been, that although this gigantic continent-wide five-year conflict had plenty of lessons to offer, the main takeaway for British commanders was essentially racist and therefore not much help: if the Chinese, who are a ragtag bunch, can fight the Japanese to a halt then the Japanese can't be that good either. Burma, if it featured in Allied strategic thinking at all, was protected by the umbrella of Singapore's security, and its location far beyond India's eastern border meant that there was essentially little to worry about. And the terrain, many believed, was impassable. The jungle too thick, too hostile, the mountains too difficult, the valleys too steep, the seasons and disease simply too demanding for any army. This cocktail of complacent assumptions, neatly stirred and served cold, went for nothing in the face of well-mobilized, well-trained and objective-driven Japanese soldiers. Why would it do otherwise, how could it?

No one had the answer – Commander-in-Chief, India, Archie Wavell, back in New Delhi, far from the madding crowd, had tried as best he could to get his head around the essential problem of fighting the Japanese, and as detached as he was could only issue orders and instructions that were irrelevant by the time they reached the men on the ground. Holding Rangoon became an end in itself: one the Japanese, determined to defeat the British by outflanking and encircling them, cutting them off from their supply lines, were happy to entertain. Similarly, withdrawal from Rangoon gave the Japanese the opportunity to exploit the chaos any such retreat would entail. On the ground, General Officer Commanding Sir Thomas Hutton dealt with the bitter inheritance of poor strategic thinking and the realities of the workings of the British Empire in India and Burma.

India, the Raj, the Jewel in the Crown, may have excited Winston Churchill's imperial imagination but in terms of spending and commitment it hadn't excited anyone much for decades. The inter-war years had seen a growth in independence movements in India, fractured and representing different pressure groups but all inevitably focused on the same thing: getting the British out. The British were beginning to feel the pressure, and although at the end of the First World War the empire had grown bigger than ever, an exhausted Exchequer – and the political establishment – didn't much fancy paying for defending the empire. Besides, the Indian Army between the wars had developed along these lines. Its main function was controlling the border on the North-West Frontier, a remnant of nineteenth-century Great Game shenanigans, or, more prosaically, internal policing. Keeping order. Empire stuff. Forty-three battalions were allotted this role. And given the growth of the independence movements all over the subcontinent, this kept the army fairly busy. In 1939, the Indian Army, comfortably occupying its colonial role, had numbered about 130,000 men – a tiny force to police the vastest of countries. It wasn't a fighting army in the way that the Japanese Imperial Army was. While there were British regiments on hand as 'stiffeners', about

44,000 men in all – and most officers who rose to prominence during the war had done time in India – the Indian Army itself was far from up to date. It didn't have many automatic weapons,* it certainly didn't have tanks. For all the criticism the British Army has had retrospectively about its use of armour, at least officers between the wars had given it some thought. In India, this simply hadn't happened – armoured cars were as far as things went. While the empire in India might on paper have offered the British colossal military and industrial resources and manpower, there had been no investment. Reforms had come in the 1920s, seeding the Indian Army with Indian officers. The best soldiers, the cream of the crop, were to be deployed as a DUKE strategic reserve, rushed to wherever the empire might need them, Egypt, Iraq or Malaya, for example – though mule companies were sent as far afield as France to join the BEF in 1940. These were the exception, though, rather than the rule in an army that was at the end of the line and the back of the queue.

Consequently, when war came and new levies were raised in India, this was again done on the cheap. Churchill's relationship with India was paradoxical. He had pushed back hard between the wars on the question of independence – he regarded India romantically as the cornerstone of the British imperial project yet he didn't rate the Indian Army as anything more than a local gendarmerie; he had no faith in its potential at all. To start with, this became a self-fulfilling diagnosis. Training was basic and, because no one expected to be fighting in Burma,

---

* The Japanese, by contrast, made sure every section was well-equipped with light machine guns.

focused on how to fight in other theatres. The plan in 1940 was to raise an armoured division and five infantry divisions – we met one of those divisions in the previous chapter. The year after, it was decided that 50 new infantry battalions needed to be raised and seven new armoured divisions: this kind of expansion in an army that had never been seen as a fighting army, and that therefore had no proper training base to meet the problems that accompanied it, was storing up all sorts of trouble for later. Just as training in the British Army was decentralized, so it was in the Indian Army, and its traditions were – for all the British talk of recruiting from 'martial races' – less martial. Units were stripped of their experienced personnel – a process rather grimly called 'milking' – so any coherence they might have possessed went out of the window.

If India was at the back of the queue, Burma was definitely the end of the line. Hutton's Burma Army, an adjunct to the Indian Army, had locally raised troops who had been poorly trained. Whatever strategic imperatives the British leadership might have been working on in January and February 1942, they were reaping what they had sown in terms of neglect of their own assets and complacency about Japanese capabilities. The boxer Mike Tyson said, irresistibly truthfully, 'Everyone has a plan until they're punched in the mouth'; the British didn't have a plan and were punched in the mouth anyway. Confusion between commanders about strategy, where to fight the Japanese, at the border, at road junctions, which territory to defend and so on – Bill Slim, whom we will meet later, looked on aghast at the British defence of territory for its own sake – were all questions rendered tragically academic by the inability of the Indian Army, Burma Army and indeed the

British Army to defeat the Japanese tactically. The men on the ground, through no fault of their own, from divisional commanders down, had not been prepared for the battle the Japanese had in mind, nor had they been prepared to fight in the jungle. Tactically, the larder was bare, so strategy would necessarily starve.

In Burma itself there was enough discontent with British rule that when the Japanese came they were able to mobilize some of the population against the British and pose as an army of liberation. Jitters and rumours about how the Japanese were able to win so comprehensively in Burma in 1942 didn't dilute the essential lessons: training had been no good, equipment inadequate, leadership had failed. The Japanese attitude to the jungle was to make the most of it rather than write it off as impassable, echoing the German attitude in the Ardennes in the spring of 1940. The British obliged by fighting along roads and at fixed positions, granting the Japanese the initiative and allowing them to control the tempo of the battle. The Japanese would move through the jungle, its cover keeping them nearly invisible, to static British positions and appear, seemingly miraculously, in the British, Indian or Burmese rear. Believing they were encircled, surrounded, had had their flanks turned, the DUKE units would tend to try to fall back, often enough in panic. In another echo of the fall of France, the Japanese had joined up their air power with the land assault, and the British were unable to counter with anything meaningful. Communications collapsed. For my money, the nadir of the campaign came on 22 February 1942, only a month after the invasion began, when Brigadier George Smyth (who had a VC from the previous war and was regarded as unimpeachably courageous), commanding the 17th Indian Division, blew up the railway bridge on the River Sittang while as many as two-thirds of his men were still on the wrong side of it. Smyth had been refused permission by Lieutenant General Hutton to withdraw sooner, and then in the confusion of battle and the delay of clear command, made his own, awful decision at 4.30 in the morning. Smyth was sacked. It was his good fortune that the Japanese wanted to capture Rangoon now that the road was open, thanks to Smyth's calamitous decision, rather than destroy his division. It escaped with some of its rifles and not much else.

So in the sense of command, what had gone wrong? Everything really – the entire system, imperial, strategic, tactical. And it went wrong everywhere in the theatre; the Japanese caught everyone with their pants right down around their ankles. Burma fell, Singapore fell, the Philippines fell. And as the blame was meted out, and efforts to make sure it didn't fall on the men began, the simple question of how on earth to fight the Japanese in Burma was grappled with. Too late, of course, and as the result of some hard lessons. Confidence was at an all-time low, and just as the Indian Army had been ill-prepared for the campaign it had had forced upon it by the Japanese, it was similarly ill-equipped for the necessary post mortem. Disjointed, decentralized (taking its cue from its parent institution), expanding like mad, the Indian Army was incapable of actually getting down on paper and collating what needed to be done, let alone then acting on these lessons. The jungle was impenetrable, the Japanese unbeatable.

Yet the following year, the strangest thing happened. A DUKE formation struck out into the jungles of Burma. It returned, battered and bruised, having left some of its wounded behind. But it had, for all the hardship, survived in the jungle. It was led by the unlikeliest of leaders, a man regarded by many as a visionary, and by just as many others as a lunatic: Orde Charles Wingate. Of all the commanders in this book, Wingate is the most Marmite. (And just to let the reader know, I can't stand Marmite.)

*

A soldier's son from a long line of soldiers' sons, it was no surprise that Wingate had entered the army between the wars. Wingate was born in India in 1903 to a Scottish family – not the gin-sipping, snooker- and polo-playing colonialists of my clichéd imagination; instead they belonged to the Plymouth Brethren, a fundamentalist Christian sect that had its origins in Dublin. The Brethren did without clergy and relied solely on scripture for guidance, one of a number of radical revisions to Christian thought of the kind that crop up during the Victorian era. Calvinist in flavour and fervour, the Brethren spent much of their time preaching, schisming and splintering, but at the centre of Brethren thought was an ascetic and austere way of facing the world. No musical instruments in church, no women in trousers, that sort of thing. Not working on the Sabbath; no fun, basically. Seriousness of mind, a feeling of being the Elect, of being in the service of Providence, as well as being outside conventional society, non-conformist. In an era of muscular Christianity, the army with its imperial mission was a good fit for such evangelism.

Wingate's father, George, had been an active imperial soldier, involved in several operations in 1895, 1897 and 1901 to quell border uprisings, but after 30 years' service, he was placed on the half-pay list and went home to Blighty, eventually settling the family in Godalming. With his retirement, George could focus on his good works as well as his seven children, keeping tabs on missionaries on the North-West Frontier as well as leading prayer in his local chapel. So young Orde Wingate grew up with belief at the centre of his family's life, the army as its culture and the Raj as its hinterland. This doesn't sound much fun, but then I am rather soft.

Wingate was sent to Charterhouse, which was the local top public school, and didn't fit in (he was excused chapel on religious grounds), didn't get on, didn't do well in his studies, didn't take part in games and embarked on a life-long habit of storing up grudges. He did do well as a cadet, but he was seventeen in 1918 and at a top public school so there was really only one direction of travel for a boy of his background.

By the time he got into the army in 1921, he'd muffed his entrance exam and had decided to go to Woolwich rather than Sandhurst, the less prestigious but more affordable option. Woolwich then was doing what it could to revert to its peacetime condition. Wingate, who by now had evolved fully as a non-conformist, scruffy and rebellious, particularly around what to wear, was the proverbial fly in Woolwich's ointment, as much for his fellow cadets, all doing their damnedest to conform with the system, as for the institution. Like so much about Wingate, his time at Woolwich is shrouded in myth, tales told out of school. Cadets would have to endure an ordeal, a form of collective punishment known as 'running' that was supposed to make the candidate consider his responsibility to the group in general. Rather than be humiliated like this, the story goes, Wingate decided to walk stark naked between the lines of cadets, demanding they strike him with their knotted towels, stunning them into silence. Then, as an encore, he dived into the cold-water tank and was carried aloft by jubilant and repentant contemporaries (I've added that last bit, but the problem is it's quite hard to get to Wingate's past – you have to jump through so many halos). He went into the Royal Artillery having passed out low from Woolwich, with very little man-of-destiny potential on show.

The Royal Military Academy Woolwich was where the Royal Artillery and the Royal Engineers trained their officers. Gunnery and engineering were very much trades within the army, so the officers Woolwich produced in theory had lower status than men who'd been to Sandhurst, even though their training was technical and scientific, exactly the sort of thing a forward-looking army might want to encourage. Between the wars, the army tried to reorganize and centralize its officer education but, as with so much reform between the wars, it never quite got around to completing it. The British tradition of military education had been patchy at best, and certainly nothing like as self-consciously intellectual as the American way of doing things: West Point, by comparison, granted its graduates degrees in the 1930s – passing out of West Point made you a Bachelor of Science. When the war came, there was no time for reform – instead there was expansion, convulsive innovation and pragmatic change – and it wasn't until 1947 that Woolwich and Sandhurst were merged. However, in the 1920s the Royal Artillery which Wingate had joined had put rolling barrages and the modern techniques it had developed during the Great War behind it and was more focused on horse riding and fox hunting: 'Proper soldiering' again. Such was Wingate's prowess on horseback that he was sent to the Military School of Equitation, though inevitably he spent his time there rubbing people up the wrong way.

*

Wingate's talent for irritation and creating consternation didn't hinder his military career. It is remarkable that throughout his life, for all his relentless grandstanding, arguing and – to use a more contemporary phrase – shithousery, he still managed to work his way through the army and, in the end, get his way with the Chindit expeditions. Because of the British Army's imperial commitments, the army was spread all over the world, each posting a locus of empire-building and patronage. Wingate was fortunate in that he had connections. Sir Reginald Wingate, his father's cousin, was Orde's guardian angel for this phase of his career. Sir Reginald's patch was Africa – he was known as 'Wingate of the Sudan'. An artilleryman by trade, with a command of Arabic, Sir Reginald had made a name for himself fighting the dervishes. He was Kitchener's* intelligence officer, part of the campaign to reconquer Sudan: the campaign that saw one-sided battles at Atbara and Omdurman. The young Winston Churchill was at the Battle of Omdurman with the 21st Lancers, trying to square the circle of being a subaltern and a journalist: he had used *his* personal contacts to get to Sudan. Wingate finished the dervishes off at the Battle of Umm Diwaykarat, another

---

* A Woolwich graduate and gunner.

typically unbalanced encounter, Maxim guns giving the
British their advantage. Wingate's column of 8,000 men
defeated the Khalifa's army of 10,000 with only three men
killed, the Khalifa losing 1,000 killed and 3,000 captured.
Wingate became governor of Sudan. Sir Reginald was a
master of imperial expeditionary warfare, especially when
the odds were so heavily stacked in his favour.

He governed Sudan from 1899 to 1916, transferring to
be High Commissioner in Egypt in 1917. This Wingate's
time in Egypt ended badly two years later – he was
replaced by General Edmund Allenby, wasn't given a
peerage, and with his reputation tarnished retired to direc-
torships, honorary military positions and intrigue. Sir
Reginald, known as 'Rex', was a famous author and carried considerable influence, and even though his time in
Egypt hadn't worked out, in the public imagination he was
the expert on Sudan. Rex was probably the right nickname too:

> Indeed, it was true to say that Cousin Rex had acted as
> the uncrowned king of the country during his period
> as Governor-General. He revelled in the social side of
> his work and turned Khartoum into a fashionable win-
> ter resort for minor European royalty and wealthy
> aristocratic travellers. Levees, balls and formal dinners
> were regular features of life at Government House and
> he took pains to ensure that he was treated as King
> Edward *VII*'s representative in the Sudan.[1]

Rex was instrumental in making sure that his bolshie,
obdurate cousin had a future in the army, as well as foster-
ing his interest in taking a role in colonial adventuring
warfare. Connections overrode character: Wingate might

be a pain in the arse but he was a connected pain in the arse, and through his cousin Rex he had discovered the power of influence, the need to court the powerful. For a young rebel stuck at riding school, Sudan offered adventure and the echo of familial glory. Any obstructions to Orde's progress in Sudan evaporated in the face of Rex's influence. In 1926, Orde Wingate went to the School of Oriental Studies to learn Arabic. The following year, with his older cousin's encouragement, he went on an expedition to Sudan, taking a six-month break from the army and doing it his way: by bicycle. When he got there, he joined the Sudan Defence Force.

Orde Wingate thrived in his cousin's former fiefdom, though he started in his usual restless Wingate way, annoying his superiors, winding up his fellow officers. Officers in Sudan had to be able to cope with the pressures of the posting – in the usual style of the British Empire, there were only a handful of men governing hundreds of thousands. They had to be single, too; the presence of women, or at least British women, was regarded as too disruptive. (Wingate left his fiancée, Peggy, at home – this relationship then petered out.) Riding, playing bridge and being a good chap were the requirements for this tough, five-year posting. Wingate found it hard to fit in, of course, though he quickly learned to keep a lid on some of his more outré conversation, particularly politics. Shutting up and listening paid off. He got into playing poker.

In Sudan, Wingate's character and interests evolved towards the man who would lead the Chindits. He was becoming convinced that he was destined for greatness, testing methods for endurance in harsh environments, as well as experiencing highs and lows of mood, sometimes plunging into melancholia. No modern diagnosis being to hand, I won't make one, but he would take to his bed when overwhelmed by despair. Sudan was a long way from the army Wingate had chafed against. It also had a completely colonial structure, officers commanding companies of Sudanese and Egyptians, and was typically decentralized. Officers were left to their own devices and had to figure out how to do their soldiering in the brutally hot (and cold) environment. This suited Wingate, who found that it gave him room to express himself as a soldier, finding ways of patrolling in difficult conditions, as well as a focus and distraction from his bouts of despair. Further intriguing with the Royal Geographical Society saw Captain Orde Wingate lead an expedition into the Libyan desert, looking for the lost oasis of Zerzura, a gruelling trip that ended in failure. He experimented with hydration in the desert, restricting his intake of water, reporting to his father that his urine was the colour of strong tea.

The Chindit expeditions, Wingate's ability to pull levers of power that others didn't have at their disposal, the determination to bend the environment to his will, were seeded in Sudan. Furthermore, Wingate's resolve to be better than those around him, his inability to suffer fools, as well as his soaring and plunging self-confidence dressed up in apocalyptic biblical language, were all in evidence in Sudan – traits that were regarded as part of the Wingate package by the men who had to deal with him in the 1940s. And another part of Wingate's inheritance from serving in Sudan was his boldly delineated colonial view on race: he was paternalistic towards his Sudanese charges in a way that could be called condescending at best.

When his five years in Sudan were up and Orde

Wingate returned to England, the Royal Artillery was giving up on its horses and becoming mechanized. Adventure this was not. Instead he went on to Palestine – aided by his Arabic and prompted by a worry he wouldn't get into the Staff College – where he became fixated religiously and politically on Zionism, befriending Chaim Weizmann (Wingate is a national hero in Israel, unusually for a Christian), filled his time with guerrilla warfare – 'Special Night Squads' – and again rubbed up his superiors the wrong way, mainly because he had opted to take sides.* By the 1940s, Wingate had mutated into a fiercely ambitious, self-possessed leader who could not take no for an answer and who specialized in private-army antics. Most importantly, he caught the eye of his boss, General Archie Wavell, who had a taste for irregular warfare.

*

After the defeats of 1942, the Indian Army and its British commanders were out of solutions and lacked the systems to collate their experiences and learn from them. Officers wrote up their accounts of what had happened to them and some were circulated; others disappeared into the ether. There were plenty of bright ideas around, but a ton of terrible ideas, too. The Arakan offensive that followed in December 1942 was a comprehensive disaster, strategically, tactically, operationally. Having been defeated by the Japanese on the offensive, the British took it on themselves to be

---

* Wingate was an inspiration to the generation of Israelis who founded the Israel Defence Forces, men such as Moshe Dayan, who had trained under him, though judging by accounts of his time in Palestine that was no barrel of laughs either.

defeated by the Japanese on the defensive. Attempting to clear the Japanese 33 Division from its defensive positions in Arakan, Lieutenant General Noel Irwin's plan was to approach the Japanese directly, in narrow frontal attacks. As the British advanced on Rathedaung on the east bank of the Mayu River, the pattern of the battle began to make itself plain. The Japanese, again using the advantages that the jungle afforded them, had built virtually invisible bunker complexes with mutually supporting fields of fire, killing zones that would make individual positions unapproachable. The Japanese quickly adapted to the tactics the British were using, of artillery barrages – which couldn't penetrate the solidly built log bunkers – withdrawing from where the artillery was aimed and waiting until the barrage blew itself out, and they were prepared to order artillery fire on any of their own positions if attacking British troops got close to them.

Tiny Japanese contingents were able to hold out and inflict brutal punishment on British formations, who tried and tried again to approach the Japanese defences frontally. A platoon could hold out against battalions, companies, brigades. Rather than use the jungle to infiltrate and surround the Japanese, the British got stuck in a rut that resembled First World War fighting. General Irwin refused the advice that he would be better off getting his men to circumvent and flank the Japanese positions or even go around behind them, and carried on feeding men into the Arakan meat grinder. Morale collapsed accordingly. Tanks were brought in, but not in sufficient numbers to make a breakthrough: the eight Valentines that had made their way to Burma found the terrain almost impossible to negotiate and the attack on 1 February 1943 failed. Even when DUKE troops got in amongst the Japanese positions they'd be forced back out again. Each time Irwin tried to get a grip on the battle, he would simply repeat his mistakes; he felt incapable of taking advice either from his peers or from those in his command. Pressure from above was of the 'how hard can it be?' variety. As the offensive went on, the Japanese saw an opportunity to counter-attack. Using the jungle to manoeuvre, they threatened to surround and destroy the DUKE brigades. Again, Lieutenant General Bill Slim had warned that getting stuck ran the risk of a Japanese counter-attack, and that failing to treat the jungle as an environment as suitable for moving formations as any other was a mistake – all the Japanese had done was figure out how. Yet again there was confusion on the part of the British command as to when to withdraw to avoid encirclement and destruction.

Irwin's battle slithered into bitter chaos. On 25 March, Major General Wilfrid Lloyd decided the time had come for him to withdraw his 14th Indian Infantry Division, which was cut off from the rest of his men, on the other side of the Mayu range, worried that if he left it too late his men would be overwhelmed or trapped by the coming monsoon. Irwin had other ideas and sacked Lloyd. The Japanese, however, weren't getting their knickers in a twist and were determined to seize the opportunity the British had delivered them. Yet again they found a way through a part of Burma that the British had written off as impassable, over the Mayu range. Tellingly, Lloyd's replacement, Major General Cyril Lomax, conferred with Bill Slim as to what to do next – Slim had after all read the Japanese intentions right. Slim reasoned that holding territory for its own sake was pointless, especially if that territory gave the enemy the chance to attack in strength. Slim was convinced that fighting the Japanese was far from impossible, that the jungle wasn't impassable and that the Japanese would be defeated if they weren't allowed to dictate terms. Trying to smash into defensive positions manned by Japanese soldiers with no intention of giving their lives cheaply was a thankless and fruitless task. Bringing the Japanese to battle on terms unfavourable to them was the only way to win: there was a glimpse of this at the end of the Arakan offensive as the Japanese in pursuit across the paddy fields of Cox's Bazaar – in India itself – found themselves vulnerable to artillery fire, as well as being at the end of their logistical capacity.

But what the Arakan offensive amounted to was another humiliating drubbing for the British and the Indian Army; the little-regarded campaign – at least back in London – had gone wrong again. Conventional methods had failed. In the scramble for solutions, General Archie Wavell had characteristically been trying less conventional means to take the fight to the Japanese. And lo! It came to pass that one man had come forward: Orde Wingate, fresh from colonial adventures new with the all-too-biblically named Gideon Force in Ethiopia, and he forced his way into the theatre, connections, monomania and a gap in the market all playing their part. The scene was set for the Chindits.

*

In 1941, Wingate had been fighting in the East Africa Campaign. It may surprise the reader to know that during the campaign in Ethiopia he had managed to rub everyone up the wrong way. Although he won a bar to his DSO (he'd won the original medal in Palestine) and the campaign to eject the Italians from Ethiopia had been a success, he had been demoted and his special outfit, Gideon Force, had been disbanded. It had been a classically colonial operation – rallying the locals against the Italian invader, proffering the idea that everyone was better off with British imperialism than anyone else's. Gideon Force had also done things on the fly, in a difficult climate, and had scored a crucial geopolitical victory. Wingate had, not unlike his experience of becoming a Zionist in Palestine, become enamoured of the cause of Haile Selassie. Sick with malaria – arguably the Atabrine he was taking for his malaria might have contributed to his poor mental health – and gloomy about his prospects, Wingate had tried to kill himself, stabbing himself in the neck. However, ever the hustler, Wingate had sent his rejected report on Gideon Force's exploits to Westminster, and it had got Churchill's attention. In mid 1941, Churchill was looking for good news and inspiring leaders, and as a self-styled maverick and free-thinker himself he possibly – having not examined Wingate too closely – thought he might be worth a punt in the Far East: for the veteran of Omdurman the name Wingate must have rung a bell. Connections paid off again and the Secretary of State for India made sure Wingate got sent to Rangoon. Winston Churchill, with his predilection for commandos and special forces, his love of the swashbuckling private armies that the British Army seemed entirely riddled with, wanted a guerrilla warfare expert – and so did Wavell.

Wingate got to work on Wavell, bending his ear with theories. Given Wavell's failure to understand the challenges the divisions and men in his command faced in fighting the Japanese in the jungle, and his lack of grip on

Bernard Montgomery in his 'Monty' incarnation: a high visibility, publicity conscious commander. Before he became 'Monty' he was doing what he could to put his men first, not out of sentimentality, but hard-headed pragmatism. It nearly cost him his job.

'Monty' – experimental head gear in evidence – shares the limelight with the prime minister Winston Churchill.

Scenes straight from science fiction – German *Fallshirmjäger* – and evidence of German tactical and technological innovation on the battlefield. They brought with them an impression of invincibility that often didn't match reality.

The consummate warrior, New Zealand's Bernard Freyberg aka 'The Salamander'. At Crete he faced an enemy whose intentions he knew intimately, however foreknowledge wasn't enough.

The 2-pounder anti-tank gun in action. Designed for combat in the close countryside of North-West Europe, dug in or tucked into a hedgerow, the open desert terrain found the 2-pounder 'pop-gun' wanting.

Soldier, poet, farmer, historian, military theoretician, birdwatcher, writer, polymath, Francis Tuker. In an army of chaps and reluctant professionals, Tuker's career was characterised by frustration as much as it was by victory.

Tuker's beloved Gurkhas. As a career officer in the Indian Army, Tuker was used to working with well-motivated professional soldiers.

Chindits showing the signs of the strain of deep penetration in the jungle, a brutal and merciless environment which invalided men as reliably as encountering the enemy.

Orde Wingate. Let the controversy commence!

Bill Slim eschewed showmanship and relied on a quiet, cooperative and steely authority to get his army into shape and defeat the Japanese in Eastern India and Burma.

Mortars in the jungle: the angle of the mortar tube suggests the enemy weren't that far away.

Omar Bradley (right) with Lieutenant Kenneth Anderson in Tunisia. Bradley was there to act as President Dwight D. Eisenhower's eyes and ears. He is noticeably more buttoned up than his British colleague.

how to respond, as evidenced in both the retreat of 1942 and the Arakan offensive, it is little wonder that Wingate managed to get his hands on a brigade pretty quickly. With his new command – 77th Indian Infantry Brigade – he began to experiment and finesse the techniques he – and only he – had in mind. Here the name Chindits springs up, though as with many things about Wingate, there are myths and confusion about where the name came from. His initial experiments were a disaster. After he insisted his men camp in the Indian jungle in August 1942, sickness gripped his battalions, and men had to be brought in to replace the men crocked by their maverick leader's training. If it is hard being a genius – and many thought Wingate *was* a genius – he certainly made it look difficult. Officers would find themselves on the receiving end of withering bollockings, sudden changes of mind, unfathomable behaviour. Some of his eccentricities sound half attention-seeking, half mad. He would let his men grow beards in the jungle, and grew a proper bushy wild-man beard himself. He'd eat raw onions. He would take briefings in the nude, though this character reference comes from 'Mad' Mike Calvert, who was to become synonymous with the Chindits himself.

> We walked for miles and talked for hours and my conviction grew that this was a man I could fight for. He was not the popular type of swashbuckling hero. One of his habits was to dictate letters as he walked up and down stark naked in the heat, and physically he was not very great. But this did not matter in the least. He had a tremendous spirit which drove him on and completely overcame any physical drawbacks. No one

could spend long in his company without realizing that he had this burning fire inside him. With his thin face, intent eyes and straggly beard he looked like a man of destiny; and he believed he was just that.[2]

What was Wingate's concept? It was – essentially – to run an old colonial-style column, the kind Kitchener had taken into Sudan to fight the Mahdi, but rather than rely on wagon trains and living off the land to sustain it, to use air power to resupply food, ammunition, medicine and everything a modern fighting column might need. Wingate believed that radio had changed everything along with aircraft. He was putting old wine into new bottles, which for me explains how he was able to appeal to politicians and soldiers who had come of age during the pomp of the imperial era. The only problem was how tough the terrain was in Burma, how merciless the climate, and as yet the Allies had nothing approaching air superiority over Burma nor the transport planes required to carry out resupply. Nor were any planes going to come Burma's way soon – it was bottom of everyone's strategic list. Wingate believed that columns could operate tactically – in the sense that they were an offshoot of the main effort, supported by the main effort – or strategically, self-contained, a hundred miles deep into enemy territory. He envisaged men wandering behind enemy lines, 'deliver[ing] fatal blows at [the enemy's] Military organization by attacking vital objectives, which he is unable to defend from such attacks'.[3] It sounds great, and he came packaged with a reputation as a guerrilla leader, with connections and the burning fire inside him. Who could deny Wingate his chance?

As it happened, there was one man who didn't think that this strategic vision of Long Range Penetration could work, that it was rather a distraction, potentially squandering resources, men and morale, that it failed to truly take into account what fighting the Japanese had been like and was nothing like the way the Japanese could be beaten. But Bill Slim's assessment would have to wait. In the free-for-all of trying to find ways to fight the Japanese that followed the rout of 1942, Wingate had been so single-mindedly focused on making his vision the solution that he hadn't much taken in anyone else's experience. Operation LONGCLOTH, his first expedition, exposed his plans' limitations in full. Because taking men into the jungle at the limits of human endurance was one thing, doing it against a first-class enemy was quite another.

Gideon Force, the Special Night Squads, slave-trader-hunting expeditions in Sudan – everything Wingate had done so far had not been against such an opponent. Rex Wingate's experience at Omdurman had been similar. Kitchener's expedition was outnumbered two to one. It was a typical imperial army – it consisted of 17,000 Sudanese and Egyptian soldiers and 8,200 British. It faced the Mahdi's army of 52,000. Nevertheless, being outnumbered didn't matter. By the end of the day, 12,000 of the Mahdi's men were dead, 13,000 wounded and 5,000 captured, for a cost to Kitchener's force of 48 killed. Firepower was the defining element at Omdurman, and discipline. With Maxim guns, modern rifles and artillery, as well as gunboats, Kitchener was able to shatter the Mahdi's army before noon. A technological mismatch had done for the Mahdi. The Japanese were no Mahdi army, and they were far more motivated and experienced than any of the

Italians Wingate had run into in Ethiopia. They were not going to offer Wingate the kind of battle he had fought before, either tactically or, if he got his way, strategically.

Operation LONGCLOTH started on 8 February 1943. Wingate marched his 3,000 Chindits into Burma, across the Chindwin River. The column struck out boldly, aiming for Japanese rail communications. Wingate's order of the day for LONGCLOTH promised his men a date with destiny:

> To-day we stand on the threshold of battle. The time of preparation is over, and we are moving on the enemy to prove ourselves and our methods. At this moment we stand beside the soldiers of the United Nations in the front line trenches throughout the world. It is always a minority that occupies the front line. It is a still smaller minority that accepts with a good heart tasks like this that we have chosen to carry out. We need not, therefore, as we go forward into the conflict, suspect ourselves of selfish or interested motives. We have all had the opportunity of withdrawing and we are here because we have chosen to be here; that is, we have chosen to bear the burden and heat of the day. Men who make this choice are above the average in courage. We therefore have no fear for the staunchness and guts of our comrades.
>
> The motive which has led each and all of us to devote ourselves to what lies ahead cannot conceivably have been a bad motive. Comfort and security are not sacrificed voluntarily for the sake of others by ill-disposed people. Our motive, therefore, may be taken to be the desire to serve our day and generation in the

way that seems the nearest to our hand. The battle is not always to the strong, nor the race to the swift. Victory in war cannot be counted upon, but what can be counted is that we shall go forward determined to do what we can to bring this war to the end which we believe best for our friends and comrades in arms, without boastfulness or forgetting our duty, resolved to do the right so far as we can see the right.

Our aim is to make possible a Government of the world in which all men can live at peace with equal opportunity of service.

Finally, knowing the vanity of man's effort and the confusion of his purpose, let us pray that God may accept our service and direct our endeavours, so that when we shall have done all we shall see the fruit of our labours and be satisfied.

O. C. Wingate. Commander
77th Indian Infantry Brigade[4]

Stirring stuff, but up against malaria and an enemy who would literally fight to the last round, could it be enough?

*

LONGCLOTH could get the same kind of write-up as the Arakan offensive. Unrealistic expectations of enemy and terrain. A leadership convinced it had the answers and refusing to take counsel. Contradictory orders, junior officers taking matters into their own hands. The enemy responding vigorously and decisively. DUKE troops' training not truly preparing them for the Japanese response. A brisk retreat with the very real threat of encirclement and destruction. The bitter tragedy of men being captured by the Japanese and the fate that befell them. On 8 February, Wingate's Southern Group was ambushed by the Japanese, losing critical supplies and equipment. This entanglement prompted Wingate to order his Northern Group – under 'Mad' Mike Calvert – to pursue and attack a Japanese patrol. He wanted his men blooded. Between 2 and 4 March, both groups were hit. At Kyaikthin, Southern Group were ambushed and panicked. Radios were lost and ciphers captured. Northern Group were attacked near Nyaungwun 'in strength' and withdrew to the Chindwin. Wingate faced one of the paradoxes his methods had thrown up for him. To cause the Japanese confusion and maximize his potential for disruption, he had divided 77th Brigade into separate columns. This had, however, dissipated his brigade's fighting power. The best option for the Chindits was to avoid the Japanese if they possibly could; whenever a Chindit column did encounter the enemy it would force Wingate to rethink his plans.

His men were sick, too: dysentery, malaria, jungle sores, exhaustion, malnourishment. In training, Wingate had been very hot on personal hygiene and health, intolerant of malingerers. His leadership style was draconian and hands-on – on one occasion he punched a junior officer for making a mistake: he was unabashed about physically encouraging his men. For Operation LONGCLOTH, Wingate had ordered that the wounded be abandoned. Even the rosiest, most hagiographic accounts of Wingate's leadership (which are all revealing in themselves) seem to take a sharp intake of breath at this. Wingate's leadership style was 'you're either for me or against me', so this left anyone wanting not to abandon the wounded against him. But this draconian discipline went further: some of Wingate's officers flogged their men for misdemeanours; he had recommended Field Punishment No. 1: tying a man to the wheel of a field gun. 'Mad' Mike Calvert preferred to find out who was up to the job through training, something Wingate seemed to have overlooked, awing his men with his personality and fire-eating.

By the end of March, all the air had gone out of the Chindit balloon. Wingate opted to abandon mules and equipment and 'save our most valuable asset, i.e. the experience we had gained'.[5] Railways had been damaged and Japanese troop concentrations had been attacked by planes guided onto their targets by the Chindits, but there was not a great deal to show for the jungle excursion. The Japanese armies didn't have as big a logistical tail as the DUKE forces, preferring to live off the land and eat less, so they were not as vulnerable to railway attack as Wingate had believed, and in any case the railways were quickly repaired. And the bill for Wingate's adventure was comparable to the misadventure in the Arakan, worse even: of the 3,000 men in 77th Indian Infantry Brigade, only 600 would ever be battle fit again. Only 2,182 made it back from Burma; 450 had been killed in combat, the rest were in Japanese hands with all that that implied. It is hard not to read LONGCLOTH now as a disaster.

There was not time at the time, however. On his return from the jungle, miraculously free of blame for the calamity he had commanded – he had expected to be court-martialled – Wingate got cracking on making sure that the Chindits were hailed as a success. Courting journalists, working hard on politicians like the Viceroy of India,

Wingate was able to present the Chindit mission as a success: his men had returned undaunted from the jungle, led by their charismatic and unconventional boss. Wingate suddenly became a jungle Lawrence of Arabia. It fired the imagination and by May – at the same time the Arakan offensive was dribbling to its ignominious halt – he was being hailed as 'the Clive of Burma' (an imperial flavour that probably suited Wingate) and the altogether exaggerated notion got about that the Chindits had achieved mastery of the jungle. Given the casualties from sickness, this was a little far-fetched. With a military and political establishment desperate for good news from the Burma theatre, Wingate and his men were just the ticket. Fame beckoned, exactly the thing you'd want to bestow on a monomaniacal self-styled radical. His attitude and methods, far from facing forward as a modernizer, were steeped in the imperial traditions of the British Army rather than the imperial realities of the Indian Army. Indeed, if Wingate resembled anyone, it was Gordon of Khartoum: messianic, imperial, driven regardless of the cost. He had become irresistible, mythic, controversial.

*

The second Chindit expedition, Operation THURSDAY, in February 1944, was of a different order to LONGCLOTH. Wingate had been granted 23 battalions of men, a division's worth. The RAF and the USAAF's ability to resupply by air was by now reaching maturity. Wingate had been wheeled out at the Quadrant Conference in Quebec by Winston Churchill as an example to the Americans that the British could fight in Burma; progress *was* being made, the Japanese were beatable, backing the British effort in Burma – about which the Americans were deeply ambivalent, it being a British reconquest of a colony – was worthwhile. Wingate had done a full charismatic number on the old imperialist, offering Churchill the thing he craved: a fighting general who wanted to stick it to the Japanese, rather than yet another general sucking his teeth and saying he wasn't sure it could be done. Wingate returned to India with Churchill's blessing, and Churchill promptly forgot all about him. Burma was at the back of the strategic queue.

This time Wingate was going to try Long Range Penetration on a strategic level. All but one of his brigades would be inserted by glider, a colossal effort quite beyond LONG-CLOTH's ambitions. The Chindit columns would be resupplied by air daily, now that the RAF had gained the air superiority it needed to be able to send Dakotas backwards and forwards over the jungle. Nevertheless, THURSDAY got off to a rocky start; because Wingate had been desperate to maintain secrecy, none of the landing zones had been recced properly – he had banned over-flying the proposed landings zones for fear of tipping the Japanese off – and they had to be switched at the very last minute. Again, the jungle tested his men to their limits, and the enemy similarly wasn't going to simply allow columns to maraud around their rear unimpeded. Again, the Chindits found themselves trying to avoid the enemy – surviving in the jungle was enough – and when they did encounter the Japanese, they lacked the artillery they needed to defeat them. The columns were too cumbersome to hit and run, and lacked the critical mass needed to inflict decisive blows on the enemy.

As the culmination of his advocacy, politicking and

hard driving was playing out, Orde Wingate, whose life was one of unwritable drama and incident, exited the scene. If the Chindits were the one-man band they were accused of being, proof of *that* concept was on hand. Doing his rounds of Chindit positions, Wingate left Imphal in a B25 Mitchell and was never seen again: the plane crashed in the Naga Hills. The pilot had protested that it was over-loaded. The Chindits were on their own. Immediately, Brigadier Joe Lentaigne, who had been prominently scep-tical of Wingate's conception of Long Range Penetration, was given command of the Chindits, and for the diehard believers the dream was over.

What was Wingate like, in person? At least, for the men he commanded? Richard Rhodes James, a signals officer in 77th Indian Infantry Brigade, saw him up close. His memoir, *Chindit*, written up from notes he had made imme-diately after his return to India, devotes a chapter to Orde Wingate. Rhodes James, an admirer of Lentaigne as well, did what he could to get to grips with Orde Wingate. He wrote:

> I remember considering seriously with my fellow offi-cers the question Is he mad? He would approach you staring straight at you with his piercing eyes and in a hard monotone fire off a string of questions. He seemed to want to wring everything out of you and you were conscious that your answers, however prompt, would always be inadequate, for his stand-ards were unattainable. He was living in the clouds and inattentive to the ways in which he clothed his spiritual self. As you looked at him – it was difficult to stare back into those eyes – you saw at first a

Bohemian who didn't mind how he looked. You felt: 'he doesn't look much like a soldier'. His appearance compared oddly with other great men of arms.[6]

While Operation THURSDAY drifted away from Wingate's plan and into the orbit of the other major players in Burma, the main event was under way, a battle that brought into play the advantages the DUKE forces possessed: air power, jungle skills and, most importantly of all, critical mass. The Japanese could be defeated, not by going out looking for railway lines to blow up or by being mobile like the Japanese were themselves, but by bringing them to battle and crashing them onto the rocks of Allied power. There was no point trying to beat the Japanese at their own game; far better to get them to play yours. In the time it had taken to mount two questionable adventures, one man had conceived what that new game should be: Bill Slim.

5

Bill Slim

No withdrawal

Bill Slim's last battle with the Fourteenth Army in Burma was not the final battle in Burma. Slim did not get to finish what he had undoubtedly started and defeat, finally, the Japanese in Burma. As fate would have it in this theatre at the edge of the British world, the final battle at the Sittang Bend – in which 15,000 Japanese were destroyed at a cost of 96 Allied troops – was fought by Slim and his army's replacements: the coup de grâce went to Lieutenant General Montagu Stopford and the newly badged Twelfth Army.* Stopford had served as a corps commander under Slim, and Twelfth Army was based on units of the Fourteenth Army, so Stopford and his men were well versed in his way of doing things and fought a Slim-style battle, leveraging the advantages that had accumulated over the three years Slim had been in charge. Slim and the Fourteenth

* Twelfth Army had spent most of its war as a deception formation, a fake army designed to fool the enemy about British dispositions in the Mediterranean, consisting of three fake British corps and one bogus Polish corps. It had fake designs on Crete, Greece and Italy at various stages of the campaign in the Med, before being transferred as a phantom formation to India to threaten Sumatra. Only when the Fourteenth Army was needed elsewhere did Twelfth Army spring, Adam's rib-like, from the headquarters of the Indian XXXIII Corps.

Army had been withdrawn from Burma in preparation for the planned liberation of Singapore and Malaya. That Slim had been given this next gargantuan and complex task was a mark of the confidence that the Allied Chiefs of Staff now, finally, had in him and the Fourteenth Army. It took them long enough.

Slim's last battle in Burma was a triumph of every aspect of his generalship. Having defeated Mutaguchi Renya in India the year before, in the epic battles at Kohima and Imphal, by letting the Japanese come to him and fight, Slim turned his attention to moving into Burma, finding the enemy there and destroying him. In late 1944, with the monsoon over and the next phase of his plan settled, Slim made his move, bridging the Chindwin River. His plan was to fight the Japanese in the open on the Shwebo Plain – based on his experience of fighting the Japanese over the last two years, he expected them to come to battle the way they had so far. Divining his opponents' intentions was far from straightforward, and when the 19th and 20th Indian Divisions made their advances over the river, they discovered that the Japanese had abandoned what Slim had assumed would be their positions west of the Irrawaddy River – his men made huge advances unopposed, up to 80 miles in five days, the kind of progress no one had expected to make.

It was clear the Japanese had opted to fight further east, so Slim, rather than proceeding as planned, completely rewrote his strategy and decided that his best option was to reorient his offensive, swapping his axis of advance from north to south, attaching the 19th Division to the XXXIII Corps and sending it on across the Shwebo Plain towards Mandalay. But he diverted the rest of the IV Corps to turn south and cross the Irrawaddy, then swing past the Japanese positions and go around their flank. With a fake headquarters transmitting dummy radio traffic to cover the IV Corps's switch, the Japanese were oblivious to the new danger of Slim's advance to and over the Irrawaddy. Allied air superiority prevented the Japanese from spotting the 350-mile trail of military vehicles as the Fourteenth Army reorganized itself and headed south down the Gangaw Valley. When Slim's men appeared at the Irrawaddy, they caught the Japanese by surprise, and because they arrived at the boundary between two Japanese armies, the response was more confused than it might have been (though Slim was unaware of this advantage). Fighting was fierce, and the entire crossing was improvised, with British and Indian troops making do with the boats they could get their hands on.

Multiple crossings kept the enemy guessing as to where Slim's main thrust would fall, while dominance in the air and with artillery closed down the Japanese options for resisting this multi-fronted offensive. Indian Army tanks pushed forward towards Mandalay, while the Japanese dug in at Meiktila, the town to its south through which Slim's southern hook would have to pass to meet his northern pincer, but were evicted in a four-day battle. The Japanese then, rather than reinforcing Meiktila, had to recapture it, and facing forces better armed, better led, better motivated, equipped and fed, they didn't stand a chance. Fighting two battles simultaneously, for Meiktila and Mandalay, the Japanese realized they were trapped in the jaws of the Fourteenth Army and, wary of another disastrous battle of attrition with Slim, abandoned the city; Mandalay was captured by the end of March. The battle for central Burma had been won and it had been won on Slim's terms. The contrast with how the campaign had begun in 1942 could not have been more dramatic.

*

While superiors had come and gone – some booted upstairs, some into training posts where they could only lose battles at arm's length – and assorted schemers in the theatre had squandered their chance, Bill Slim had, since the disasters of 1942 and 1943, figured out how to beat the Japanese. He had been fortunate: others had furnished him with plenty of lessons, though he had also learned from his own mistakes. When victory came in 1945, a victory forever overshadowed by the mushroom clouds of Hiroshima and Nagasaki, it was his supreme commander, Mountbatten, who got to style himself 'Mountbatten of Burma', but it was Slim who had masterminded the battles in 1944 and 1945 that had brought the Japanese Fifteenth Army to its knees, nay, destroyed it. It was the biggest single military defeat the Japanese army had endured, far greater than any of the island-hopping encounters with the Americans, worse than any reverses in China; for many Japanese the shame was deeper still for losing to an army made up mainly of Indians. Moreover, Slim had done the whole thing on a shoestring, and without the chiefs of staff in London and Washington ever really getting what he was doing. Even after his great victories in 1944, when his long-term adversary Mutaguchi crashed his Fifteenth Army onto the rocks Slim had prepared for him, back in London, Alan Brooke hadn't entirely grasped what Slim had achieved. Slim had defeated two opponents for the price of one: the Japanese and the jungle. In his memoirs – a parade of modesty and self-effacement – he says of the jungle and others' understanding of it: 'I often wished afterwards that some of my visitors, who measured distances on small-scale maps, and were politely astonished at the slowness with which I proposed to advance, had walked to my headquarters instead of flown.'[1]

Slim had to fight his battles on a strict timetable. As well as being the strategic poor relative, Slim's campaigning was further confined by the monsoon. The best part of half a year had to be written off as the opposing armies in Burma took an imposed breather: time to reassess, retrain, rethink, adapt. Slim's campaigning season could not have been more unlike that of the European theatre – the monsoon curtailed his opportunities to take the battle to the Japanese far more dramatically than the winters did in Europe. European winters presented challenges to the fighting but combat didn't stop. The winter of 1944/5 was notable for the epic Ardennes Offensive – where poor weather granted the Germans a temporary gap in Allied air superiority and allowed them one last, bitter, pointless hurrah in the defence of the Reich. In Burma the weather ruled supreme, and the opportunities for grand gestures and decisive campaigns were restricted.

The monsoon season in Burma runs from late May to the start of November, a month or so later in India – five months when rain falls so heavily that fighting becomes impossible. Winter, such as it exists, was the best time to fight in Burma and eastern India; from mid November to mid February temperatures might settle in the 20s (degrees Centigrade) – Rangoon averages at 25 during the winter. Then the weather changes in anticipation of the monsoon: from the middle of February it gets hotter and hotter, with temperatures in February averaging 40 degrees in Rangoon, benefitting from being on the coast, and 45 degrees inland at Mandalay. By May the heat is unbearable. When the monsoon finally comes (it isn't exactly punctual but has average arrival dates), the temperatures drop to around 30 degrees but the rain is intense. In some places 1,200 millimetres of rain fall in the first month. Moving a large, modern and mechanized army in these conditions was, needless to say, extremely challenging, and neither side found a way to conduct strategic operations during the monsoon; small-scale infiltration and reconnaissance were still feasible during the monsoon but moving an army about in these conditions was impossible.

Any major fighting had to have reached a conclusion by May, then, or would have one forced upon it: certainly weather dictated the tempo of the Allies operational method, reliant as it was on its air power for supply. By 1944, this element was essentially academic for the Japanese; they had ceded air superiority to the Allies early in the year: when the monsoon came it was their chance to escape the deadly clutches of Slim's strategic machinations. The monsoon deadline meant that campaigns would peter out or crescendo in a frantic attempt to achieve something decisive before poor weather dominated everything. So with the weather making things nigh-on impossible for half of the year, what of the terrain?

The terrain offered its own challenges for both Indian Army methods and British Army thinking. Mountainous throughout, with plunging valleys and vast rivers, Burma was a hugely difficult battlefield. The option of an integrated mechanized approach, as on the battlefields of

Europe or the North African desert, simply didn't exist, and attempts to stick to roads could and did come unstuck. Mules were more use than lorries in vast stretches of Burma. Criticism aimed at the inter-war army for not giving enough thought to a mechanized enemy in Europe rarely extends to slating the same military thinkers for not considering a defence of Burma at all, let alone against a rampant and well-trained Japanese opponent. Post-First World War thinking was that the (great big expensive) naval base at Singapore would provide a deterrent defence for the eastern end of the empire. British imperial power would radiate its vibes from Singapore and no one would dare take it on. So Burma was in effect a new theatre, and although the British had fought Burma into submission in the nineteenth century, memories didn't extend that far back, And defending the place was nobody's priority; even in 1941, the War Office assured the governor of Burma that he didn't need any more troops to defend the country, as there was no possibility of invasion.

Whichever new theatre a soldier was deployed to presented a whole new set of problems; experience gained in other theatres was perhaps of little help. At the core of soldiering was training, but working out what that training should be was a problem in itself. The lessons of the desert or of North-West Europe did not necessarily apply. The Indian Army was also expanding like crazy, with new soldiers who needed motivating, in a period of rapid growth and mobilization in the face of the Quit India campaign, the attempts of Gandhi and others to disrupt and destabilize the war effort (ironically exactly the sort of thing the pre-war Indian Army would have had to deal with). Essentially, the Indian Army was having to reinvent itself, in anticipation of the post-colonial era that was to follow. Rather like the influence of the Beveridge Report on British troops and their morale in the second half of the war, the deal between these new Indian levies and the empire was the promise of what was to come once the job had been done: independence.

Being at the very end of the Allied line rather precluded the use of the armour in the way it had been deployed in the desert: there could be no swanning around looking for a punch-up. Besides, such swanning or whatever armoured role there would be would, until the last year of the war, have to be carried out with tank types that had become obsolete in the Western battlefield. Outdated by Panzer standards, Valentines and Lees in particular did a lot of the donkey work in the jungle, the Lee with its mixed armament – a 75mm artillery gun and a 37mm lighter gun that was very effective against massed Japanese infantry – proving to be an excellent weapon at the Battle of the Admin Box.* To supply an army in the field – though 'field' doesn't get anywhere near to describing the Burmese terrain – roads would have to be cut and built and, more crucially as the answer to supply became a question of air power, airstrips prepared. Hills and valleys and *chaungs* – small rivers – as well as vegetation filled the landscape with obstacles. As in the desert there was little infrastructure, but unlike the desert the landscape

---

* Obsolescence in the technology-hungry Western theatre didn't mean a tank was unsuitable for the jungle: the Australians made great use of comparatively ancient Matilda II tanks in their campaigns. Though they had long been ineffective against German armour, their 2-pounder gun and thick armour made them ideal for busting Japanese defensive positions.

didn't allow easy passage once you were offroad. What villages and settlements there were were far apart and there were none of the amenities of a European battle-field; it wasn't like France with villages with petrol pumps. And though the inhabitants lived in fear of the Japanese, they were, as often as not, not necessarily well disposed to the British.

Slim had read the land and read the way the Japanese chose to fight in it. Because Japanese supply lines were lighter and more stretched than those of the British, the best way to disrupt and defeat them was to do everything you could to hold them up, delay and engage them. Fight-ing the Japanese would force them into using their ammunition and expending their resources, and thwart their attempts to resupply by capturing Allied stuff; the Japanese armies travelled light in anticipation of capturing future supplies or centres of supply. To stymie this hand-to-mouth strategy meant rethinking what you held and why and where you kept it. Again and again in 1942, Slim had despaired at the way Harold Alexander prioritized territory over engagement or consolidating in a way that would hold the Japanese up. When Rangoon fell, it came as a blow to an army that had pinned its hopes on holding it rather than defeating the Japanese. The Japanese emphasis on circumventing British roadblocks, evading the 'front line', and the loss of nerve it provoked in British leaders left their response flat-footed and unimaginative. Slim knew that panicked last-minute retreats were no substitute for aggression and orderly straightening of lines; he was also smart enough to know that when men got back to India at the end of a thousand-mile retreat from Burma, the last thing he should do was characterize them as defeated.

They had done their best in a situation that wasn't of their making, and when they had licked their wounds, regrouped and addressed how best to beat the Japanese, that was exactly what they would do

Slim took defeat personally. His memoirs are bald in addressing what that defeat meant, and worth quoting at length:

> In preparation, in execution, in strategy, and in tactics we had been worsted, and we had paid the penalty – defeat. Defeat is bitter. Bitter to the common soldier, but trebly bitter to his general. The soldier may comfort himself with the thought that, whatever the result, he has done his duty faithfully and steadfastly, but the commander has failed in *his* duty if he has not won victory – for that *is* his duty. He has no other comparable to it. He will go over in his mind the events of the campaign, 'Here,' he will think, 'I went wrong; here I took counsel of my fears when I should have been bold; there I should have waited to gather strength, not struck piecemeal; at such a moment I failed to grasp opportunity when it was presented to me.' He will remember the soldiers whom he sent into the attack that failed and who did not come back. He will recall the look in the eyes of men who trusted him. 'I have failed them,' he will say to himself, 'and failed my country!' He will see himself for what he is – a defeated general. In a dark hour he will turn in upon himself and question the very foundations of his leadership and his manhood.[2]

As we will see later, while George S. Patton projected his ideas of manhood onto others, Slim reflected them back onto himself. And unlike Montgomery, he was entirely open to the possibility that he might make mistakes.

*

The question of what could have been done differently in 1942 is worth asking, but it merits the response 'not much'. Training, and the morale that sprung from it, as well as the ability of DUKE leaders to realize their strategy *because their soldiers were well trained*, were absent in the Burma Army, low down in the imperial pecking order. Burma was annexed in 1886 after decades of pressure, skirmishing and open warfare: the First Anglo-Burmese War (1824–6) was hugely expensive and almost bankrupted British India. Two subsequent wars ate into Burmese autonomy. Rangoon, the colony's capital, offered the empire a waypoint between Singapore and Calcutta. Agriculture dominated – British rule redirected the Burmese economy away from subsistence agriculture and towards the export of rice to Europe. There was oil, too. Indian labour migrated into Burma, adding more racial tensions to the mix of internal ethnic differences. An emerging independence movement was focused around Burmese Buddhism – the Young Men's Buddhist Association had been founded in 1906 and was firmly nationalist, in reaction to British rule.*

To an enemy keen to undermine British rule, Burma was ripe for exploitation, for divide and rule, for creating chaos and collapse, for making the most of civilian unrest. British rule had soured things sufficiently to make defending the country pretty tricky. Of course, none of this

---

* The YMBA remains pretty fruity: in 2021, it supported the military coup in Myanmar.

tricky, sticky stuff mattered if British imperial strategic plans worked out and the Japanese were deterred by Singapore. All of this was reflected in the forces available to Wavell to defend Burma. Like the Indian Army, the Burma Army's role had been internal policing. It lacked automatic weapons, while the Japanese infantry section was well provided for. And, as the Japanese bested the British, Burmese loyalties frayed fast. The British contingent in Burma was similarly poorly trained and ill-equipped, so their effectiveness as a stiffener was limited. The lack of confident decision-making Slim saw in his fellow officers, their lack of resolve in resisting the Japanese tactic of swinging around and getting behind the British would have to be replaced with aggression, tenacity and an understanding that in the close quarters of the jungle there was no front or rear. The British Army was going to have to get itself out of the habit of being beatable, just as it had in the desert.

Plenty of solutions to the problem of taking back Burma were posited from elsewhere. Time and again, British strategic planners had floated amphibious operations as the way to recapture the Burmese capital, Rangoon, and time and again the proposed operations were cancelled on the grounds that the shipping and landing craft simply couldn't be spared: Burma wasn't enough of a priority. Meanwhile, Slim used the monsoon breaks to get on with perfecting the Fourteenth Army, training it to fight the Japanese aggressively and break the spell the Japanese had cast over his men as well as his superiors, gearing a predominantly Indian army to the reconquest of Burma – landing craft could wait. When seaborne landings did finally come good in 1945, Slim had successfully pursued, outmanoeuvred and destroyed the Fifteenth Army to the point where the amphibious landings were surplus to requirements. The RAF sent a Mosquito over Rangoon to take a look at the state of the city. On the roof of the jail there was the message: 'JAPS GONE. EXTRACT DIGIT'. The Japs had gone because Slim, to the incredulity of the chiefs of staffs, had inflicted on them a colossal defeat. Slim hadn't waited for them to make up their minds about what to do in Burma, he'd just got on with it.

*

Defending India, part of an empire that the British public had turned its back on, had none of the traction politically or strategically that fighting in North-West Europe possessed. India tended to be where senior officers were booted upstairs, a dumping ground for officers who had had a 'mare in the Western Desert. As the war developed calamitously in 1942, India unexpectedly became a front line. An officer corps full of duds and imperial lifers would not be up to the task: if the disasters of 1942 were showing anything it might be that.

Slim didn't fit in this category at all – his inter-war years were spent teaching at the staff colleges in Camberley and Quetta, drawing on his pre-First World War life as a teacher. Crucially, he had chosen India; Slim made the transfer to the Indian Army after the First World War deliberately. In his spare time he wrote short stories and poems under a pen name, Anthony Mills. 'I See Death', for instance, owes a weighty debt to Kipling; it's a story of fakirs and dire predictions, promotions and mysterious death foretold, consuls and colonels. It's firmly set in British India and it opens:

It's my job to recognize a dangerous man when I meet him and I think I'm pretty good at it. I'm not such a fool as to say every thug has a face that labels him, but you can't be superintendent in an Indian city for as long as I have without developing a sort of sixth sense that warns just as it warns the mongoose of the hidden snake.[3]

He presented a modest exterior, too: while he undoubtedly did develop a self-conscious and recognizable style in what he wore, there was none of the attention-seeking peacocking that some of his contemporaries adopted. That is, if he did craft an image in the way Montgomery and Patton had, he did so much more subtly, and therefore successfully. Slim excites little of the antagonism that they do. Like both of those two inglorious hams, he made sure he met his men as often as he could, but he did it in a soft-spoken and unshowy style, drawing them into his confidence rather than seeking to radiate it, or irradiate his men with it.

Slim had one thing going for him that many of the officers who had fought the Japanese in 1942 had lacked: luck. Without luck, Slim would never have been in command of the Fourteenth Army in 1944 when the Japanese offered him the chance of victory by deciding to march on India. His war had started badly. He had been fighting in the East Africa Campaign, in command of the 10th Indian Infantry Brigade, and was wounded in Eritrea when his position was strafed – he returned to India for a staff job. When he had recovered, he moved to Iraq; the British were based in Basra. Iraq had been obtained by the UK as part of the spoils of the collapse of the Ottoman Empire and began the 1920s as the British Mandate of Mesopotamia. One of the reasons the First World War might have felt like unfinished business for the empire-hungry Axis powers is that the British Empire had expanded further still as a direct result of it: in imperial terms, it was plain – wars worked. But Iraq was a huge drain on British resources. In 1920, the Iraqi Revolt made it obvious that Britain would have its hands full dealing with the newly founded Kingdom of Iraq – a typically British piece of imperial bodging: Iraq was independent, but the British weren't going anywhere. After a decade of puppet-state status, Iraq became a fully independent kingdom in 1932, but with the RAF still knocking about. The chaos might sound familiar to us today: Kurdish groups, Yazidis, Shia and Sunnis all attempted to assert themselves within the new Iraqi polity. Iraq was a huge headache for the British, and their attempt to control the place on the cheap manifested itself in the country falling under the RAF's remit. With planes dropping bombs on places, the Iraqi populace would learn not to mess with the British and the status quo. The decade of unrest between Iraq becoming a kingdom and the Anglo-Iraqi War of 1941 suggests the RAF weren't all that successful with this strategy.

Slim's luck gave him the command he needed to prove himself in Iraq. 'It was good fun commanding a division in the Iraq desert,' he wrote.

> We had bought our beer in Haifa and drunk it on the shores of the Caspian. We could move, we could fight, and we had begun to build up that most valuable of all assets, a tradition of success. We had a good soldierly conceit of ourselves [. . .] The desert

suits the British, and so does fighting in it. You can see your man.[4]

Slim's command had come to him through good fortune. Recovering from the wounds he had sustained in East Africa, Slim was put on the staff at Indian GHQ. Iraq fell within Delhi's remit, and Slim was involved with planning; then in May 1941, he was dispatched to Basra as the local chief of staff. Then came the twist of fate: the man commanding the 10th Indian Infantry Division was taken ill, and Slim was promoted to take over. His boss, Lieutenant General Edward Quinan, had been charged with securing Iraq, Syria and Lebanon and displacing the colonial Vichy forces. Quinan's reputation for attention to detail was legendary, so he must have had great confidence in Slim to divert him from a staff job to command. This suited Slim – he had little taste for staff work. By the time he was done in Iraq he had been mentioned in dispatches twice and had found doing things his way, thinking on his feet and making do with what he had at his disposal, suited his temperament as a soldier – he had taken risks and improvised in the campaign to capture Deir-ez-Zor, surprising the enemy and taking the town within a day. Well-trained men accustomed to their environment and a bold manoeuvre forcing the enemy into confusion had worked wonders for Slim. The transfer to Burma that followed put him on the receiving end of what had worked so well for him in Iraq. The retreat of the Burma Corps in 1942, the disasters that befell the Indian and British armies, were explicable rather than a mystery. Alexander, who had been sent to save the situation, was, Slim said later, facing 'a task impossible with the means provided'.

The next year, Slim, kept out of battle by Lieutenant General Irwin, was able to observe where, again, they were going wrong: Irwin had fought his battle to the point where he had destroyed his men's morale. Poor morale was the symptom, poor training was the cause. Poor training, in the end, came from poor leadership. Slim needed to offer his men a new spiritual foundation that could withstand both jungle *and* an enemy that had a completely different outlook on death. He needed to foster aggression – he knew he could not motivate his men with the notion that they were fighting for the British Empire: his Indian soldiers wanted out of the empire, his British men knew the thing was done. Instead they were fighting to 'destroy the Japanese Army, to smash it as an evil thing'.[5] The Japanese had obliged him by treating both British and Burmese appallingly – they were no beneficent liberator. Now, with cause defined, Slim needed to equip his men with the means to this end.

*

Slim offered eight points, and in some ways it seems astonishing that some of these needed to be written down. But as the Arakan offensive ground itself into stalemate and then peril, Slim – sidelined by Irwin and then later blamed by him for how Arakan had gone, something of a reach given that the disaster Irwin had commanded was terminal for his career in Burma – was able to take the time to perfect his training method for XV Corps. Here the lack of centralization in the British and Indian Armies came into play – Slim was able to enforce his way of doing things rather than having to conform to existing standards, standards which had come up horribly short.

I. The individual soldier must learn, by living, moving, and exercising in it, that the jungle is neither impenetrable nor unfriendly. When he has once learned to move and live in it, he can use it for concealment, covered movement, and surprise.[6]

This was taking the perceived Japanese advantage head-on. Characterizing the jungle as neither impenetrable nor unfriendly was a radical proposition – until Slim proposed this it's exactly what the jungle was. In the wake of the 1942 retreat, different officers had tried to formulate their own solutions to the issues of jungle warfare, but there had been nothing as empathic as this plain statement about the jungle. Having outlined the problem, Slim offered the solution. How to master the jungle? Patrolling.

II. Patrolling is the master key to jungle fighting. All units, not only infantry battalions, must learn to patrol in the jungle, boldly, widely, cunningly and offensively.

The only real way of knowing for sure where the enemy was, and possibly divining his intentions, was patrolling. The jungle offered opportunities for concealment that favoured patrolling and reconnaissance; however, the emphasis on patrolling pushed more responsibility onto junior officers and NCOs, Keeping a unit coherent in the jungle was very demanding: maps if they existed weren't much use, getting lost was easy. Leadership was key, according to *Military Training Pamphlet No. 9 (India)*, aka *The Jungle Book**:

* The cartoon cover of this manual shows a Japanese soldier (no stereotype spared) writhing in the grasp of a hand dubbed 'good training'.

The hardship of jungle operations demands the highest type of leadership. The difficulties of control necessitate decentralization, which results in increased importance of small-unit actions. Because of this, junior officers and non-commissioned officers must possess outstanding initiative, boldness, and determination. Similarly, the development of self-reliance on the part of each individual is an important training objective.

Training had to ensure that everyone, cooks and clerks included, could patrol and, if it came to it – which it most likely would, going on past form – fight.

Having tackled the questions raised by the jungle, Slim moved on to the Japanese.

III. All units must get used to having Japanese parties in their rear, and, when this happens, regard not themselves, but the Japanese, as 'surrounded'.

This fundamental point addressed the problem that had bedevilled the British in 1942, and towards the end of the first Arakan offensive in 1943. Japanese speed of movement through the jungle had foxed everyone, Slim included, but by making sure everyone was trained to fight – especially in the British 'rear' – the Japanese could be held up and defeated. This was put to the test at the Battle of the Admin Box at Shinzweya in February 1944, when a Japanese formation advanced through Frank Messervy's 7th Indian Army Division. Messervy's headquarters was overrun (not for the first time in his career) and he was caught in his pyjamas. Everyone, from teeth to tail, became part of Messervy's fighting force, and the

Japanese had no answer to it. Once entangled in battle from every angle, they were held up long enough for reinforcements to arrive and destroy them. Messervy and his headquarters troops evaded the Japanese through the jungle – further fruit of their renewed jungle training – and he was able to take command of the battle. It delivered Slim and the Fourteenth Army, and indeed the British Empire, their first unambiguous victory in Burma after two solid years of disaster. Nor did it require spinning like Wingate's efforts of the previous year.

> IV. In defence, no attempt should be made to hold long continuous lines. Avenues of approach must be covered and enemy penetration between our posts dealt with at once by mobile local reserves who have completely reconnoitred the country.

Although Slim's ambitions were far from defensive – and with the war being fought inside India itself, it wasn't as though he could aspire to anything other than the reconquest of Burma – this fourth point addressed much the same issues as its predecessor. Long continuous lines offered the Japanese more opportunity to create confusion, infiltrate and isolate. Compact coherent formations could respond more decisively. Getting strung out along a road and dismantled piecemeal had been the story of 1942. Slim knew he could not afford to repeat this tactic.

Another tactic that couldn't be repeated was the bitter frontal slanging matches that Irwin had insisted on using in the Arakan in 1943.

> V. There should rarely be frontal attacks and never frontal attacks on narrow fronts. Attacks should follow

hooks and come in from flank or rear, while pressure holds the enemy in front.

Frontal attacks had achieved nothing in Arakan against well-concealed defensive positions. But if the Japanese had taught the British the futility of frontal attacks, it wasn't a lesson they had learned themselves. When Slim's methods came into play in 1944, and the Japanese had to deal with DUKE forces that were prepared to stand and fight, exploit the terrain and fight a war of jungle manoeuvre and counter-attack, their answer was repeated mass frontal attacks. Accounts of all the major engagements of 1944 describe Japanese infantry attacks as punctual, repetitive, predictable. Men would gather in large numbers in the same place and at the same time of day, call out threats and insults, and then charge. Once guns and mortars had been ranged these attacks would be not just repulsed but shattered. The hideous and bloody fighting at Kohima, where the British famously held on at the opposite end of the tennis court to the enemy, was made tactically more straightforward for the DUKE defenders by the Japanese, in the supposedly Einsteinian definition of insanity, trying the same thing over and over again and expecting different results. Had they been more tactically astute they might have broken the DUKE forces at Kohima.

Irony loiters at the scenes of 1944's battles. Mutaguchi's march on India had been inspired by studying British tactics – it was Wingate's disastrous adventures in LONG-CLOTH the previous year that had convinced Mutaguchi that he could strike a strategic blow by driving columns into the jungle, and get to India if he was able to create enough offensive momentum. Slim had used the enforced monsoon break to consider how to deny Mutaguchi that momentum. He had also considered how to make the Allied advantage in armour – Japan had not joined the tank race in any serious way – count in the jungle. Deploying tanks in bits and pieces in the Arakan had failed. Getting armour to Burma had been difficult enough, a symptom of the lack of importance accorded to the theatre. Squandering them, losing them in indecisive actions, might mean the supply would dry up altogether. Slim's attitude to kit had always been that his men would make do with what there was rather than what might be available in the future. Talking to the Press Club in 1946, he said,

> No boats? We'll build 'em! No vegetables, we'll grow 'em! No eggs? Duck farms! No parachutes? We'll use gully [dirt-cheap jute]! No road metal? Bake our own bricks and lay 'em! No air strips? Put down bithess [improvised hessian strips soaked in bitumen]! Malaria, we'll stop it! Medium guns busting? Saw off three feet of the barrel and go on shooting! Their motto, 'God helps those who help themselves.'[7]

Therefore Slim, who had had little experience of tanks as an Indian Army hand, nevertheless made his mind up about how they would be deployed in the Burmese battlefield. Concentration of force, the simple and deliberate lesson of Heinz Guderian's triumph in France in May 1940, was the principle Slim applied.

> VI. Tanks can be used in almost any country except swamp. In close country they must always have infantry with them to defend and reconnoitre for them.

They should always be used in the maximum numbers available and capable of being deployed. Whenever possible penny packets must be avoided. The more you use, the fewer you lose.

Legendary Panzer commander Guderian would have approved: 'You hit somebody with your fist and not with your fingers spread' and 'strike hard and fast and do not separate'. Slim understood what armour offered, perhaps more profoundly than Guderian, who described logistics as 'the ball and chain of armoured warfare', an attitude that sowed the seeds of disaster for the Germans in the Soviet Union. Slim knew he could only do as well as his logistics would allow.

In the style of an Orders (O) Group, with orders being repeated, Slim came to repeat himself: there were no non-combatants in jungle warfare. Patrolling mattered, at all times. The best way to know the whereabouts of the enemy was to patrol; being in contact with the enemy meant you knew where he was, after all. Everyone needed to be able to fight, and patrolling was the lubricant in the fighting machine.

VII. There are no non-combatants in jungle warfare. Every unit and sub-unit, including medical ones, is responsible for its own all-round protection, including patrolling, at all times.

If these seven points were followed, then the eighth would surely follow.

VIII. If the Japanese are allowed to hold the initiative they are formidable. When we have it, they are confused and easy to kill. By mobility away from roads, surprise, and offensive action we must regain and keep the initiative.[8]

Slim had delivered the foundations for how he would beat the Japanese, and in the British and Indian Army style, it had taken a general to formulate a way of doing it and then do what he could to instil his method in the men he commanded. In this he shared a great deal with Montgomery, who had determined that to get the best results from his men he would have to be autocratic. As both Slim and Montgomery ascended to the top in their very different theatres, they had drawn the same conclusion, but the chief difference was that Slim wasn't interested in openly playing the autocrat for his men.

Slim's successes on the battlefield had come when he – as he was happy to admit – had not taken counsel of his fears. More importantly still, when he was left to his own devices he was able to get his men to fight resolutely and bring the enemy to its knees. Similarly, just as Montgomery had Brooke's backing, Slim had the backing he needed. Mountbatten, Auchinleck and Wavell had all given Slim the tools he needed to finish the job. Mountbatten was prepared to bat for Slim when he needed resources or simply moral support. Auchinleck with his Infantry Committee in 1943 had helped to equip Slim with soldiers who had been trained for the jungle – in particular, putting a stop to 'milking' units of their experienced officers and NCOs to create new formations. Wavell had set this process in motion in late 1942, but the Indian Army had immediate operations to stage and institutional inertia to get over before the changes bore fruit. Later on, as new faces arrived in the theatre, Slim had Mountbatten's backing to the extent that he was able to ignore Leese almost entirely. That the British system of command had the flexibility in it to allow a general to take control of things was Slim and Montgomery's good fortune. But it was vulnerable when senior men didn't know what to do and had insufficient grip on the men they commanded. What you had to do was ride out the bad times and have the luck, the timing and the patronage, and hope that you got to the point where you had the leeway to impose your will on the theatre you found yourself fighting in. And Slim's theatre came with the extra challenge of the jungle.

*

Published in September 1943 by the Military Training Directorate, the fourth edition of *Military Training Pamphlet No. 9 (India): The Jungle Book* marked a turning point in training. Collating the Indian Army's experiences in 1942 and Australian experience of fighting in Malaya, it set out to centralize and standardize jungle training. The Australians had published a pamphlet of their own in May 1942 and in November of that year established a jungle school in Queensland. The Indian Army took note, and Wavell asked if he could pick Australian brains. *The Jungle Book* draws heavily on the Australian pamphlet, and extends it. Point 2 of its preface reads:

> In principle there is nothing new in jungle warfare, but the environment of the jungle is new to many of our troops. Special training is therefore necessary to accustom them to jungle conditions and to teach them jungle methods.

The preface goes on to explain how, although there is nothing new in jungle warfare, it's not like anything else the Indian Army or the British has done before.

3. Woodcraft, silent movement, concealment, deception, keen eyesight and hearing, and above all good marksmanship and superb physical fitness are the requisites of jungle fighting.

4. Experience shows that command must be decentralized so that junior leaders will be confronted with situations in which they must make decisions and act without delay on their own responsibility. The ability to make sound decisions can only follow from thorough training and continuous practice.*

5. Since both jungle fighting and night fighting are characterized by limited vision and difficulties of maintaining control and direction, they have much in common with each other. If, therefore, units are unable to train under jungle conditions, a high standard of night training must be achieved and will prove to be an excellent preparation for jungle fighting.

The Jungle Book tells its own story of how fighting in the jungle was a problem to be solved, and the new seriousness being applied to tackling this. A mark of this seriousness comes in the first section, which deals with tactical doctrine, the use of infantry, artillery, sappers and so on, attack, patrolling, defence et cetera, in exhaustive multi-paragraph detail. Patrolling runs to several pages, reflecting Slim's emphasis on it. Again and again, *The Jungle Book* stresses that the jungle is a battlefield that demands

---

* *Auftragstaktik*, anyone?

resourcefulness in leadership; commanding a spread-out formation taking several lines of advance in country with visibility of not much more than 20 feet took great skill and concentration. Frontal attacks got a short paragraph; flanking attacks, which were 'more difficult than the front[al] attack but [. . .] may often be more decisive', got ten. And then we come to Point XI, which addresses the question of withdrawal. It states simply (and the caps are theirs): 'THERE WILL BE NO WITHDRAWAL.'

*

But it was disease, rather than an enemy, that was the toughest nut to crack. The jungle itself was an incredibly unhealthy, dangerous place: 'an enemy behind every rock', as the modern jungle manuals say. In the jungle were mosquitoes, mites, flies ('important mechanical carriers of intestinal diseases and yaws'), lice, fleas, bloodsucking leeches, rats, chiggers ('carriers of "scrub typhus" '), centipedes, cockroaches, scorpions, poisonous snakes and crocodiles. Elephants too were a problem: men would be run into by families of elephants crashing their way through the jungle. Compare and contrast *The Jungle Book* with the notes for servicemen that have been republished and become novelty stocking fillers in recent years ('the French are a proud people', that sort of stuff) – the European theatre didn't offer any of these immediate life-threatening challenges. In terms of illness, in the jungle a soldier might expect to encounter malaria, elephantiasis (filariasis), intestinal diseases, dengue fever, typhus fever, typhoid and paratyphoid fever, gonorrhoea, syphilis, granuloma inguinale, fungal infections, tropical ulcers, parasitic infections; 'heat exhaustion, sunstroke, and pneumonia may affect small numbers of troops'.*

Top of the list, always, was malaria. 'In 1944, for every man evacuated with wounds we have one hundred and twenty evacuated sick, the annual malaria rate alone was eighty-four per cent, per annum of the total strength of the army,' wrote Slim.[9] The War Office pamphlet, the prosaically named *Malaria: A Pamphlet for Officers*, makes its point and shows its priorities: 'malaria can ruin your health permanently; it can destroy the fighting efficiency of an army'. There being a war on, it was perhaps the latter that was the main issue. The pamphlet goes on to say: 'In some ways malaria is more formidable than the human enemy. Its sphere of activity may cover the whole theatre of operations. It is always threatening you and you can never afford to relax your watch.'

Measures against malaria were multiple, and they were not just the duty of the medical officer: 'every man from the commander to the private soldier must play his part. There must be no shirkers. The same strict discipline is demanded as is required in battle.' In its way, the defence against malaria took on the same character as the need for every man to be trained to fight. Later the pamphlet states: 'Under active service conditions in the field, personal protection is the most important of all methods of malaria prevention. Failure to observe personal protective measures is tantamount to self-inflicted injury and demands strong disciplinary action.' Malaria had an added complication: men

---

* These are listed in the American equivalent of *The Jungle Book*, almost gleefully.

who had been bitten became 'infective' – mosquitoes biting a man with malaria would pick it up themselves and potentially pass it on. The infected man had to be isolated, the manual said.

Slim's solution sought to help treat the man with malaria and make things a lot less complicated logistically. The strain that malaria – along with everything else a man could catch in the jungle – placed on medical services was colossal. Men sent to recuperate in India took up vital railway space and were out of commission for longer. The Malarial Forward Treatment Unit dealt with men as soon as they had been infected: rather than a long, exhausting and potentially reinfectious round trip, they would be being treated within 24 hours and, if treatment went well, back with their unit within three weeks. Losing Malaya had meant that the default treatment for malaria, quinine, was in short supply and was replaced with mepacrine. Men had to take their mepacrine – units were surprise-tested to check that they were. Commanding officers whose men fell below the 95 per cent standard were sacked. The autocrat in Slim made sure of it: 'I only had to sack three; by then the rest had got my meaning.'[10]

*

Using all of these new methods and tools re-energized the Fourteenth Army. But in the end, the enemy had to be beaten and, in the case of the Japanese fighting in Burma, killed. The Allied preponderance of firepower, supply, the use of 'boxes' (an idea that had travelled to India from the desert, where, paradoxically, they had not worked) as solid bases from which to destroy the enemy, either with aggressive offensive action or unmoveable defence, were all very well, but fighting an enemy that might retreat, eventually, but would never surrender meant victory had to be pursued to the enemy's last round.

Winkling out the last man took guts for the men of the Fourteenth Army, regardless of firepower. Other wars have been lost by armies that outgunned an opponent who was unprepared to sell its lives cheaply. Slim was able to keep his men going, even when the fighting was at its worst, because he had put their welfare at the centre of his approach to battle.

With the defensive battles of 1944 at Kohima and Imphal won, Slim pursued the retreating Japanese into the monsoon and then beyond. The epic battles fought in the spring of 1945 brought together every aspect of what Slim had perfected with the Fourteenth Army. It was time to plan for the final routing of the Japanese from Burma. The offensive battles of 1945, in which Slim out-thought and outfought the Japanese, diverting his own forces in a dazzling armoured hook around the enemy flank and over the Irrawaddy. showed that the defeats of 1942 and 1943 were dim and distant memories. Slim's army was a different army altogether. If Slim had had to build a new army from the Indian Army in the wake of the defeats of 1942, in the United States the task was even bigger: an army was having to be built from scratch.

6

Omar Bradley

The GI General

In 1971, when the USA was up to its bloody neck in Vietnam, Omar Bradley spoke about leadership to the US Army College. Whether he was talking about his experience of command in the Second World War or addressing the quagmire in Indo-China – most likely both – the speech is a revealing read. As an army group commander from 1 August 1944 to VE Day, Bradley commanded more troops than any general in American history: 4 armies, 12 corps, 48 divisions – in all 1.3 million troops: he'd be someone you listened to. Bradley offers a heady cocktail of bromides, he talks about how you're only as good as your plan and your plan is only as good as your implementation of it: 'While it takes a good staff officer to initiate an effective plan, it requires a leader to ensure that the plan is properly executed.' He makes a dig at a former vice president of an 'industrial company' who was only ever a staff officer and never saw combat; he cautions that it is 'a grave error for the leader to surround himself with "Yes" men'. He says leaders need to be physically fit, stubborn, able to manage problems they do not understand: 'One doesn't have to be a tank expert in order to use a tank unit effectively.' The leader needs to be an all-rounder. He needs a plan – 'any good plan, boldly executed, is

162

better than indecision' – though he caveats, 'There is usually more than one way to obtain results.'

Bradley's shopping list of leadership attributes, and he accepts that some people are born leaders, centres on confidence: creating it, radiating it, inspiring it. He then turns to a story that, for a man reputedly modest, reflects rather well on him and how he believed his men saw him:

> Just before the invasion of Normandy in 1944, a story went around in some of the amphibious assault units that went ashore that they would suffer 100 per cent casualties – that none of them would come back. I found it necessary to visit these units and talk to all ranks. I told them that we would, naturally, suffer casualties, but that our losses would for certain be manageable and that with our air and naval support we would succeed. After our landing, a correspondent told me that on his way across the Channel in one of the leading *LSTs* he had noticed a sergeant reading a novel. Struck by the seeming lack of concern of the sergeant, he asked, 'Aren't you worried? How can you be reading at a time like this?' The sergeant replied: 'No, I am not worried. General Bradley said everything would go alright, so why should I worry.'

He also said a general needs 'LUCK'. And he used capitals. Omar Bradley was not as confident in his use of the pen as, say, Patton, and would usually have speeches written for him, but those capitals feel like his.

*

When, after a spot of diplomatic dithering, Britain and France declared war on Germany in September 1939, honouring their commitment to Poland, the USA was doing its utmost to look the other way. Foreign adventures – at least in Europe – were not something the American political establishment could sanction; convincing the electorate of the need to get involved in another war would be impossible. For all the strategic arguments there might be for America to involve itself in this new European war, the political reality was the president knew this was beyond his reach, defying political gravity. Besides, America would be getting involved anyway, taking vast orders for manufacturing planes, rifles and all the kind of materiel that the British and French needed. This new war would dovetail nicely with the New Deal.

The American establishment had drawn from its First World War experiences conclusions similar to those of the other main Allied players, except it had the luxury of distance. Isolationist America was in a sense not much different from Ten Year Rule Britain, except it did not have an overseas empire (the Philippines don't count for some reason). America's nearest neighbours, Canada and Mexico, had settled their differences with the US – Mexico had, during the First World War, been on the receiving end of some heavy flirting by Germany that came to nothing for Mexico but resulted in America's entry into the war, and Canada had been an ally alongside America, despite being a part of the empire the Americans so despised. What this meant was that by 1939 the US Army was essentially a paper formation, its officers a tiny cadre – the US Army was more like a think-tank than anything that might be able to field tanks. What soldiering the US Army was actually doing resembled, if anything, the kind of imperial garrison duties that the British Army undertook, but on a far smaller scale: guarding the Panama Canal and keeping a US presence in the American non-colony in the Philippines. It seems staggering now, with the hindsight of the decades after the war, that the US Army in 1939 was the seventeenth largest in the world. And while American policy in the 1930s gravitated towards trying to help the Chinese in their struggle against Japan, the notion that the USA might field an army was preposterous. The declaration of war in Europe didn't much change that. The US was staying out of it, no matter what Nazi Germany might appear to be, or do next.

However, that didn't mean that President Roosevelt was going to do nothing. On 1 September 1939, he made an important and consequential appointment, directly in the wake of the news that Germany had invaded Poland, though not because of it: General G. C. Marshall was formally appointed US Army Chief of Staff. This was to be expected – he had been in place as deputy – but it was appointing Marshall that set the tone and direction of the truly astonishing military expansion that was to follow. Marshall established his relationship with Roosevelt there and then: he told the president he would need to be able to speak frankly to him, disagree, give him what he had to hear rather than what he wanted to hear. Marshall insisted on being called 'General', and he made a point of not laughing at the president's jokes.

The numbers make the expansion the US underwent all the more amazing. In 1939, the US Army comprised 189,839 officers and enlisted men. The British Army by the end of that year, as recruitment and expansion got going after the collapse of the Munich agreement, stood at 1.1 million men – and by the summer of 1940 another

550,000 men had joined. Five years later the British Army was at its largest with 2.9 million in all ranks. The growth of the US Army leaves the British for dust – by the end of the war 11 million men had served in the US Army (during the First World War it had grown to 3.6 million, so this expansion was of a different order). Other numbers tell the story of how the US completely transformed itself militarily. Between the wars, the tank arm of the US Army was wound down. At the same time that the British Army, instructed by its politicians not to anticipate another European war, was mulling how to become a fully mechanized force, the Americans were turning their backs on tanks altogether, much to the chagrin of the men who had embraced this new form of warfare during the Great War: for example, George S. Patton. By the end of the Second World War the US had produced 90,000 tanks – many of which were exported to the United States' allies – but as a measure of what that meant for the Americans on the battlefield, the counter-attack the US Army put in after the German Ardennes offensive in January 1945 drew on the more than 7,000 tanks that the US armies in North-West Europe had at their disposal.

These numbers don't just speak for themselves, they holler from the rooftops of something truly profound; especially given that in 1939 US tank production of its main type, the M2 light tank, totalled eighteen. The 11.6-ton M2 was armed with a machine gun, in contrast to tanks like the 46-ton M26 Pershing, which went into service only five years later boasting 90mm tank-busting ordnance. During exercises in Louisiana in the summer of 1940, which started two days before the German attack on France, Belgium and the Netherlands, the US Army had made do with trucks with 'TANK' painted on their sides and next to no planes. These Louisiana Manoeuvres seemed farcical in comparison with the German war machine. Cynics could take heart from the fact that the US Army was no longer seventeenth in the world – it had gone up a place with the destruction of the Poles. This all underlines what a dazzling achievement American rearmament was, and it does make you wonder just how poor an appreciation the German and Japanese governments had of their distant potential foes.

Marshall's strength was as an administrator – he had not commanded men in combat. In the First World War he had worked on 'Black Jack' Pershing's staff, where he had drawn his own conclusions about command: orders didn't need to be perfect, they needed to be delivered on time. Much of how the Americans had fought in the Great War had displeased Marshall; he didn't like waste, he wanted his men involved in the decisions that were being made for them, he prized the democratic involvement of his men. Expanding the US Army on the scale and at the speed required needed someone able to navigate Washington politics, who could be taken seriously by the president and the army, rather than a tactical genius. As ever with these kinds of appointments, not everyone was delighted. Marshall brought his people with him into his revolutionary shake-up of the US Army. Omar Bradley was one of them, along with George S. Patton,* Mark Clark, Jacob L. Devers and Ike Eisenhower. The US Army was to be cast in George Marshall's image.

---

* Though Patton had favoured one of Marshall's rivals, it didn't seem to affect his career.

Nevertheless, isolationism prevailed in Washington. As the Phoney War unfolded and the shock of Poland's rapid defeat faded, received political wisdom drifted towards the notion that the new war in Europe would blow over somehow, that there was no more fighting to come. Roosevelt and Marshall faced opposition from every angle; even the Secretary of War, Harry Hines Woodring, was opposed to reforming the army. (This didn't stop him saying in later life that Marshall's appointment had been his idea. Politicians, eh?) Two weeks after war broke out in 1939, Charles Lindbergh, his platform afforded him by a heady mixture of public fame and sympathy, urged America to stay out of the war between white people, for the sake of white people, because the real war would be with the 'Asiatic hordes'. If this was him predicting war with Japan, he was indeed prescient, but it also displayed a nakedly racist appreciation of what the stakes were in Europe; he also warned against 'enemies within' in a way an anti-Semite might understand. Public opinion in the spring of 1940 was firmly set against entering the European war – 96.4 per cent of Americans polled were opposed to war. It was in the face of all of this that Marshall set about expanding and reforming the army.

The relationship between the state, the army and its veterans, however, was extremely fragile. A new model would be needed. Veterans of the First World War – many of whom were still in hospitals suffering from long-term injuries sustained in the Great War – had marched on Washington in the run-up to Roosevelt's election in 1932. Calling themselves the Bonus Army, they demanded justice for their service. In 1924, the Hoover administration, strapped for cash, had awarded veterans a bonus that was not redeemable until 1945 (one for fans of irony, that). The

Bonus Marchers camped in Washington; the police couldn't move them on. Troops were then deployed against them – the Chief of Staff Douglas MacArthur had no compunction about charging the Bonus Marchers, who thought the troops were parading in sympathy. Cavalry and tanks were deployed: cavalryman and tank enthusiast George Patton doing his bit, alongside Ike Eisenhower, who had advised MacArthur against it. The camp was cleared at bayonet point and with tear gas, and was understandably electorally damaging for Roosevelt's predecessor, Herbert Hoover. There were fears of communist infiltration, understandable in the wake of the Russian Revolution; this paranoia put the willies up the Hoover White House far more than the possibility that the state might be doing long-term political damage to its relationship with the fathers of the sons it might need to recruit in the event of another war.

This may have backfired on Hoover – Roosevelt certainly thought so – but Roosevelt had not sided with the veterans either, also refusing to pay the proposed bonus sooner. Nevertheless, rather than sending the army to the albeit slightly smaller Bonus March that met in Washington the next year, he sent his wife. Eleanor Roosevelt went down to the Bonus Camp and led a singalong and somehow defused the situation, offering the men a place in the newly instituted Civilian Conservation Corps, the president's New Deal voluntary work scheme for unmarried men between 18 and 25 years of age, loosening the qualification requirement so older men and men with families could get work. The CCC's role was to keep men in work and improve the country's infrastructure and resource management: forestry, roads, dams, parks, mosquito control as well as disaster relief – manual outdoor labour, enrollees living in camps where they were working. At its largest, the CCC had 300,000 people enrolled – 3 million people in total served with the CCC, including what was called the Indian Division, keeping Native Americans in work, as well as segregated camps for black Americans, though blacks weren't allowed leadership roles. Enrollees were paid $30 a month; crucially, they had to send $25 home. It was better paid therefore than the army. The CCC, nicknamed Roosevelt's Tree Army, was massively popular with the American public, polling very positively, and it was claimed enrollees benefitted from the physical work and being outdoors. Education and training were built in for the CCC recruits, so they didn't go in one end and come out the other having learned only how to wield a shovel.

Roosevelt intended the CCC would be a means to create future national wealth. Dust Bowl Depression America seemed the perfect time for such a social experiment, and Roosevelt saw an opportunity. It quickly became clear that young Americans needed as much care as the country's blasted environment. The Army Surgeon General performed a survey in the late 1930s of 100,000 enrollees, finding that poverty had taken its toll – 75 per cent were what the army regarded as underweight, prone to illness and disease. This served as a forewarning for what the army would be dealing with if young American men were drafted. Little wonder then that the CCC, like the army, as part of its induction, put enrolees through a regime of fitness training, inoculation, discipline and proper food. Men who had served with the CCC would return home transformed: muscular, tanned, self-assured. The CCC offered masculinity, associated with the outdoors, and a fresh-air life not unlike the life of a soldier. Only the pay was better.

Inevitably, for all this hearty outdoorsy transform-the-American-wilderness stuff and the general improvement of the feckless (I'm trying to capture the spirit of things here, rather than agree, you'll understand), the CCC was regarded by some as un-American. Un-Americanism is, of course, in the eye of the beholder – like beauty, often subjective. From the left it felt un-American because of its similarities to the *Arbeitsdienst* in Germany; the charge was it was a fascist scheme of work camps. On the right, well, you guessed it: the CCC was fomenting communism for much the same reasons. Camps were hotbeds of radicalism and antagonistic to democratic values. The White House countered that the CCC was a melting pot for all American ethnicities where men were bound together by honest toil; Jews, Poles, Italians, Slovaks could all say they were Americans thanks to their work with the CCC. This played well with the right, though of course as an idea it had its limits. This angle fitted the White House and public opinion well, but the extent to which it was true was debatable. If you were black, the CCC didn't represent a chance to be brought into the American national community at all. The New Deal didn't welcome all ethnicities to its new labour-born civic family.

Beyond Eleanor Roosevelt's offer to the Bonus Marchers in 1933, the CCC became entangled with the army. With further irony, Douglas MacArthur was put in charge of the CCC camps. He grumbled about how this would affect US Army readiness, but given how tiny the army was, what wouldn't? Plenty in the army quickly took to the CCC, though, and the relationship was fruitful. For MacArthur, it presented an opportunity for empire-building; he liked the idea that the CCC essentially offered the army

300,000 partially trained recruits, their bodies hardened by manual labour, disciplined in quasi-military command. To his frustration, he didn't get all that far in turning the CCC into a military reserve, but the organization nevertheless offered the army plenty to get its teeth into. How officers performed in running CCC camps became a good barometer of their leadership skills. In contrast to MacArthur, George Marshall made the most of the experience, in particular the challenges that the expansion of the CCC in its first year offered him as an administrator, having to coordinate a vast and sudden influx of enrolees (not unlike what would happen to the army only a few years later). The CCC forced the army to come face to face with civilians in peacetime, to mobilize them, organize them, put them to national use. As the effects of the Great Depression diminished, the need for the CCC tailed off, but not before the army had benefitted from the experience of training men and itself. One of the officers who did well in the CCC – indeed, who loved his time with it – was Major Omar Bradley.

*

A bright lad, son of a schoolteacher, Omar was born on 12 February 1893 and grew up in poverty in Missouri. He was working as a boilermaker when he applied to West Point – coming second in his application; the candidate who came first didn't take up his place, so Bradley got through by default. Though no one was to know it at the time, the class that Bradley graduated from in 1915 had a dazzling future ahead of it. Known now as 'the class the stars fell on', it delivered a fundament of future generals, from staff officers to a presidential commander-in-chief.

Bradley loved every minute of it, his memoirs talk of sports, friends, 'Duty, Honor, Country', as well as of 'a smiling golden-haired Kansan, Dwight D. Eisenhower'.[1] Bradley even relates that he thought the merciless hazing that the class underwent had its merits in that it bound them together. Mutual support was important, too. Bradley claims he coached his roommate through his first year in maths and science. He excelled in sports and, now he was eating properly, put on weight. The 1914 West Point base-ball team that Bradley played in was made up entirely of generals of the future. Team sports took up so much time, he felt they affected his grades:

> However, I have never regretted my sports obsession for a moment. It is almost trite to observe that in organized team sports one learns the important art of group cooperation in goal achievement. No extracurricular endeavor I know of could better prepare a soldier for the battlefield. West Point sports also gave me an excellent opportunity to take the measure of many men who would serve with, or under, me in World War II.[2]

His love of team sports is key to understanding Bradley's attitude, his personality, his approach to command. He was interested in being a team player; even when he was in command positions his attitude was that he was a team player; his role was to bring out the best in the men he regarded as his teammates. That he was born dirt poor, won a scholarship place and loved to play team sports with his classmates is the core of who Bradley was and what he felt the army had to offer to ordinary Americans like him.

Bradley was a keen athlete in a class of athletic excellence. His first posting was to the Mexican border; then, when America entered the First World War, he was sent to guard copper mines in Montana, a posting he regarded as miserable; then the war ended before he could get to France and fight. In March 1919, he was earmarked for a trip to Vladivostok in command of 1,000 troops for duty in Siberia; this posting evaporated quickly enough. After the war, he earned a reputation as a trainer, teaching at West Point, and above all for being dependable, catching George Marshall's eye. Marshall reckoned you could give Bradley a job and leave him to get on with it. During his time in the CCC, Bradley ran the six all-black companies at Fort Benning:

> men who had arrived from the poorest farm areas of Georgia and Alabama. We organized them, issued clothing, established pay accounts [. . .] gave them physicals and a couple of weeks 'training,' then shipped them to camps in the field. Some of these men had not had a square meal for at least a year.
>
> The army's magnificent performance with the *CCC* in the summer of 1933, undertaken so reluctantly, was one of the highlights of its peacetime years. It all ran with clockwork precision; the *CCC* itself was judged first rate. It was a good drill for us, like the rapid mobilization of 1917 – and another rapid mobilization that, unknown to us, lay only seven years ahead.[3]

Bradley's enthusiasm for the CCC put him in the camp of believers within the army, and bound him to Marshall rather than MacArthur. It also acclimatized him to having to work with citizens rather than soldiers when war did finally arrive. The CCC went a long way to attuning the US Army to its future recruits. Bradley later summarized his time with CCC with a who's who of US Army Second World War command talent:

> These had been four wonderful and constructive years. I had not only participated in a revolution but had made or renewed and cemented many friendships with infantry officers who would play leading roles in the years ahead: George Marshall, Joe Stilwell, Bedell Smith, Joe Collins, Matt Ridgway, Pink Bull, Buck Lanham, Forrest Harding and scores of others. The Marshall years at Fort Benning have been flippantly described as his 'nursery school' for the generals of World War II.[4]

When war came to Europe, Bradley was at the War Department, very much one of Marshall's guys, and he admired his boss's style, dry as it was, calling him

> austere, cold, aloof, succinct, prudish [. . .] he never addressed anyone by his first name [. . .] yet, off duty Marshall had a discernible warmth and moderate sense of fun. He loved to ride, to fox-hunt, to stage elaborate pageants and parades, to gather his officers and their wives for tea and cakes, to entertain and write to children he knew.[5]

Bradley, who lived a plain life, not drinking or smoking, clearly admired his mentor's austerity, and perhaps emulated it. Their association would be critical to the development of the army and the invention of the GI.

Marshall had an extremely difficult year in 1941. Newspaper stories about plummeting morale amongst recruits in army camps were leapt upon by isolationists and non-interventionists (the two being interchangeable, and comprising elements sympathetic to the Germans as well as straightforward pacifists). An army with no enemy to fight was necessarily difficult to motivate. There was tension around the question of extending men's time in the army – with no war to justify the measure, Roosevelt had to bargain hard with Congress. In mid August, an article in *Life* magazine about how the US Army was essentially aimless caused Roosevelt and Marshall further disruption. Men were reported as saying they didn't believe the president when he said the country was faced with a national emergency: the article claimed that morale was rock bottom at the precise moment the president wanted to extend army service. The War Department publicly denied it, worried that the *Life* article and the debates in Congress were in themselves lowering morale amongst its new recruits.

The *New York Times* decide to commission its own report; Hilton Howell Railey, a mercurial journalistic adventurer who had written for the *Times* from the front line in the Great War, as well as promoting Amelia Earhart – he had phoned her to ask her if she would like to fly the Atlantic – was commissioned to debunk the *Life* article. Unfortunately, Railey's conclusions were even more pessimistic – and given a sneak preview, the army banned their publication. Riley had found chaos, drunkenness and what he called disloyalty. The National Guard in particular came in for heavy criticism. Marshall decided that the solution lay in officer training – from there all else would follow – and he wanted the best people identified and trained accordingly, rather than relying on the tradition of businessmen nominating themselves as colonels and running regiments that had operated in the previous war. Marshall promoted Bradley, sent him to Fort Benning and ordered him to devise an officer training scheme that would deliver men who could lead and train. Bradley based his Officer Candidate School on West Point principles of hard work and a sense of honour, and the idea that each candidate had the potential to rise to the very top, regardless of who they were, if they had the talent and put in the graft.

Bradley was working inside the guts of the new army, intimate with its developments and Marshall's ambitions, and radically re-energizing officer training. He had his ear to the ground as developments in armour were pushed for by people like Patton, who had made a name for himself in the Louisiana Manoeuvres (these manoeuvres had been keenly followed by the papers, reporting on the results of the battle exercises as if they were real battles. Bradley had worked on the staff and planning side of the Louisiana Manoeuvres rather than in command, not grabbing headlines like Patton). Bradley also paid keen attention to the nascent airborne establishment at Fort Benning under William C. Lee; the Americans had been as shocked and stimulated by German use of parachute and glider-borne troops as the British, and like their British counterparts they overlooked just how disastrous some of these operations had been. But what Bradley wanted really was command, to get out of the War Department, get away from research and development and put into practice his ideas about how to train citizen soldiers. In late December 1941, he got his chance.

*

America's forced entry into the war meant that all the tip-toeing the Roosevelt administration had done around the America First movement (super-isolationist, the movement that had started out as pacifist was pretty quickly consumed by proto-fascists), the Future Veterans movement, a satirical take on how badly veterans had fared, and other anti-mobilization opponents, like anti-British Irish representatives, could now end. In 1941, the US Army had run another series of manoeuvres, which revealed how short of kit they were and how hard it was to train men without it. The army decided to reactivate three of its First World War divisions: the 77th, 82nd and 85th. The numbers in themselves speak for Roosevelt's ambitions for colossal expansion in the army. Bradley was assigned the 82nd Division – and some readers will have got ahead of me here: it was later converted to an airborne division and duly became glamorous and famous, taking part in operations and adventures of legend. But not under Bradley. When he got the job, he assembled a staff around him, including Matt Ridgway, who would go on to command the 82nd once it had its jump wings. The 82nd was to be established at Camp Claiborne ('almost overnight') and, as Bradley described it in his memoir, 'was to be a new experiment in mobilization [. . .] the challenge was large; the danger of failure, or even disaster, lay everywhere'.[6] Again, modesty prevents Bradley from saying immediately that it was a success and the springboard to his further promotion, but the 82nd worked well for him. His CCC days came in handy: the division was built around a cadre of 10 per cent of men from the 9th Division – 700 officers and enlisted men – then the rest of the division were draftees, civilians, not volunteers, men who had been scooped up by circumstance. Bradley describes his concerns – that day one for a draftee is the worst, the most nerve-racking day, that the sudden arrival of 16,000 men all at once having to adjust to a life of 'hurry up and wait' might lead to devastating morale problems.

So this is how the 'GI General' made his GIs:

> I conceived the notion – radical at the time – that we would do everything within our ability to make the draftees feel they were coming to a 'home' where people really cared about their welfare. This is not to say we intended to coddle the recruits. In fact, we intended to be tough as hell on them, but in an intelligent, humane, understanding way. At the same time, we would evoke and build upon the 82nd's illustrious history, giving our conscripts the impression that they were not only coming to a home, but a famous, even elitist, one.[7]

Bradley prioritized fitness, shocked as he was by the state of the draftees: one-third of the men were below par physically. His complaints sound entirely modern, and like those of any officer having to deal with drafted men rather than volunteers:

> Some of our draftees could not walk a mile with a pack without keeling over. Most were overweight and soft as marshmallows. Only a very few were capable of the hard sustained physical exertion that we knew they would experience in combat.[8]

Officers had to do the same training as the men – Bradley tells of an occasion when he fell from the obstacle course rope into sewage (Matt Ridgway loved this incident so much he put it in his memoirs as well). Bradley, without combat experience, searching for tactical wisdom, looked to the history of the 82nd – their most famous soldier was Sergeant Alvin York, who had fought an astonishing personal action during the Meuse–Argonne offensive in October 1918. York had gone forward in a small party to try to knock out a German machine-gun position on Hill 221. His party managed to get into the German lines but were counter-attacked – York fought a pitiless close-range battle, killing at least 25 men with his rifle and his pistol and taking 'only' 132 prisoners. He won the Congressional Medal of Honour* and with that came colossal fame. Between the wars, he had served as a superintendent with the CCC; then, when war seemed on the cards again, York stuck his head above the political parapet as an opponent of isolationism. Bradley asked York to come to talk to the 82nd, and picked his brains about his heroic action. York explained to Bradley what a close-range affair it had been: most of his shooting had been at 25 yards; Bradley set up a shooting range as part of an assault course; men would run through the course and then engage can targets at short range. It was a million miles from the static long-range shooting the US Army had favoured up to that point.

Bradley's formula worked – he was team-building, and drawing on his team's historic experience. It worked so well that he was immediately reposted to the 28th National Guard Division, which, rather than raising him, needed saving. The 82nd was earmarked for conversion to airborne,

---

* And the French Légion d'Honneur, Croix de Guerre, Médaille Militaire, the Italian Croce al Merito and the Montenegrans didn't miss out either, awarding him the War Medal, plus many, many more.

which was deemed a bit too paratrooper and not GI enough
for the GI General's skills. Bradley spent four weeks figuring out what was wrong with the 28th: everything, pretty
much. The officers were too old; command structures were
incoherent and inconsistent; the men were unfit, prone to
going home when they ought to be in camp. Again, Bradley's modesty suggests he really wasn't sure, when he
initiated a top-to-bottom reorganization of the division,
whether he would face 'meek compliance or mutiny'. He
decided he would give the 28th the 82nd treatment, working on route marches, building up the distances, weeding
out the men who weren't fit enough, joining the route
marches himself. Bradley spent the rest of 1942 with these
National Guardsmen, and while he took great satisfaction
in a job well done, he must have begun to wonder whether
he would ever get into battle. He was also getting the kind
of press that would infuriate flashier commanders: he was
seen as ordinary, straight, solid and stable, ungimmicky,
though also as someone who was a true leader, who inspired
devotion. Certainly Bradley was devoted to his command –
his family only saw him on Sundays. When Operation
TORCH began in November 1942 and the new US Army
met its first full-scale test in combat, Bradley was still training National Guardsmen. The 28th practised amphibious
landings anyway, an experience Bradley would file away as
useful at the time and which would be crucial later. He had
been in the army for 31 years before a combat command
came: this expert trainer, staff officer and civilian handler
supreme was off to serve in North Africa with his old classmate Eisenhower.

When he got to Africa, he found that what Eisenhower
wanted him to do was fix the II Corps, which had been

defeated by Rommel in the Kasserine Pass. A rude awakening for everyone in the US Army, now they had passed from the world of theory into the world of practical warfare. Lieutenant General Lloyd Fredendall was fired and returned to training in the US – like Bradley, he was one of Marshall's men; Marshall's patronage had got him the command but it hadn't spared him the sack. Bradley was installed by Eisenhower as George Patton's deputy; his real task was as Ike's eyes and ears in Patton's (very successful) shake-up. Interestingly, Bradley immediately identified what he thought was the problem with how the US Army had performed in Tunisia: the Louisiana Manoeuvres. Bradley believed that the manoeuvres had offered the army a bum steer:

> In maneuvers, when two forces meet, the umpires invariably decide that the smaller force must withdraw, or if greatly outnumbered, it must surrender. And while the umpires deliberate, the men simply stand or sit about idly. No means are provided for giving proportionate weight to the many intangibles of warfare, such as morale, training, leadership, conditioning. There have been many cases where, in my opinion, forces have surrendered unnecessarily. According to the umpire rules, they were probably justified. I believe that very few circumstances arise where surrender is actually justified. A greatly outnumbered force can accomplish wonders by vigorous and aggressive action.[9]

Useful and instructive as they had been for the logistical and organizational experience of full-scale operations, the manoeuvres had missed out these intangibles. Leadership truly mattered, morale was central to the execution of leadership, aggression was essential. These were the lessons of the battlefield. When the Tunisian campaign ended Bradley was given command of the II Corps, and Patton returned to the I Armored Corps to prepare for the invasion of Sicily. Bradley cleared house, sacking the people he didn't think were up to snuff. This was Bradley's great promotion, his moment of ascent that meant he had entered the major leagues. Next came Operation HUSKY, the invasion of Sicily. If this was an Allied rehearsal for an eventual amphibious invasion of north-west France, then it was Bradley's rehearsal too. Solid, stable, dependable, in Marshall's image, working closely with his classmate Dwight D. Eisenhower, the GI General.

*

The writer Ernie Pyle – 'as you may know, I am concerned mainly with the common soldier – the well-known GI'[10] – who worked in what would be called an embedded style nowadays,* spent time with Bradley, saw him close up; it was he who coined Bradley's nickname: the GI General. Bradley wasn't a man for spending much time with his men, though, preferring to stick with his staff, so what did Pyle mean? In 1943, the term GI was only just emerging to describe the everyman American soldier; in the Great War they had been known as 'Doughboys', but by the Second World War this had started to shift. GI meant 'Government Issue', or 'General Issue', coming by way of the 'Galvanized Iron' markings on logistical items. I think

---

* Pyle was killed by Japanese machine-gun fire on the island of Iejima, off Okinawa, in April 1945.

it is in this sense that Bradley is 'General Issue' – he is the standard for generals, the dependable, unflashy, solid general, quite unlike some of the characters around him. His style was one of calm confidence, and having the confidence of those around him, above or below, coupled with an almost studied ordinariness: as a man from the West Point class of 1915, he must have known he was anything other than ordinary. This is why he ascended as far as he did: he kept his head down and got on with it, kept his beefs pretty much to himself. Bradley did threaten to resign when he and Ike were taken by surprise by the German Ardennes Offensive in the winter of 1944 – easily their biggest blunder of the war – because Eisenhower decided to move Bradley's First and Ninth Armies to Montgomery's command to shore up the Allies' left flank. Bradley by this point had had his fill of Montgomery and was incensed. This incident doesn't make his memoirs.

Pyle liked, no, adored Bradley, and this was clearly genuine as he was quite capable of expressing disdain for people he encountered, and the higher-ups he didn't like he would simply omit. Pyle spent three days with Bradley on Sicily, watching the general and taking in his style, and devoted a chapter to him in *Brave Men* entitled 'Brass Hats'. Pyle had to concede that Bradley liked to keep things so unflashy that he wasn't great copy when Pyle first encountered him at a press conference – Ernie Pyle took his time warming to Bradley, who didn't seem much interested in generating headlines for hacks.

His time spent with Bradley didn't make things any easier:

General Bradley is a hard man to write about in a way, just because he is so damn normal. He wears faintly-tinted tortoise-shell glasses. It would be toying with the truth to call him handsome. Instead of good looks, his face shows the kindness and calmness that lies behind it.[11]

Bradley was clearly comfortable in the uniforms the US Army had chosen, which were meant to reflect civilian workwear and be democratic and practical in their styling rather than militaristic. According to Pyle – and the reference would offer a contrast to those in the know about how other generals liked to dress up – 'He didn't even own a Sam Browne belt or a dress cap.'[12] Were it not for his helmet, the pictures of Bradley in his long waterproof mac on his way to Normandy could be of a senior executive on the Staten Island Ferry. As for his manner:

> He can be firm, terribly firm, but never gross or rude [. . .] To me General Bradley looked like a school-teacher rather than a soldier. When I told him that, he said I wasn't so far wrong, because his father was a country schoolteacher and he himself had taught at West Point and other places.[13]

And he was austere:

> The general didn't smoke at all. He took his cigarette rations and gave them away. He drank and swore in great moderation [. . .] He had three bottles of champagne that somebody gave him, and he saved those to celebrate the capture of Messina.[14]

Good times. But underneath the dust-dry austerity and the normality, there was Bradley's inner self-discipline and ultimately his determination to cut out the chaff:

'Despite his mildness the general was not what you would call easygoing [. . .] They didn't get the traditional Army bawling-out from him, but they did get the gate [fired].'[15]

*

Bradley had been at the core of the efforts to build a new army, through 'the class the stars fell on' at West Point, the CCC, the War Department, Fort Benning and the Officer Candidate School, the 82nd Division, and in the process he had built himself, the GI General. After the war, he said it was the CCC that had saved the army, and then, once the war came, the men of the CCC had gone on to 'save the world'.[16] Before the breakout in Normandy, Pyle wrote of Bradley: 'There wasn't a correspondent over there, or soldier, or officer I ever heard of who hadn't complete and utter faith in General Bradley. If he felt we were ready for the push, that was good enough for us.'[17]

If you were on Bradley's team, you had complete and utter faith in the man; in the US Army of the common man, their leader was one of them. But the American tradition of the rugged individualist also found its expression at the highest level of command. Leadership as legend-building: Patton.

7

George S. Patton

American man of war

Operation OVERLORD – the centrepiece of the Western Allies' summer of 1944, after the ejection of the Germans from North Africa and the invasion of Italy – was the next clear, logical – nay, obvious – step in the Allied grand strategy and promised to deliver the great showdown in the West. In the four years since the calamity of the fall of France, the Allies had learned a great deal, from their enemies and from themselves – these lessons would now be applied on a new front.

OVERLORD was an operation in which the Allies played to their industrial strengths and leveraged their advantages, another amphibious offensive, sustained from the sea by the Allied navies, and protected from the skies by their air forces, which had been preparing the airspace over France for several months. The landings in North Africa and Sicily – as well as the Dieppe landings, often thought of as the rehearsal for D-Day but really just one of a string of amphibious operations the Allies undertook in the preceding years – had offered the Allies the chance to develop some muscle memory, but it was OVERLORD that demonstrated comprehensively the one thing the Allies and the Germans both knew: that the Allies possessed massive material superiority over the Germans. Gigantic, boggling, stratospheric, complex superiority. The Germans were fully aware how far behind they were; they faced an opponent which had a seemingly endless supply of everything imaginable that came from distant factories and farms untroubled by bombing (though because its material wealth was necessarily complex, the Allied way of war was therefore vulnerable to being disrupted). But this didn't seem to deter the Germans, even as the pressure of fighting in Italy and on the Eastern Front and over the skies of Western Europe mounted. Whether their motivation was political indoctrination; a feeling that they had their backs to the apocalyptic wall and that Germany, shattered by pitiless heavy bombing as it was, needed defending; or simple totalitarian ruthlessness, the Germans clung on, well after they had doubtless lost. Without the means to win the war, German resistance became an end in itself.

Yet despite this colossal material advantage, motivating and maintaining the morale of these Allied troops was as central to the Allied effort as arming and fettling them was; although of course arming them well, keeping them well-fed and cared for with that same enviable abundance was as important a part of that same motivational process as any. Morale was a Möbius strip – troops did well if their morale was high and their morale was high if they did well. The Allied victory often gets put down to the Allied material preponderance and not much else, the Germans simply overwhelmed by stuff (sometimes this is framed as despite the Germans being tactically that much better than the Allies, almost as though it wasn't a fair fight, which seems a peculiar way to look at it, and sometimes seems tinged with a sort of 'if only' sentiment), but soldiers need something to fight for, something to be motivated by, no matter how much stuff they might have at their disposal. And one Allied commander who had very, very firm views on how men should be motivated, and who notoriously acted on those views, was about to re-enter the fray: George S. Patton.

*

General George Smith Patton is more than just a general, more than a mere commander, much, much more than a man in olive drab poring over his maps in his tent, or, better still, in his boss's tent pointing out where his boss has gone wrong. He's bigger than that. He's bigger really than anyone else in this book.* He's huge. He's a totem, a self-created archetype, he's his own gold standard, he's a movie star, but again he's more than that: Patton is the star of his own movie. He's the bloke with stars on his helmet in a way that no one else with stars on their helmet can match. Of all the commanders in this book, he is the only one that got a movie all to himself: *Patton* (what else?). Montgomery gets a film about his double, M. E. Clifton James repeating his wartime role, but not about himself – by the time British war movies got around to Monty, they weren't much interested in anything other than quirky 'with hilarious consequences' shenanigans. Like Monty, George Patton is instantly recognizable, which is just the way he wanted it, for his men and for his own reputation, tied together as these concerns were. He fancied himself a symbol, believed that being one suited his command style and, more importantly, benefitted his men. Patton the symbol rather than the man is the American way of war, with all that that entails.

It does cut in more than one direction: to his detractors

* Though he's still going to have to make do with just a chapter.

he's too reckless, careless, profligate; to his fans he's a seasoned paragon used to beating up the likes of Monty for
being 'too slow' or 'too cautious' or, worse even than however
you might characterize Montgomery's battlefield performance, being some sort of trumped-up self-regarding popinjay
(the last of these is the stickiest of wickets of the full mote/
beam variety for Patton fanboys). Montgomery regarded
Patton as a lover of war – and Patton would have agreed;
his diary is full of declarations about how war is the making
of a man, how dull life after the war will be, and in his
periods of inaction he mithers and moans. What both men
have in common is they have escaped the academic reser-
vation, even managed to give serious popular military
history the slip, and exist outside either, because of their
image-conscious approach to leadership and their inability
to keep their opinions to themselves. They are set up as
rivals, but that doesn't really fit the reality, except in Sicily
during Operation HUSKY: by the time the Allied campaign was up and running in Western Europe they weren't
in comparable roles – Montgomery, as the commander of
DUKE land forces, occupied a far more political role than
Patton ever did, with all the reputational risk that that
entailed. And although the Allied war effort was a collective undertaking, using larger-than-life characters in the
telling of the history remains irresistible, and both men
amply oblige. Yet like so many historical figures, indeed
like anyone you might have a first impression of, the more
you learn about Patton, the further he gets from view, the
flimsier these descriptions appear, the less they fit the man.

Nevertheless, if you want to make him into one, say, an
all-American Hannibal, Patton is reliable as a totem
because his story ends at the zenith of his career – he's a

Jim Morrison or Jimi Hendrix* of American generals, taken in his prime, his greatest achievements safely sealed by his death. His death in 1945 ensured neither he nor subsequent events could step in and trip up his legacy. Unlike his supposed rival, Monty, whose 1950s memoirs were so wonky with regards to the truth and at the same time so outspoken about his allies' shortcomings, that they enraged and revealed in equal measure, tarnishing whatever reputation he might have left. Patton's death deprived the world of the prospect of this ultimate warrior crashing about causing trouble during the Cold War.

Before he died, Patton had done what he could to make his feelings known about the Soviet Union (he had appraised the Red Army and found it wanting: 'I have no particular desire to understand them, except to ascertain how much lead or iron it takes to kill them'[1]) but he had had the misfortune to be venting these feelings about the Soviets during the short-lived window when no one was much interested in doing any more fighting. He also along the way expressed views about Jews that honestly I'd not care to repeat, the kind that make you wonder whether he was fighting for the right side and that are hard to put down simply to him being a product of his times, though of course that is what they are. Patton, if nothing else, was an incredibly well-read and considered man, so that he might hold those views seems shocking. Had he lived he might well have led an army in Korea, though whether MacArthur would have tolerated such a headline-grabbing European-theatre general muscling in on his battlefield in his part of

---

* Take a moment to imagine his reaction to hearing his reaction to being compared to these two longhairs.

the world – Patton was one of Ike's guys, after all – has to sit alongside the kind of idle speculation you might have about what a Jim Morrison/Jimi Hendrix collaboration would have been like. Terrible, I reckon, and we'd all know all about it, and would rather it hadn't happened. The 'Patton survives the car crash' alternate universe would possibly be less contained than his wartime career.

The crash itself, on 9 December 1945, was precisely the way Patton would not have wanted to go – and when the time came, he knew it. He'd been relieved of his command as governor of Bavaria, a job it is surprising that anyone imagined he might be suited to, being seen as too politically accommodating to former Nazis – he said that if he had to exclude all Nazis from public office it would be equivalent to excluding all Republicans and Democrats. Public opinion wasn't ready for this baldly pragmatic view, at least not yet. Reporters badgered and bugged Patton about what he meant, tried to get him to lose his temper: he was distrustful of the press, which he much preferred when it was amplifying his image rather than questioning it. Patton, in his diaries at least, dug his heels in, couldn't see why anyone thought he had said anything wrong, and grumbled about communist and Jewish undermining of Germany's rebuilding. However, without the imperative to keep the square peg in the round hole – Patton was a brilliant battlefield commander but a lousy politician-soldier – Ike let him go. Coming home from a hunting trip with his chief of staff the day before he was due to return to the US, his car collided with a truck. Patton, who wasn't wearing a seatbelt – hell, of course not; it was the 1940s – hit his head on the glass partition, cut his forehead and broke his neck, damaging his spinal column. No one else in the car was

hurt; even the hunting dog was fine. Paralysed and unable
to breath easily, Patton was put into spinal traction, and
gradually deteriorated. His wife, Beatrice, was flow over
from the US to see him. He asked the doctors to tell him
the bad news: he would never be able to ride a horse again.
As he lay on his deathbed, thousands of messages, letters,
cards and telegrams came for him, from everyone from
President Truman to veterans' associations and including
offers of medical help. Twelve days after the accident, the
man who said 'the more I see of people the more I regret I
survived the war'[2] was dead.

But Patton, thanks to Hollywood, which happily
indulged his fondness for his self-image and turned him
into an Oscar winner, lives on, 'transfigured' as his biographer Martin Blumenson has put it.[3] He has entered the
pantheon of the immortals, become a name that outshines
all his peers, even that of his more famous (and responsible) commanding officer. Eisenhower, after all, went on
to be president, but when looking at the war generals, Ike
is presented as much as an embattled diplomat-soldier as
he is a supreme commander – it is Patton who is the
commander supreme (and no diplomat). And it is understandable why Patton has had so much posthumously
invested in him. Patton's movie fame, the surest way to
deliver a real man into the realm of legend, happened at
the peak of the Vietnam War, when American post-war
martial values and sense of military purpose were being
tested to destruction. A reassuringly straight-talkin' general who whupped the enemy's ass at the cinema was just
the ticket, literally. By 1969, the Vietnam War had
degenerated into a squalid struggle against a foe that
seemed not to be getting the message about American

military might;* an epic war film with the Germans taking a dutiful pasting from a general who lived a similarly
epic life is what you might call propaganda. (It was that
or *Kelly's Heroes*, *M*A*S*H* or *Catch-22*, I suppose.) With
Patton having met his untimely demise, the movie was
comfortable playing fast and loose with its depiction of
the man, in the way a modern film would at least claim
it would not. (Though, wait a second, Winston Churchill
took the Tube according to *Darkest Hour*.) For example, the
movie promotes Patton to a four-star general well ahead
of schedule, and the wardrobe department filled their
boots by making him wear his dress uniform and Sam
Browne belt along with all his medals, which he eschewed;
the film's opening shot lingers on his medals, his riding
crop, his sash. But that's showbusiness!

Had Patton lived to see this film it might, perhaps, have
been sauce for the goose; having spent his career not
worrying too much if he rubbed people up the wrong way,
his posthumous triumph over his rivals might have felt fit-
ting, even if it does border – in the author's view – on the
preposterous. Given that Omar Bradley advised on the
film,† perhaps that would have been fine with Patton – had
he lived, would Patton have advised on it himself, causing
the filmmakers headaches? But the film hoovered up

---

* The Vietnam War, of course, poses a problem for the proponent of the
you-can-win-if-you-have-more-stuff argument: the Americans had plenty
of stuff, but they still couldn't win.

† Bradley's second wife, Hollywood scriptwriter Kitty Buhler, persuaded
Bradley to get involved in the film, and made sure that he was well
rewarded, cut in on a percentage of the profits. The irony of Bradley
making money out of a film about a man who couldn't much stand him is
pretty delicious.

audiences, acclaim, Oscars and didn't tell us much about what the man was like beyond the image he had sought to project. And why would it?

*

Patton's crowning moment – the relief of Bastogne and the Third Army's lightning turnabout to snuff out the German offensive in the Ardennes – speaks for Patton's talent for rapid movement, and behind it his skill in assembling and training a staff capable of responding to his energetic approach to battle. For his detractors, this triumph is offset by his costly, grinding campaign in Lorraine in October and November 1944. His problems that autumn and winter were the same problems that all Allied generals faced: immense pressure on supply lines, stiffening German resistance and the worsening weather as the traditional campaigning season ended. Though he would have been loath to say so, Patton ran into the same kind of trouble as everyone else on Eisenhower's broad front, and his flashy mobile-warfare genius was not much in evidence. The disastrous raid on Offlag XIII-B, when he sent a task force to liberate the prisoner-of-war camp his son-in-law happened to held in, in late March 1945, was the kind of escapade that could completely ruin a general's reputation, but Patton wasn't around to make excuses once he had died and so it doesn't seem to damage him. Attempts at the time to turn it into a full-blown scandal fizzled out.

Patton was a cavalryman in the American tradition. In Britain, this might mean an upper-class officer, a countryman especially, a toff. Patton's father was a soldier-turned-attorney general, well-to-do, connected, monied – his family on both sides had been soldiers of battles past. They also claimed ancestry from aristocrats of varying grandeur. His grandfather George S, Patton, Jr, had been a Confederate colonel during the American Civil War, and died of his wounds after the Third Battle of Winchester in 1864 – the third battle he had been wounded in. One of his younger brothers, Waller T. Patton, had been killed at Gettysburg the previous year. Omar Bradley, Patton's great colleague and rival in later life, described Patton as

> the most fiercely ambitious man and the strangest duck I have ever known. He appeared to be motivated by some deep, inexplicable martial spirit. He devoured military history and poetry and imagined – in the spirit of reincarnation – that he had fought with Alexander the Great, Genghis Khan, Caesar, Napoleon [. . .] Although he could be the epitome of grace and charm at social or official functions, he was at the same time the most earthily profane man I ever knew. I sometimes wondered if this macho profanity was unconscious overcompensation for his most serious personal flaw: a voice that was almost comically squeaky and high-pitched, altogether lacking in command authority.[4]

Bradley had, of course, made sure that Patton was long dead before he published this view.

Soldiering gripped the young Patton's imagination, and the boy could afford to pursue his dream of being a soldier; he was full of military fervour and, despite his dyslexia (contemporary diagnosis of Patton's literacy problems, known at the time as congenital word blindness, comes from his biographers), he devoured military literature. As he worked his way through cadet school and West Point, the young Patton faced down his intellectual limitations and did what he could to excel. He excelled in the martial arts and pastimes: this led to a place on the American Olympic team as a pentathlete. He didn't win a medal, but his shooting, fencing, equestrian and athletic skills were undeniably world class. Patton was determined to make his mark as a soldier, and in the tiny US Army he was able to cut through. After the Olympics, he trained with the French cavalry and became the US Army's top swordsman – redesigning the cavalry sword and entrusted with rethinking American cavalry combat techniques and tactics, characteristically making them more aggressive, just in time for the First World War. Long before he became a famous general, Patton was making his mark, building a legacy.

However, the American government had other priorities. While the US wasn't an imperial power, absolutely not, the Philippines were a US territory, and US Army units were stationed there to keep the peace, though it was definitely not an imperial commitment, no, sir. Lieutenant Patton had no desire to go to the Philippines, so he swerved that, and instead fought in one of the more local border emergencies, riding against Pancho Villa in 1916, as part of the Mexican punitive expedition (yes, they did call it that). He innovated in a way that indicates the direction of travel of his thinking, using motor cars to move his men and surprise the enemy: Patton had updated the notion of cavalry for the motorized age, and made the necessary logistical adjustments that entailed – mechanics, spares, fuel. In this he was genuinely pioneering: he had seen the future of armoured manoeuvre warfare, and yet as a cavalryman he was open to the idea of replacing horses, an inevitability that some of his British contemporaries were trying to avoid.

Patton had also ensured the patronage of 'Black Jack' Pershing – soon to be the commander of the American Expeditionary Force – which enabled Patton to get himself out of the more boring jobs, such as procuring horses, and into combat. The Great War gave him the chance to experience the birth of armoured warfare – by the end of the war he had set himself up as the man who understood this stuff better than anyone else. He was frustrated in his pursuit of perfecting mobile warfare – which he conceived as a weapon in its own right rather than in support of infantry – coming up against an isolationist American government that could see no enemies beyond its borders and certainly not in Europe. Who needed a mobile tank force beyond the theoretical? In this, the US Army suffered in the same way that the British Army did – while there were people doing the thinking that was to come in handy in the 1940s, the people writing the cheques to pay for any experiments that needed to be done couldn't justify the expense. Patton's inter-war military career was perhaps typical of the men who became US Army generals – part of a small cadre of men, he both got to know and like as well as get on the nerves of many of the names who would feature as leaders in the next war. But a born soldier like Patton was only ever going to be thwarted by peace. Patton regarded war as a test of character, one that he had already passed. Would – if and when* it came again – anyone else?

The thing that Patton truly loved was combat – or

* Patton had a boat called *If and When*, named for when he would get to sail it – if and when he got back from war.

rather 'battle', in the abstract as well as in reality. And he was gifted in expressing this love. Patton had a way with words, especially in public; for all his struggles with reading and writing as a child, he had mastered words, and unlike the grousing he did in his diaries what he said in his speeches is well worth looking at. And the most famous speech he made, which covers the lot, his thinking about war, his men, the enemy, as well as demonstrating in its full glory his way of expressing it, is his address to the Third Army before it embarked for Normandy. Patton had been doing two jobs in England; as well as being appointed to command the Third Army, he was also nominally head of the FUSAG – First US Army Group, a phantom army at the centre of the Allies' BODYGUARD deception plans. This fake army transmitted false radio messages about its activities for the consumption of the Abwehr, detailing phoney preparations in East Anglia in the hope that the Germans would interpret them as the preparations of an invasion force tailored to a landing in the Pas de Calais. The previous year, Patton had run into the kind of trouble that he seemed to attract: he had struck men suffering from combat fatigue, calling them cowards. He'd also been careless in what he'd said before the invasion of Sicily: at the airfield at Biscari, 71 Italians and two Germans were shot in cold blood, and the man accused, Sergeant Horace T. West, cited Patton's suggestion that prisoners should not be taken in his defence. Tough talk could have consequences. And it did, after all, cost him his job, though not for the deaths of these prisoners of war. Rather it was the treatment of his own men that was his undoing.

*

While in Sicily, Patton's attitudes to combat and specifically to battle fatigue betrayed him. Visiting a field hospital on 3 August 1943, he was confronted with a soldier who had been treated for 'exhaustion'. Private Kuhl's notes said: 'Psycho-neurosis anxiety state – moderate severe (soldier has been twice before in hospital within ten days. He can't take it at the front, evidently. He is repeatedly returned.)'[5] He had been sedated and had diarrhoea. Writing to Patton later, Eisenhower expressed dismay:

> I hope you can assure me that none of them is true; but the detailed circumstances communicated to me lead to the belief that some ground for the charges must exist. I am well aware of the necessity for hardness and toughness on the battlefield. I clearly understand that firm and drastic measures are at times necessary in order to secure the desired objectives. But this does not excuse brutality, abuse of the sick, nor exhibition of uncontrollable temper in front of subordinates.[6]

Unfortunately for Patton, the report that was attached suggested that Patton had done exactly what Ike feared:

> Lt. Gen. George S. Patton, Jr., came into the tent with the commanding officer and other medical officers [. . .] The General spoke to the various patients in the receiving tent and especially commended the wounded men. Then he came to Pvt. Kuhl and asked him what was the matter. The soldier replied, 'I guess I can't take it.' The General immediately flared up, cursed the soldier, called him all types of a coward, then slapped him across the face with his gloves and

finally grabbed the soldier by the scruff of his neck and kicked him out of the tent.[7]

And he'd done it more than once. A week later, he slapped another soldier, Paul G. Bennett. Colonel Donald E. Currier, who had witnessed Patton's tantrum, said that Patton asked Bennett what the problem was:

> The man replied, 'It's my nerves' and began to sob. The General then screamed at him, 'What did you say?' The man replied, 'It's my nerves, I can't stand the shelling any more.' He was still sobbing. The General then yelled at him, 'Your nerves, hell; you are just a Goddamned coward, you yellow son of a bitch.' He then slapped the man and said, 'Shut up that Goddamned crying. I won't have these brave men here who have been shot at seeing a yellow bastard sitting here crying.' He then struck the man again, knocking his helmet liner off and into the next tent. He then turned to the admitting officer and yelled, 'Don't admit this yellow bastard; there's nothing the matter with him. I don't have the hospitals cluttered up with these sons of bitches who haven't got the guts to fight.' He then turned to the man again, who was managing to sit at attention though shaking all over and said, 'You're going back to the front lines and you may get shot and killed, but you're going to fight. If you don't, I'll stand you up against a wall and have a firing squad kill you on purpose. In fact,' he said, reaching for his pistol, 'I ought to shoot you myself, you Goddamned whimpering coward.'[8]

His diary confirms his blood-curdling views on men who felt they could not go on, infamously saying they should be shot. Combat stress, shell shock, PTSD, names that overlap and exclude one another as each belongs to its own era: these are conditions as old as war itself. That Patton, whose reading about war was so extensive, who had immersed himself in every detail of campaigns ancient and modern as best he could, should have behaved as though it were a simple question of cowardice is perhaps surprising, but Patton's style did not allow for sympathy.

There seems to be a pattern of armies being forced to rediscover combat fatigue, or 'Nostalgia' or 'Old Sergeant's Disease', each time a new war begins. At the start of the Second World War, the US Army based policy on the conclusions it had drawn from the First. The understanding was that men without the character to withstand combat could be weeded out with a series of state-of-the-art psychiatric tests, and that looking at the composition of a man's character would be enough. The rejection rate was 18.5 per cent. Of the 18,000,000 men examined by the US Army during the war, 29 per cent were rejected for physical reasons – over 5 million. Another 970,000 were rejected on the grounds of being temperamentally unsuited to war.

Their confidence in this technique meant that the army was poorly prepared for what followed – lots of men with combat fatigue. By 1943, it was becoming clear that the army had got it quite wrong: it was, the army conceded, impossible to predict who would suffer psychological stress that would manifest itself as 'combat fatigue', and a vague estimate was placed on what a man could be expected to tolerate: 60 to 240 days in theatre, a range that seems to have the defining characteristic of not being definitive. By the Normandy campaign it had been revised: a rifleman – and it was the infantry that were bearing the brunt of the fighting in France – was expected to last maybe 30 days before entering a state of collapse. In Italy it had been noted that even combat veterans – men whose stout character had been proven by experience of combat – were starting to crack. Anxiety, fear, heightened awareness – all necessary survival instincts – were overwhelming soldiers, regardless of who they were.

Fear was something the US Army made sure it surveyed. Figures from the Pacific – where the US Marine Corps had had a rude awakening regarding combat fatigue at Guadalcanal – with 500 marines going home incapacitated, paint a bitter picture. Violent pounding of the heart, a sinking feeling in the stomach, shaking or trembling all over, feeling sick, cold sweats – these were common symptoms. Fear was everywhere, fear of death, of being maimed. It was centre stage in men's daily lives, in the field or in anticipation. And it was impossible to predict who would be affected and how.

Psychiatric breakdown in battle is nevertheless hard to quantify, and rarely comes up in the ledger of the casualty costs of war, certainly not in the mid twentieth century. It is an internal wound. Lost limbs are easier to count. Yet for all that, combat fatigue was the US Army's largest single category of disability discharge. While it is difficult to measure, attempts since the First World War to categorize and qualify it have been made. There are categories: fatigue cases – soldiers who are 'simply' tired, exhausted from the mental and physical effort of being in battle, through lack of sleep and physical exertion. The expectation is that if a soldier in this state isn't removed from the battlefield he will face immediate collapse, crying fits, self-isolation from his fellows, sweats, palpitations, hypersensitivity to noise. By 1944, the US Army had adopted a simple treatment for this: removal of the man to an aid post to the rear of the front, an injection of sodium amytal to knock him out for a 48-hour sleep, a hot meal, shower and fresh uniform, and a chat with a doctor. The Americans recovered 50–70 per cent of their 'simple' fatigue cases this way. Officers had differing views of this, of course – and over in the British Army this matches Spike Milligan's experience when he broke down in Italy in early 1944 – however, he was one of the ones this treatment didn't work for.

Beyond 'simple' fatigue it gets worse. Confusional states, delirium, dissociation, not realizing where you are. Conversion hysteria – and hysteria is a term that crops up in much of the discussion of combat fatigue, often with pejorative overtones – is a state in which the sufferer's fear reaches the point where it manifests itself as another symptom, amnesia, deafness or blindness, for instance: 'the mind literally forces the body to become incapacitated'.[9] Then there's anxiety states: giddiness, fainting, the shits (aka 'emotional diarrhoea'[10]); obsessive and compulsive states, shakes and tics – but the soldier knows they are related to his fear and regardless can't stop them; and, finally, character disorders – the manifestations of a soldier's fears become so ingrained they become who he is. His symptoms become embedded.

It wasn't until the end of the war that the US Army had caught up with how best to treat its men, and even then different officers had different opinions on the question. For those who had faith in the screening process, anyone who had made it through to the army and couldn't fight must be a coward, rather than someone who might be suffering from combat fatigue – as anyone might. Patton's outburst had revealed him and the extent to which he empathized with his men – while the stress he might be under was the stress of command, he could not wholly relate to them as young men on the modern battlefield. The press decided to sit on the story, though they took it to Eisenhower, sensitive to the possibility that Patton might be court-martialled for striking one of his men. But the story leaked, and Ike – with a heavy heart – relieved Patton of his command. He wasn't on the bench for long. His appointment to command the Third Army showed how much Patton was valued as a general – he just couldn't be trusted with the headline job of the invasion: Bradley beat him to the punch, commanding the American component of OVERLORD.

*

Still, Patton wasn't twiddling his thumbs while waiting for OVERLORD to happen. Appointed to command the brand-new Third Army on 22 January 1944, Patton and his staff had to get his army on track in time for their despatch to France. As the UK filled up with troops from the US and Canada, room needed to be found for them to train, ranges for them to fire their weapons established. As new divisions came under the Third Army's wing, Patton sought to make himself visible to the men under his command – part of how he burnished the reputation that shines so brightly now. The Third Army's equipment had to be reviewed and sorted – some had been shipped ahead of the men, some had come with the men, some was yet to arrive. In order to know what his army could bring to bear in terms of combat strength, this was something Patton had to have intimate knowledge of. Being in the know about the location of the OVERLORD landings, he read about the Norman Conquest in order to familiarize himself with William the Conqueror's campaigns. The Roman roads that criss-crossed Normandy hadn't changed so much since the Middle Ages. Industrious, tireless, hungry for combat, Patton got his army into shape. And besides the tons of paperwork he must have had to process, and the doubtless ruthless grip he had on his staff, Patton's essential attitude to battle and bravery hadn't changed since the scandals of Sicily.

So, before Patton's Third Army departed for France, he talked tough. The speech that survives as a transcript[11] – and there is some doubt and confusion around whom he gave the speech to, whether it was always in this form – most likely dates to 5 June 1944, D-1. It's got the lot, and to deliver his peroration he would be turned out as 'Patton', polished helmet, riding boots, clenched jaw, though not in front of a house-sized Stars and Stripes as in the movie (a filleted version of this speech opens the film). 'Be seated,' he said. And then into the valley of rhetoric he rode:

> Men, all this stuff you hear about America not want-ing to fight, wanting to stay out of the war, is a lot of horse dung. Americans love to fight. All real Ameri-cans love the sting and clash of battle. When you were kids, you all admired the champion marble shooter, the fastest runner, the big-league ball players and the toughest boxers. Americans love a winner and will not tolerate a loser. Americans play to win all the time. That's why Americans have never lost and will never lose a war. The very thought of losing is hateful to Americans. Battle is the most significant competition

in which a man can indulge. It brings out all that is best and it removes all that is base.[12]

'A lot of horse dung'. Are we really to believe that's what he said?* The trouble with this address is that as soon as it had been delivered a row broke out within the US Army about the language Patton had used. Omar Bradley regarded the profanity in Patton's speech as beneath a general in the US Army, but their relationship was characterized by friction and rivalry, Patton regarded it as an essential way of communicating directly with his men. Given the explosion of profanity that accompanied the drafting of millions of men into the forces, Bradley's approach seems performative at best – but even in war ideas of propriety seemed to matter. Patton thought otherwise, believing that being in command and communicating with his men required the right amount of seasoning:

> When I want my men to remember something important, to really make it stick, I give it to them double dirty. It may not sound nice to a bunch of little old ladies, at an afternoon tea party, but it helps my soldiers to remember. You can't run an army without profanity, and it has to be eloquent profanity. An army without profanity couldn't fight its way out of a piss-soaked paper bag.[13]

QED. He swore like a trooper because he liked his troopers and wanted his troopers to know he was one of them; like everything Patton did, it was calculated, rehearsed, deliberate. He wanted his men to grasp the nettle, and if that meant he used words that would sting, then what of it?

* Some versions go with 'baloney'.

He was also happy to address what might be most immediately on any soldier's mind: 'You are not all going to die.'

Patton went on to offer a prediction, though quite where he got the numbers from is questionable: 'Only two per cent of you right here today would be killed in a major battle.'

The Third Army lost 16,596 dead, with 96,241 wounded and 26,809 missing in action: a total of 139,646. By the end of the war the Third Army had received vast amounts of replacements: 110,000 men had been brought in to keep it going. Patton knew that this was what his men were in for, but it was the kind of assertion a general might make to get his men's confidence.

> Every man is scared in his first action. If he says he's not, he's a goddamn liar. But the real hero is the man who fights even though he's scared. Some men will get over their fright in a minute under fire, some take an hour, and for some it takes days. But the real man never lets his fear of death overpower his honor, his sense of duty to his country, and his innate manhood.[14]

Patton had cut to the chase, talking directly about death, about fear, and tying how you dealt with them to manhood. *A real man's innate manhood.* Patton hadn't let go of any of his core beliefs regarding combat and bravery that had got him into so much trouble the previous year when he had slapped and bawled out men who had combat fatigue. It was exactly this kind of motivational technique that the Allied armies had sought to move away from. Patton didn't hold with the idea of combat fatigue; he believed that men who couldn't return to the front line were malingerers at best, cowards at worst. He didn't seem to consider the effect on the other men at the front line of his insistence that men who were in a state of nervous exhaustion were cowards; NCOs and officers might find it easier to maintain unit cohesion with anyone who was cracking up – or, as Patton would have it, malingering – sent away from the front. Worries about how combat stress was contagious were prevalent in Allied units, though many were also sceptical that it even existed. Opinion was divided. Patton's wasn't. Patton confided in his diary that he thought that companies should deal with this themselves, try the men for cowardice and execute the guilty. The US Army was not in a capital punishment mood when it came to desertion – it hanged men for rape and murder, it executed only one man, Eddie Slovik, for desertion during the Second World War,* so Patton was very unlikely to get his way with those he regarded as cowards.

Patton then moved on to how his men had been made.

> All through your army career you men have bitched about what you call 'this chicken-shit drilling.' That is all for a purpose – to ensure instant obedience to orders and to create constant alertness. This must be bred into every soldier. I don't give a fuck for a man who is not always on his toes. But the drilling has made veterans of all you men. You are ready! A man has to be alert all the time if he expects to keep on breathing. If not, some German son-of-a-bitch will sneak up behind him and beat him to death with a

---

* Slovik strikes me as unlucky more than anything else; he protested not his innocence as such but that he was being made an example of. He wasn't wrong.

sock full of shit. There are four hundred neatly marked graves in Sicily, all because one man went to sleep on the job – but they are German graves, because we caught the bastard asleep before his officer did.[15]

Drill certainly was something men bitched about: they always have done, they still do. But in saying this, Patton showed his understanding of his men, he tied even the things his men regarded as chickenshit to their warrior spirit, to how it afforded them the means to suffer a different fate to their enemy. And it's hard to fault Patton here: no man wants to be beaten to death with a sock full of shit. But it wasn't just about the individual. After all:

> An army is a team. It lives, eats, sleeps, and fights as a team. This individual hero stuff is bullshit. The bilious bastards who write that stuff for the *Saturday Evening Post* don't know any more about real battle than they do about fucking. And we have the best team – we have the finest food and equipment, the best spirit and the best men in the world. Why, by God, I actually pity these poor bastards we're going up against.[16]

The *Saturday Evening Post* was probably the right magazine for Patton to pick as an example of the home front not really understanding the actual front. The most widely circulated fortnightly magazine in the US with 4 million subscribers, with its covers by Norman Rockwell and others, the *Saturday Evening Post* offered (often fictionalized) accounts of wartime heroics, though tempered there with an everyman idea of the doughboy, Rockwell's creation 'Willie Gillis'. It was comfortably middle class in its outlook, unlike Patton and his men. The imaginary Gillis used to get mail asking after him, so how switched on the readers were is up for debate. But Gillis was a 'storybook combat fighter'. Having dealt with death and journalism, Patton moved on to his key message: teamwork was key.

All the real heroes are not storybook combat fighters. Every single man in the army plays a vital role. So don't ever let up. Don't ever think that your job is unimportant. What if every truck driver decided that he didn't like the whine of the shells and turned yellow and jumped headlong into a ditch? That cowardly bastard could say to himself, 'Hell, they won't miss me, just one man in thousands.' What if every man said that? Where in the hell would we be then? No, thank God, Americans don't say that. Every man does his job. Every man is important. The ordnance men are needed to supply the guns, the quartermaster is needed to bring up the food and clothes for us because where we are going there isn't a hell of a lot to steal. Every last damn man in the mess hall, even the one who boils the water to keep us from getting the GI shits, has a job to do.[17]

For all his reputation as a blood-and-guts general, this passage illustrates clearly Patton's understanding of how the US Army actually worked, how the long tail that the Americans had kept the sharp end going. Keeping GIs from getting the shits was, after all, essential to the army's success. However, Patton wasn't averse to a bit of rhetorical bait and switch: boiling water was important, bravery more so. Even to the point of creating a warrior nation.

Each man must think not only of himself, but think of his buddy fighting alongside him. We don't want yellow cowards in the army. They should be killed off like flies. If not, they will go back home after the war, goddamn cowards, and breed more cowards. The brave men will breed more brave men. Kill off the goddamn cowards and we'll have a nation of brave men.[18]

This – rhetorical, of course, at least I hope it is – could be straight out of *Mein Kampf.* Or *Starship Troopers.* Either way, it's tough talk. You can see this being something he might say to a man with 'exhaustion' in a field hospital. But rather than leaving us to wonder what he might mean by brave, Patton tells his audience:

One of the bravest men I saw in the African campaign was on a telegraph pole in the midst of furious fire while we were moving toward Tunis. I stopped and asked him what the hell he was doing up there. He answered, 'Fixing the wire, sir.' 'Isn't it a little unhealthy up there right now?' I asked. 'Yes sir, but this goddamn wire has got to be fixed.' I asked, 'Don't those planes strafing the road bother you?' And he answered, 'No sir, but you sure as hell do.' Now, there was a real soldier. A real man. A man who devoted all he had to his duty, no matter how great the odds, no matter how seemingly insignificant his duty appeared at the time.[19]

Of course, this merry tale includes Patton as the thing his men truly fear. But again, he makes it clear that his army operates as a whole. Although he doesn't say 'there's no I in team', he might as well, but it is *his* team he's talking about. The men under Patton's command weren't an army of equals as far as he was concerned – unlike Bradley, he was the scion of privilege, and the extent to which Patton was self-made was in terms of the image of himself as a born leader that he had created.

Supply was central to victory: Patton had understood this long before he came into contact with the enemy; on manoeuvres in 1941, he had left money for fuel at gas stations and been penalized by the umpires on the exercise. This story found its way into the papers, helping to establish his reputation as a win-at-all-costs man. He'd also defied the umpires on the Louisiana Manoeuvres who had deemed his tank knocked out, and gone ahead to claim victory, despite being 'dead'.

> And you should have seen the trucks on the road to Gabès. Those drivers were magnificent. All day and all night they crawled along those son-of-a-bitch roads, never stopping, never deviating from their course with shells bursting all around them. Many of the men drove over 40 consecutive hours. We got through on good old American guts. These were not combat men. But they were soldiers with a job to do. They were part of a team. Without them the fight would have been lost.[20]

Patton knew men driving trucks were every bit as important as the men on the front line. On exercise in Louisiana he had – along with the rest of the US Army establishment – started to get to grips with the sheer scale of the logistical effort they would be undertaking, fighting a war across two oceans. While you might find the origins of the American 'tradition' of fighting on a broad front in the Civil War, the exigencies of running a campaign on the other side of the Atlantic maybe offer a better explanation as to why Eisenhower picked that way to fight the war in Europe. Patton knew this. He also knew what his men really wanted: even if all he himself really wanted was to fight.

> Sure, we all want to go home. We want to get this war over with. But you can't win a war lying down. The quickest way to get it over with is to get the bastards who started it. We want to get the hell over there and clean the goddamn thing up, and then get at those purple-pissing Japs. The quicker they are whipped, the quicker we go home. The shortest way home is through Berlin and Tokyo. So keep moving. And when we get to Berlin, I am personally going to shoot that paper-hanging son-of-a-bitch Hitler.[21]

Patton here was reflecting on what was on everyone's mind in the Germany-first US Army: Japan. Japan was next, everyone involved in long-term planning in the US Army knew, to the point of it being unspoken. Even before **OVERLORD**, the US Army was considering its manpower issues for 1945 and how it could maintain an army large enough to take on the ultimate strategic goal – the invasion of Japan. Getting to Berlin and personally shooting the paper-hanging son-of-a-bitch in Berlin might not mean going home. At least not yet. Back to business. Was he too tough? Did he care?

> I don't give a damn about such complaints. I believe that an ounce of sweat will save a gallon of blood. The harder we push, the more Germans we kill. The

more Germans we kill, the fewer of our men will be killed. Pushing harder means fewer casualties. I want you all to remember that. My men don't surrender. I don't want to hear of any soldier under my command being captured unless he is hit. Even if you are hit, you can still fight. That's not just bullshit either. I want men like the lieutenant in Libya who, with a Luger against his chest, swept aside the gun with his hand, jerked his helmet off with the other and busted the hell out of the Boche with the helmet. Then he picked up the gun and he killed another German. All this time the man had a bullet through his lung. That's a man for you![22]

Patton's emphasis on how aggressive fighting would in the end save the lives of his men – for all its technicolor gory detail – suggests that the thing he really was trying to do was keep casualties down, that he envisaged fighting a campaign that would do everything it could to ensure a quick and less costly victory.* This speech sits interestingly on the edge of Patton's private and professional presentation of his views on warfare. While in his diaries he might rage about cowards and sons of bitches and the inadequacies of those around him, and this language bled into this kind of stump speech, his orders to the Third Army on the eve of the invasion had considerably less emphasis on advancing constantly and holding the enemy's balls. In his letter to his corps commanders on 20 May 1944, he had

---

* Though he found, like most Allied commanders, that this balancing act was almost impossible to manage as the winter of 1944 drew in and German resistance stiffened.

said that haste and speed were 'not synonymous'. Moreover, hasty attacks did not 'produce speedy successes or speedy advances because hasty attacks are not coordinated attacks'. At the same time a unit 'must never halt because some other unit is stuck. If you push on, you will release the pressure on the adjacent unit, and it will accompany you.' Patton was calling on his corps commanders to be flexible in the same way that he was asking his men to be tough and resolute; he was appealing to their sense of loyalty and duty, but with the same core motivation – getting the battle won so that they could go home. Or, as he had also said, so they could 'kill Japs'.

And, of course, Patton was operating in another role as the face of the BODYGUARD deception plan. Hence his next line: 'Don't forget, you don't know I'm here at all. No word of that fact is to be mentioned in any letters. The world is not supposed to know what the hell they did with me. I'm not supposed to be commanding this army.'[23] For someone keeping a low profile, Patton had caused consternation when he made a speech at Knutsford in April saying that the British, Americans and Russians were the people who ought to run the world – something he regarded as a dry statement of fact. But Patton's glamour and the air of secrecy around him were something he could repackage for his men with glee.

> I'm not even supposed to be in England. Let the first bastards to find out be the goddamned Germans. Some day, I want them to rise up on their piss-soaked hind legs and howl 'Ach! It's the goddamned Third Army and that son-of-a-bitch Patton again!'
>
> [. . .]

(left to right) Omar Bradley, Dwight D. Eisenhower and George Patton: the GI General, the Supreme Commander and the American Man of War. Bradley's sartorial style echoing that of his classmates, Patton wearing whatever he pleased.

For all his ruthless individualism, George Patton knew that teamwork was everything.

By the time the US Army was fighting in North-West Europe it had begun to address the question of combat fatigue: who could cope with the battlefield was essentially unknowable. Any man might collapse under the strain of modern war.

As the end of the war approached Patton began to wonder what he would do with his life. Fate intervened.

Lieutenant Colonel Alastair 'Jock' Pearson. A legend of the airborne fraternity, Richard Gale relied on officers like Pearson to pull things together and propel operations. Pearson excelled at this in Normandy, as he had done in North Africa and Sicily.

Major General Richard Gale. 'Windy' Gale raised the 6th Airborne Division, its sole focus the D-Day landings. He fostered a spirit in his officers and men that sought to embrace chaos.

'Windy' Gale ensured that everyone in his division was briefed on its tasks, in the expectation that parachute landings might go awry. For all the complexity in its preparation, delivering men by air rarely went to plan. D-Day was no exception.

White kept a diary –
against the rules – and
sketched when he could,
capturing the squalor
of the life of the fighting
infantryman.

MORNING 'CUPPA'   PLATOON HQ. IN AFFERDEN WOODS.

The 52nd Lowland Division finally
arrived in Europe at Walcheren Island,
below sea level.

The gliders of the second lift on the
evening of D-Day.

Peter White (centre row, second from left): artist, pacifist, infantryman and officer.

An amphibious Sherman DD-tank. Both lateral thinking and ingenious engineering would get tanks ashore on D-Day.

Percy 'Hobo' Hobart. He raised Britain's three most famous armoured divisions, and the third one was a charm.

The 79th Armoured Division's insignia: without the glasses a resemblance perhaps?

Then there's one thing you men will be able to say when this war is over and you get back home. Thirty years from now when you're sitting by your fireside with your grandson on your knee and he asks, 'What did you do in the great World War Two?' You won't have to cough and say, 'Well, your granddaddy shovelled shit in Louisiana.' No sir, you can look him straight in the eye and say 'Son, your granddaddy rode with the great Third Army and a son-of-a-goddamned-bitch named George Patton!'

All right, you sons of bitches. You know how I feel. I'll be proud to lead you wonderful guys in battle anytime, anywhere. That's all.[24]

When his men finally embarked for France, Patton, who called himself in his diary 'an emotional soldier', was able to tell himself he had spoken to the Third Army in the style he intended to lead them, inspiring and profane, yes, but with as firm an appreciation of what he would need to do for them as they had of him. This was leadership as legend and the legend persists.

8

Alastair Pearson

Go to it!

In the years that followed the war a search for explanations as to how it had been fought, won and lost began. One of the enduring puzzles that the Western Allies faced, looking back, was the German ability to fight on in the face of overwhelming odds. It seemed the Germans were mobilized beyond their circumstances, able to organize and reorganize under colossal pressure, to improvise and adapt, to maintain coherence in even the most chaotic situations. As the Cold War developed, it became a pressing question: how had the Germans done it? And especially, how had they done it on the Eastern Front, fighting the Soviets? – a question that had immediate relevance. The Germans were happy to offer an explanation and, of course, because of the political sensitivities of the Cold War and the need not to be beastly to the Germans, the explanation was not one of political motivation but of something more militarily profound, and applicable to the Western way of doing things: the doctrine of *Auftragstaktik*.

Auftragstaktik translates literally as 'mission tactics' but it's not tactics as such; as a concept it has since transmuted into the NATO concept of Mission Command. What it is is simple enough: the idea that soldiers, officers, NCOs, would be trained to the point where they could act on their own initiative rather than waste time and senior officers' patience with requests for instructions. Orders should be kept simple and succinct so as not to complicate or constrain; the intent of those orders is understood implicitly. This ideal of soldiering came direct from Prussian military tradition and theory, and after the war became the coveted way of doing things. How had the Prussians arrived at this?

German strategic thinking was traditionally focused on speed, not because of German strength but because, even in this single continental theatre, of its weakness. This thinking was not confined to the Second World War. These quick wins had been how Prussia under Bismarck had gobbled up its neighbours, clobbered and neutralized its powerful rivals and unified Germany. France had fallen to exactly this kind of military operation in the Franco-Prussian War in 1870, and everyone knew it. Knockout blows, Schlieffen plans, Manstein plans, Blitzkrieg, BARBAROSSA, these were all conceived as ways to win wars quickly because German military and strategic thinkers knew that as a central continental power Germany needed to get things over with militarily before its (often much larger) opponents woke up to the danger. And that politically as well as economically short wars are easier to sustain – Hitler's pre-war geopolitical strategy relied on quick and therefore cheap wins while Britain and France made their minds up what to do about a resurgent Germany.

To make sure that things ran smoothly and quickly, German thinking centred on how leadership functioned. The 1933 Field Regulations stated: 'Leadership in war is an art, a free creativity based on a foundation of knowledge. The greatest demands of war are made on the personality.' The changes that had prompted the search for a way to command men more creatively had been technological. Since the foundation of the Prussian military academy in the early 1800s, artillery had become far more lethal and small arms had dramatically increased in range. This meant that the kind of massive columns and blocks of troops that had characterized the Napoleonic Wars weren't practicable any more, formations that could be more tightly controlled with calls and drums and bugles were obsolete. Men had to be dispersed, but they had to be commanded too. Helmuth von Moltke pushed *Auftragstaktik* forward as a doctrine, and by 1888 it was German practice that rather than write specific orders, commanders should let their subordinates know what needed to be achieved and then let them get on with it. German officers and NCOs therefore were instilled with the idea that they should get results rather than follow orders. Furthermore, if things went wrong, you were supposed to find a solution yourself rather than ask and wait for orders as to what to do next; equally, the same applied if things went well.

> A favorable situation will never be exploited if commanders wait for orders. The highest commander and the youngest soldier must always be conscious of the fact that omission and inactivity are worse than resorting to the wrong expedient.[1]

In training, there was the apocryphal tale of the major who had messed up during the Franco-Prussian War. The major tries to explain his way out of the situation by saying he'd only being obeying orders, orders from a superior, so, in effect, orders from the King. The legend states that Prince Frederick Charles replied: 'His Majesty made you a major because he believed you would know when not to obey his orders.'[2]

It was this attitude that led to men like Heinz Guderian disobeying his orders regarding where to cross the Meuse in May 1940 and exploiting the (surprising) French collapse that followed. It was also this spirit that led him to recklessly overextend his lines in the summer of 1941 during Operation BARBAROSSA at Yel'nya. The problem with the idea of carrying on if things went well was how to judge what things going well meant. *Auftragstaktik* relied on being prepared to take risks, and risks meant casualties. Fall GELB, in the summer of 1940, relied on commanders like Guderian seizing the initiative, taking risks, pushing on regardless and getting the job done. It cost – the Germans suffered 27,000 men killed, 18,400 missing and 110,000 men wounded. By our contemporary standards a huge butcher's bill, though compared to the First World War – and this was what counted – not so bad, and it had delivered a quick victory.

The practice of *Auftragstaktik* throws up questions beyond tactical efficiency (and on the Eastern Front in particular, it seems the Germans were relatively tactically efficient, but that could well be because the Red Army wasn't quite as interested*). Those with an ear to British

---

* On the Eastern Front, the German Army continued to inflict about 50 per cent more casualties than it suffered itself, even in the final days of the war. A good later example is the first major operation of the Zhitomir–Berdichev Offensive in January 1944, when the Soviets threw 7 armies and 2 tank armies (totalling 830,000 soldiers, 1,125 tanks and 11,387 guns!!!) against a single Panzer army. Even though massively outnumbered (even when later reinforced by elements of the 1st Panzer Army) and without aerial superiority, German counter-attacks led to a cohesive defensive position

culturally received ideas about Germany and German conduct of the war might be surprised to hear that German
officers were supposed to know when not to obey orders.
Popular conception of the Nazi defence of what happened
in the concentration camps or the *Einsatzgruppen* is that
people were 'only obeying orders'. In which case, if you
were from an *Auftragstaktik* culture, then surely you knew
when not to obey them? And in which case, if these were
not orders they felt they should disobey, then these kinds of
orders must have seemed to make sense. Couple the 'you
know what to do' culture of *Auftragstaktik* with the notion of
'working towards the Fuhrer' that Ian Kershaw put forward in his epic biographies of Hitler, and you have a recipe
for ideologically driven murder that doesn't require detailed
orders: if the understanding is that partisans are enemies,
and Jews are enemies, Jews can be shot as partisans,
whether they've done anything in the way of resistance or
not. And for all of this there was still the idea that '*ein Befehl
war ein Befehl*' – 'an order was an order', especially if it was
a *Führerbefehl*. Disobey those at your peril.

In contrast, the British have been characterized as
using *Befehlstaktik* – the very opposite – you would complete
your orders and your orders would include how you were
to go about it. So you'd only go as far as it said you should
on your map, you'd radio for orders if things turned out
differently, and so on. Without a unity of doctrine, which the
British Army didn't possess when the war began, orders
were meant to bridge the gap by explaining to officers

---

eventually being restored, with the Soviet army losing 7 full divisions and
700 tanks. But then maybe trying to measure the Eastern Front against
anything that has happened before or since is essentially futile.

what needed to be done. In ideal circumstances, the German Army would train its officers and senior NCOs so that they could take over the job of the man two ranks above him – platoon commanders would be trained in how to run a battalion. That way, supposedly, everyone knew what everyone else's role was, so would be able to improvise more efficiently.

However, by the time of D-Day in June 1944 the men who had been trained in *Auftragstaktik* during the 1930s, especially in the rank and file, were long gone; they'd been squandered in the invasion of the Soviet Union, captured or killed in the desert, chewed through in Italy. Just as British politics drove strategy and strategy shaped tactics, so political decisions, and their strategic consequences, affected tactical performance. Hitler's inability to quit while he was ahead, his overestimation of what his armies were capable of, the overconfidence in Blitzkrieg (in as much as it existed as a technique with his horse-drawn army) led him into the Balkans, the desert and, fatefully, Russia. France could be defeated on relatively short supply lines: France was a far more developed, modern country, with roads, petrol stations and so on. It also, like Britain, had an army and a population that wasn't necessarily that keen on fighting at any cost. Unlike Britain, it didn't have somewhere to withdraw that army to and figure out what to do next. The Soviet front was huge, undeveloped, the Soviet Army unsentimental about how many men it lost in resisting, even ineptly. And not one of those Soviet soldiers was a voter. You can have as much *Auftragstaktik* as you like in that situation; losses inevitably mounted, the German army didn't deliver the quick victory and smashed itself, its doctrine, its trained men and its tactical know-how on the

Soviet steppes. And in the absence of *Auftragstaktik* as an explanation of the German willingness to fight on, political motivation, nationalism, ideology and all those things no one wanted to talk about after the war in Germany must be back in the frame.

*

On the night of D-Day, the British 6th Airborne Division (which included a battalion of Canadian paratroopers) landed on the Allied eastern or left flank. The division had been raised with the Normandy invasion in mind it had been formed from parts of the 1st Airborne Division which had fought in North Africa and Sicily (more of which later). If the 6th Airborne is famous for one thing it is the daring capture of the bridges over the Caen Canal and the Orne River – the former known as Pegasus Bridge – and the assault on the Merville Battery that overlooked Sword Beach, a few miles from the bridges. These extraordinary actions are well rehearsed in D-Day accounts to the point where they have become tourist attractions, but there was more to the 6th Airborne's D-Day than a company-sized glider landing and a battalion neutralizing enemy artillery. Its role was to secure the entrances and exits to the lodgement on the eastern flank north of Caen – so as well as taking the two bridges that offered the enemy a short cut to the landings at Ouistreham sur Mer, there were bridges further east to be destroyed, and high ground in between to be held. Due to be relieved the following morning, the 6th Airborne wasn't going to have to hold on stranded for too long, but with only about 6,000 men it had a lot of ground to cover. Its commanding officer, Major General Richard 'Windy' Gale, had told his men to expect chaos but was confident, for all the complexity of some of their tasks that first night, that they knew what they had to do. His motto, not entirely unlike *Auftragstaktik*, was: 'Go to it.'

Gale, who was approaching his 48th birthday on D-Day, had been in the Machine Gun Corps in the First World War, which had been formed to try to bridge the machine-gun gap with the enemy, and had come to airborne forces full of no-nonsense grip. Machine Gun Corps men were specialists who were attached to infantry battalions as firepower stiffeners, so Gale's experience in the Great War had been all about technical innovation and tactical flexibility. Gale had become a Machine Gun Corps man rather by accident – he thought he had signed up for a course, not a new regiment. He had fought at the Somme, Ypres and the capture of the German hillfort at Whyschaete (known to the British as Whitesheet) in June 1917, on a ridge that ran back to Messines, where a windmill stood proud above the ground around it, making it an excellent defensive and observation position and offering a perfect killing ground to whoever held it.* Gale won an MC during the German Spring Offensive in 1918. He had got through the war unwounded, though he had had to rest at one point to recover from exhaustion and gum disease. Between the wars, he had been to India, studied at Quetta and become convinced of the importance of mobility and manoeuvre in warfare, rather like Francis Tuker. After the fall of France, Gale had been killing time

---

* A crowdfunded excavation there in 2018 found it full of scores of German dead, piled deep in shell holes, the tiled floor of the mill still showing ripples from the shell fire the British had plastered it with: a sobering sight for this author at least.

waiting for the invasion, but his talent for training caught the eye of Alan Brooke, who offered him the job of commanding the nascent 1st Parachute Brigade – yet another of example of Brooke's sound skill in talent-spotting. He left the 2nd/5th Leicesters behind and got on with trying to get airborne forces into some kind of shape. In this new line of work you needed sharp elbows, to deal with the Air Ministry and the RAF, who didn't want to be diverted from their efforts to provide aircraft, and the other very ambitious and ruthless officers who had gravitated to all the various embryonic special forces that had sprung up.

After raising the brigade and getting it into shape, Gale then went into the War Office, where his job mutated into formulating doctrine for airborne forces – Churchill's memo hadn't gone to the trouble of detailing exactly how airborne soldiers would be used, whether men were best delivered by parachute or glider, what kind of operations they would be useful for – all while dealing with the RAF's obstructive reluctance to let the army use its precious aircraft. The RAF, having won the Battle of Britain, was hard to argue with in terms of strategic planning – and the bomber offensive, though it was yet to get properly under way, took priority. And anyway, the argument went, what could you do with parachute troops beyond smash-and-grab raiding until you had larger formations? After a year of wrestling with paperwork and Air Ministry bureaucracy, Gale was ordered to raise the 6th Airborne Division (so numbered to create the impression that there were at least six airborne divisions rather than just two), with the single aim of making what would become Operation OVERLORD work. Raising the brigades and battalions, training the men, planning the operations, rehearsing for the invasion became Gale's all-consuming work. If he knew one thing, he knew he would need officers who would be able to hold things together no matter how the landings turned out.

Airborne forces had been founded in 1940. In the chaos that followed the evacuations from Dunkirk and the rest of France, the British government nevertheless made plans for the future and those plans were unabashed about stealing ideas from the victorious enemy. This came right from the top. Despite abject disasters like The Hague, the impact that German *Fallschirmjäger* and glider-borne soldiers had had on Churchill's imagination prompted a memo to the Chief of the Imperial General Staff, 'Pug' Ismay, demanding a force of airborne troops: 'We ought to have a corps of at least 5,000 parachute troops [. . .] I hear something is being done already to form such a corps, but only I believe on a very small scale.'[3] At the same time, Churchill also demanded the creation of the Commandos, raiding troops to strike back at occupied Europe – for all their rivalry, paras and commandos were born of the same impulse and had the same midwife. Indeed, at the very beginning, commandos and paras were pretty much interchangeable. Just don't mention that in their company nowadays.

The so-called Special Service brigades were formed, training was outlined and men were recruited from other units, as often as not to the annoyance of the officers there losing motivated soldiers. For an organization as fond of abbreviations as the army, it is perhaps striking that they missed what Special Service abbreviated to, at least to start with. No. II Special Service brigade was designated airborne and became No. 2 Special Air Service, though it was no relation to David Stirling's later efforts – he appropriated the title. In the immediate scramble of recruitment, empire-building and improvisation that followed, parachute formations were put together and word got out that men were needed. These new and undeniably glamorous units were a magnet for big characters – men who had fought in the Spanish Civil War, on either side, men with errant disciplinary records and so on: blokes up for a scrap. For this reason they were viewed with suspicion by the rest of the army. Ambitious and motivated men would leave their units in the hope of a more exciting or at least different wartime career. And jump pay. The RAF could barely conceal its hostility.

Organization in the infant airborne force was chaotic, and potentially deadly, given the need for men to jump out of aircraft using equipment that was to all intents and purposes experimental. Training and development over the summer of 1940, perfecting the static-line parachute drop techniques with dummies, only went so far, and fatalities drove things along in an environment alien to our modern health and safety standards. It was trial and error that was central to delivering a workable parachute. The team at the newly established Central Landing School had adapted an RAF training parachute with a static line, fixed to a point in the aircraft, so that it would open automatically rather than with a ripcord – it took the death of Driver Evans in July of that year to configure a 'chute that was reliable and safe enough for the army, though men carried on undergoing terrible mishaps, like being snagged on the tail wheel of the bomber they were jumping out of or worse. Even as the techniques were refined, new recruits had to learn how to jump, and officers were no exception.

Attitudes to health and safety at this time are probably best described as pragmatic – the need to come up with a way of delivering men into the battlefield by parachute overrode everything else. Rather than disrupt testing after one fatal accident, one of the officers placed his colleague under arrest, investigation pending, and then carried on jumping. It was a school of hard knocks, broken teeth and noses. Jumping through the hole in the floor of the Whitley bomber carried the risk of snagging your parachute on the edge of the hole and smashing your face on the exit, known as 'ringing the bell'. Other bleak nicknames were a 'Roman candle' or 'streamer', when a man's 'chute didn't deploy properly and down he would go to his death. A reserve parachute was not worn.

*

As Gale assembled the 6th Airborne, he inherited officers from the 1st Airborne Division as well as taking on newcomers. One of those veterans of North Africa and Sicily was Alastair Pearson. Stories swirl around Pearson. He was a titan of airborne legend, in a profession not exactly short of legendary figures. Tireless, and seemingly completely immune to enemy action – the one wound he did collect in Normandy was on his hand, from a Sten gun that went off accidentally when he landed on the night of D-Day – Pearson had, according to his admirers, an uncanny knack for knowing what the Germans might do next, a sixth sense. 'Windy' Gale said of Pearson: 'as a leader he was second to none; men would follow him anywhere and do his bidding with a zest that was grand to see. Quiet and calm, he possessed immense courage. He had, too, an amazing tactical sense.'[4] Pearson liked to patrol aggressively, to stay in contact with the enemy and to wear him out. This demanded a lot from his men, so Pearson would lead patrols himself, even taking a party to rescue wounded men caught behind enemy lines a few nights after D-Day. On this jaunt he encouraged his men to sing on their way back towards their own lines to make sure they weren't fired on by their sentries. He was cunning, courageous, verbally as well as physically direct – several cheery tales relate of Pearson literally giving his men a boot up the arse when he felt it necessary, choosing to lead from behind in this instance. Alastair Pearson was a man suited to war, in particular to leading a battalion. And it was at the battalion level that the 6th Airborne did its fighting in Normandy.

A battalion commanded by a lieutenant colonel in the Second World War on paper numbered between approximately 600 and 1,000 men – though the complement could and did vary. Parachute battalions tended to number around 650 men, their strengths varying depending on how many men were fit, how many were in the land-borne administrative tail and how many might have made themselves absent. Parachute battalions, on account of their function as a battlefield flying-column, had to do a lot of waiting around; keyed-up, elite men, psychologically selected for their qualities of aggression, suffered from discipline problems born chiefly of boredom. The battalion, made up of rifle companies, which are in turn made up of platoons, answers up to its brigade and its headquarters (or in the case of the US Army, the regiment, and there were inevitable exceptions to the way things were done in the DUKE armies), but it is the last large unit that, on the battlefield, tends to behave as a unitary body.

Or at least it appears as such on the maps depicting

battles. The battalion commander would very often have to lead from the front in a way a brigadier might not. His headquarters didn't involve as many moving parts as a brigade HQ – at the start of the war in France, battalions were the last stop for radios – British formations did not have radio coverage within their battalions, so a lieutenant colonel was where the buck stopped locally. Commanding a battalion was necessarily less abstract than generalship, and required direct tactical grip: personality and the ability to generate loyalty were paramount, and what loyalty a battalion commander could establish amongst his men very much depended on the man himself. A man like Pearson would do more than attend O ('order') groups, he would hustle his battalion into action. Alastair Pearson was a battalion commander par excellence in this regard, driving men in a personally vigorous style not untypical of men in airborne forces, though of course this style was found on battlefields all over the world, and the casualty figures reflected it. This kind of leadership was personally perilous, and there were many men who had a similar attitude to Pearson whose luck wasn't as good as his when it came to getting through the war unscathed.

Being a lieutenant colonel in itself was very dangerous. Infantry officers suffered higher casualty rates than their men; little wonder as subalterns were expected to urge their men on and set an example in the worst of situations, and often enough – depending on how combat-savvy they were – would be specifically targeted by snipers. Company commanders, captains and majors were similarly exposed to danger, and turnover at the sharp end was high. In British units 65 per cent of officers could expect to be hit – 50 per cent of other ranks. In the 50th (Northumbrian)

Division, 16.5 per cent of officers were killed, 8.7 per cent of other ranks. This meant a one-in-ten chance of dying; they suffered a total of 452 officer casualties and 6,002 of other ranks. The 15th (Scottish) Division's figures were worse: 72.2 per cent of officers expected to be hit, and 28.7 per cent of them were killed. Other ranks did better but the figures aren't exactly reassuring – 62.9 per cent of other ranks were hit and 16.8 per cent killed. In Normandy, the 6th Airborne Division suffered 4,457 casualties; 821 were killed, 2,709 were wounded and 927 were reported missing. They were only in Normandy from 6 June to 26 August, just eleven weeks. The numbers mark how hard the fighting was, even on the 'quiet' left flank of the OVERLORD lodgement, a flank that tends to be overlooked compared to the battles around Caen during the same time.

Pearson had come to airborne forces two years before D-Day and had brought with him his experiences of fighting in France in 1940. He had sailed to France with the 6th Highland Light Infantry in the abortive second BEF landings in June 1940. After the Dunkirk evacuations, Churchill had made an effort to reassure the French, and doubtless himself, that the British Empire hadn't just cut and run in the face of defeat, sending General Alan Brooke (soon to be Chief of the Imperial General Staff) back to France on a predictably short-lived abortive adventure.

Pearson's brigade embarked for France on 7 June as part of the 52nd Lowland Division, landed at Cherbourg on the 8th and route-marched south. Pearson, a keen Territorial officer, quickly discovered how unfit his men were, and made a mental note that if they ever came back he would make sure they were much, much fitter. This time in France was brief, and the 6th Highland Light Infantry didn't see much action, but while he was there, Pearson nearly killed the commanding officer of another Highland battalion – he'd been told to shoot at anything that approached the crossroads he was holding. The 0.55-inch round from the Boys anti-tank rifle went right through the staff car, but didn't hit the colonel or his adjutant inside; Pearson successfully pleaded that he had only being doing as he'd been ordered and avoided a charge. But it had been a literal near-miss: the Boys might have had a poor reputation as an anti-tank weapon, but it could go straight through a car easily enough. (Hurling its bullet at 2,450 feet per second, 1,670 mph, the Boys worked well enough on earlier light Panzers, but as the war progressed acquired peashooter status.) By 17 June, the 52nd Division's situation had deteriorated and it was forced out of France in yet another British evacuation. Characteristically, Pearson was one of the last to leave, having persuaded a Glaswegian trawler to take him (and his equally characteristic purloined motorbike) back across the Channel. He rejoined his unit near Bedford and right away got into the business of making his men fitter, preparing for the expected invasion.

Two years later, in 1942, Pearson, hungry for adventure (and doubtless bored witless waiting for an invasion), decided he wanted to join a friend in the Special Boat Service, at least according to his biographer. Given the chaos surrounding special forces, this begs the question: which SBS? At the time there was more than one outfit that bore those initials, all working in cool rivalry in different obscure corners of the army, navy and marines, offering a magnet for the inspired, super-motivated, would-be superhuman. And, more prosaically, men 'who could swim', an essential requirement for volunteers. It wasn't until after the war that they were amalgamated and badged as they are now. Somehow, in all this confusion, Pearson ended up being interviewed for airborne forces rather than the SBS. At interview, he clearly made an impression on Richard Gale: Pearson was immediately made second in command of one of the new parachute battalions, though no one was quite sure which one; on arriving at the 1st Parachute Battalion's depot, he was told he was at the wrong headquarters, was sent over to the 2nd, and then back again.

Even two years into its existence, not everyone got all the training they needed on arrival at the embryonic parachute regiment. Pearson's first task as 2i/c of his battalion was to take part in a parachuting demonstration for the press, even though he had never parachuted before. These sorts of displays were a mixed blessing – while they often impressed MPs, ministers or journalists, they sometimes ran the risk of exposing a shortage of equipment or trained men. Demonstration drops could be underwhelming; often things went wrong: men landed in the wrong place and on one notorious occasion a man's fingers were caught in a glider door, causing a shriek of soldierly profanity which the Queen pretended she hadn't heard. These exercises were a distraction from the main business of training, but on this occasion substituted for Pearson's training. As the aeroplane took off, Pearson made essential small talk. He asked the other men in the plane how many jumps they'd done – one said twenty or so, another 50. They were old hands. Pearson – to his fellow parachutists' disbelief – admitted he'd not done any jumps and did anyone have any advice, please? He was rapidly filled in on parachute drill and told to follow the most experienced man on the plane who, fortunately for Pearson, worked as part of the parachute training scheme. The advice was simple enough: 'Do what I do,' he said, and Pearson jumped as instructed, managing not to break anything in front of the waiting photographers. Three more jumps earned Pearson his wings without having to do the full training that other parachutists would have: he'd shown his mettle. Pearson was the right kind of chap and was in.

*

What kind of chap was he? Born on 1 June 1915 in Glasgow, Alastair Pearson had come through private schools in Scotland and taken a job at his uncle's bakery. He was middle-class, he had excelled at sports at school, loving rugby. Pearson had joined the TA in the years between school and the war. At the outbreak of war, the Highland Light Infantry had been given things to guard: the shipyards on the Clyde, distilleries. His battalion had been thinned out by men being kept back for their reserved occupations, and when the unit returned to Glasgow from its French excursion, soldiering became much more difficult with the men being nearer home – discipline became an officer's main business rather than fighting. Pearson's thirst for action, central to his character, made a move to the more exciting world of special soldiering inevitable. He had a speech impediment: he couldn't say his 'l's – one of his nicknames was 'Bwast', from his favourite mispronounced curse. Another nickname within airborne forces was 'Jock', testament both to his Scottishness and their sheer lack of imagination, perhaps.* There was one thing

---

* Search for Pearson on Wikipedia and that's who he comes up as: 'Jock' Pearson.

that had the potential to derail Pearson's military career: his thirst. Drink lurks in many of the Pearson anecdotes: Alastair Pearson may have been a character, an officer with a capacity for hard work, hard training and with a knack for taking risks, but with that came hard drinking. After a particularly epic bender in Salisbury, he was confined to camp for 28 days – this was when he was second in command of the 1st Parachute Battalion, a high-profile drunken exploit that could have easily ruined his career. Fortunately for Pearson, pissed buccaneering officers were cut some slack at this stage of the airborne force's development, slack that would pay off when they were sent to North Africa. And in the milieu of parachute forces' officers' messes, heavy boozing was part of the culture.

After the war, Pearson lectured on leadership, and had a characteristically direct view on it – while bemoaning in properly fogeyish style that we didn't produce leaders any more. He said this:

> Now, what is leadership? Expressed in its simplest terms, a leader is a person who can get people to follow him, or, as Field-Marshal Montgomery put it: 'Anyone who has the capacity and the will to rally men and women to a common cause and the character which will inspire confidence.'[5]

Pearson was blessed with this quality; in his lecture he laid out what else a leader needed. Courage, principally. Pearson believed that there was no man alive who wouldn't like to be described as brave, and in this he lived up to his own aspiration. But why did courage matter so much? 'Because courage is not merely a virtue but is THE virtue. Without courage, there are no other virtues. Faith, hope and charity, and all the rest, don't become virtues unless you have the courage to exercise them.'[6]

*

In the winter of 1942, the campaign fought by the 1st Parachute Brigade, dispersed and fighting in battalion-sized battle groups, was ill-thought-out, based on intelligence that was patchy at best, its objectives confused and the plan for the men's extraction something that had been left to be sorted at a later date. It was an inauspicious start for British airborne forces deploying at larger than company level, though before North Africa, the results of parachute operations had been at best mixed. On 10 February 1941, a small parachute raiding force from No. 11 Special Air Service Battalion had been dropped into Italy to demolish the Tragino Aqueduct, which ran into Taranto, a key naval city for the Italians, as well as Brindisi and Bari – Operation COLOSSUS. X Troop – specially comprised of volunteers, though, naturally, *everyone* in the battalion had volunteered – flew to Malta with all of its kit in the aircraft that were to drop them in Italy. On seeing them off with a suitably stirring address, the head of Combined Operations, Admiral Sir Roger Keyes, was heard to mutter, 'What a pity.' The operation had been conceived as a blow to the Italian war effort via its infrastructure; destroying the fresh water supply to Taranto would disrupt the Reggia Marina. However, COLOSSUS had been conceived on the weakest of intelligence: when the men landed they discovered not one but two aqueducts. Navigation proved an issue for the RAF that night, X Troop's drop was scattered, one party of sappers carrying explosives did not make the rendezvous. The men who did reach their objective quickly realized to their dismay that the explosives they had brought with them would not damage anything more than one of the spans of the structure, as the aqueduct was constructed differently to expectations. They blew up what they could, then set out on their optimistic escape route, the plan being to trek some 50 miles in alerted enemy territory to the coast, where a submarine, HMS *Triumph*, would pick them up. Unfortunately, before they even set off *Triumph*'s skipper had decided to abandon his part of the mission – one of the aircraft flying the paras to Taranto had had to ditch in the sea near the appointed rendezvous site and he decided it was too dangerous. Rounded up as they attempted to escape, the men from X Troop were captured, and the Italian speaker attached to them from SOE was murdered. The survivors became prisoners of war until Italy surrendered. The aqueduct was repaired quickly. In early 1941, this was the best that British airborne forces could do.

More than a year later, on 27-28 February 1942, Operation BITING, led by John Frost, one of Pearson's big drinking buddies, was a great success – a Würzburg radar set had been dismantled and snatched for the scientific military intelligence expert R. V. Jones's boffins to examine – all but one of Frost's men had returned alive and the promise of parachute operations seemed alive again.* A company-sized operation, BITING's success

---

* In November 1942, running concurrently with the operations in North Africa, it was the turn of glider-borne pioneers to try to make an impact: the heavy water plant at Telemark in Norway was the target. This raid, Operation FRESHMAN, was a total failure; gliders containing 34 sappers crashed off-target and one of the tugs was lost. November was perhaps not the best time to attempt a North Sea crossing with tugs and

however tacitly acknowledged the limitations of airborne operations: it was on the northern French coast, much more navigable for the RAF than an aqueduct in the Italian interior, easier for the Royal Navy to control the extraction, and it stands out in that it ran smoothly. Frost's men were well rehearsed, and he didn't find he had to adapt the plan the minute he arrived in France – for a start, almost all of C Company were dropped in the right place. Frost had to improvise one aspect of the extraction: the covering party that was supposed to hold the beach was held up by the Germans, but with the rest of his men he was able to make the beach safe for the landing craft that came to collect them. Still, BITING was a huge success. Frost was awarded a Military Cross and was invited by Churchill to address the War Cabinet. Parachute operations were safe from the axe, expansion would continue. The next operations would be bigger than BITING, seeing airborne troops deployed not as raiders but as something else. Though as what had yet to be established.

The 1st Parachute Brigade under Brigadier Edwin Flavell – another one of Gale's people – embarked for North Africa as part of Operation TORCH, despite there not really being a role for them yet. In the rush to build an airborne force, which had been a singular pursuit for the people doing the building, their ideas had not been communicated to other parts of the army, which had been getting on with their own reorganizations and problem-solving, as well as rather a lot of fighting in multiple theatres. What did you use airborne soldiers for? Being a novelty was coupled

---

gliders. The men who survived the crash landings were murdered one by one by the Germans in line with Hitler's Commando Order.

with being an unknown quality: proponents of airborne were desperate to get into battle, so were prone to saying they could do anything. First Army had not factored an airborne element into Operation TORCH, but now here they were, ready and eager to be used. In this haste to get into combat, some of what were to become the hallmarks of airborne operations began to surface: shortage of aircraft, poor intelligence manifesting as an essential cluelessness about what the enemy might be up to, matched by an almost boundless optimism about what lightly armed paratroopers could do on what was their first large-scale foray behind enemy lines. Plans shifted, objectives changed.

*

The planned first drop on 15 November was cancelled, but the following day, the 1st Parachute Battalion were dropped behind enemy lines. A measure of the lack of planning was immediately evident: as his battalion flew into battle on its first drop in anger, Pearson's boss, Lieutenant Colonel James Hill, had to stand at the door of the aircraft and choose a suitable drop zone. 'This is not a good method when early enemy opposition is expected,' says the official history. Setting the scene for the operations in Tunisia, it reads:

> [Both] operations were hampered by the lack of time and transport and by the comparative inexperience of both the troops and the air forces [. . .] only a limited amount of transport was available as First Army had been unable to allot shipping space for any of the brigade's own transport. *Air photographs were nonexistent* [my emphasis] as these particular operations

had not been foreseen and only one small-scale map of Souk-el-Arba was available for the whole battalion. Information was extremely vague. But both these operations offered good chances of again forestalling the enemy if they were carried out quickly.[7]

Optimism even after the event. Landing at Souk-el-Arba unopposed,* Hill then proceeded to look for trouble – capturing buses and moving up to Beja, putting out feelers to find out how the Vichy French forces in the area were going to react. The history notes that 90 per cent of supplies were recovered despite 'the attempts of local Arabs to steal them'.[8] Hill improvised his battalion's operations from there on. His style was to improvise and confuse his opponents – he wasn't shy of using blatant deception either. He seized Beja from the French by parading his troops twice through the town, once in helmets, then again in red berets, with a trolley covered in tarpaulins that the French were told was a new anti-tank weapon. Guerrilla-style action suited Hill's situation; the battalion was not nearly heavily armed enough to properly disrupt the enemy strategically but was too large a presence to go ignored by the Germans or, more importantly, unemployed. This paradox didn't cramp Hill's style. He set about creating the impression that he had far more than a battalion at his disposal: he did this with vigorous patrolling and the whole battalion working flat out. He lacked artillery support and tactical air cover so was having to operate purely as light infantry. Once an understanding with the French

---

* One man was injured by a Sten gun misfiring: a pattern forms. Another man was strangled by his rigging lines.

was settled, the Senegalese colonial forces decided to side with the British, and Hill turned his attention to Sidi N'Sir, hoping to take on a mixed German and Italian armoured unit, a tough nut to crack for such lightly armed troops, but one that Hill, ever ambitious, was keen to pull off. The assault that followed was full of the dash, initiative and deadly chaos that went with airborne operations. During the moonlight attack, a column of 27 sappers were killed when their anti-tank explosives blew up by accident, ruining the surprise as the detonations echoed around the German/Italian hill-top positions. Lieutenant Colonel Hill and his men stormed the peak anyway, putting all those who didn't surrender to the bayonet but finding only a handful of tanks. In the fighting Hill – at the centre of things as ever – was hit in the chest by a burst of machine-gun fire as he clambered on top of one of the tanks. So Pearson came to command the battalion, and with that battlefield promotion came the beginning of the Pearson legend.

*

Pearson fought a buccaneering and courageous series of battles. By the end of it he had been awarded the DSO and Two Bars. He picked up where James Hill had left off and was a relentless patroller, always checking his men's positions. When confronted with the notion that his plan to capture the hill at Mansour was madness, he replied, 'War is usually madness.' He consistently led from the front, though not always with deadly results – in that same assault, Pearson, charging up the mountain away from his headquarters, ran straight into a pair of Germans. He drew his pistol and tried to unload it at the Germans. It was empty but they surrendered, intimidated as they were – the legend tells – by Pearson's presence.

The battalion then stayed in the line and fought as regular infantry, fighting with the 6th Armoured Division as well as in an ad hoc formation called Y Division. The quality of the paratroopers as infantrymen was now amply demonstrated. Even though it wasn't really clear how to deploy them in their role as airborne forces, they provided First Army with a useful reserve, earning the whole of the 1st Parachute Brigade essential combat experience, albeit expensively, even if they were being used in a role at odds with the one they had supposedly been raised for. They would have to wait for Sicily and Operation HUSKY to put that to the test properly.

In Sicily, Pearson and his battalion were part of the second wave of airborne landings that accompanied the invasion. The first wave of glider landings had been almost totally calamitous. George Chatterton,* who had co-founded the Glider Pilot Regiment, outlined and overseen the pilots' training, had begged his CO, the 1st Airborne's mercurial Major General George Hopkinson, to at best rethink or at worst cancel the glider landings. The landing areas were small rocky fields with stone walls; glider pilot training had – for safety reasons – focused on circuits of airfields rather than landing in terrain full of obstacles; moreover, Chatterton's men had trained on different gliders to the aircraft earmarked for Sicily. The glider pilots had been hanging about for three months and had not

---

* His memoirs are an entertaining how-I-won-the-war-and-had-the-last-laugh romp. He bangs a lot of tables and persuades his superiors that they're all wrong and he's right.

been in the air since their epic effort to bring gliders to North Africa across the Bay of Biscay via Morocco, an incredible piece of flying that had seen crews ditch in the sea, get picked up and try again. Hopkinson didn't care.*

Hopkinson left Chatterton alone for half an hour to make his mind up as to whether he wanted to stay in his post or figure out what to do. Conflicted, Chatterton opted for the latter, put on a brave face and flew a glider into Sicily himself, leading Operation LADBROKE literally from the front, consoling himself afterwards that his gliders had caused the enemy great confusion and that a great deal had been learned. After all, you learn from your mistakes.

And mistakes were pretty much all that were on offer. It's hard to overstate how much of a cock-up LADBROKE was. The glider pilots had truly been landed in it. Flying American gliders they'd not trained with, towed by crews they were unfamiliar with, flying at night when few had done any night flying – and those that had had only been allowed by the RAF to land on flarepaths, landing at night without flarepaths being deemed too dangerous. As a means of deception, the glider force appeared to be heading for Sardinia but took a right at Malta, an epic journey that strained the pilots further. The landings were a total shambles. Whatever could go wrong did go wrong. Given the task of delivering the 1st Airlanding Brigade to Eighth Army's right flank at Syracuse, many of the gliders, including Chatterton's, were cast off too early into a strong wind and ended up in the sea: 252 men were drowned. Of 145 gliders sent on the 400-mile trip from Tunisia, only 52 made

* Chatterton's memoirs tellingly describe Hopkinson as 'short'.

landfall; only 4 managed to make accurate landings on their LZs (landing zones). Gliders were supposed to be the tactically efficient way of delivering men to the battlefield, avoiding the potential problem of landing spread out, like paratrooper landings. In Sicily they were nothing of the sort.

If you couldn't get the gliders where they were meant to get to, what was the point? The Special Raiding Squadron, a rebadged Special Air Service outfit commanded by the legendary man of war Paddy Mayne, had simply sailed up to the coast to take their objectives, all landing in the right place together. They picked up some stray glider-borne men, including, to his chagrin, Chatterton, with none of the fuss the airlanding men had expended. One glider detail heading for the Ponte Grande, a bridge on one of the exits from the Eighth Army's landing area, fared typically for the night. Of eight gliders, only one landed safely on target; another that had found its way to the Ponte Grande hit a wall and exploded, killing everyone on board. The men of the South Staffords, at least those who had made it to the Ponte Grande and hadn't ended up in the Mediterranean, with a steady drift of stragglers attracted to the sound of battle, held onto the bridge for as long as they could despite the Italians' best efforts to remove them, and were relieved by the Eighth Army only half an hour after they had been forced from their positions. The glider landings had been chaotic and expensive: comprehensively oversold. Chatterton in his memoir related how his pilots had done their job magnificently, but even he couldn't say that things had gone according to plan. It is perhaps striking that the following year glider operations happened for OVERLORD at all.

All this underlined how the newfangled business of

airborne assault was not much more than a huge, deadly experiment. Parachute forces weren't much different – what they had in common now with glider forces was their first main deployment had been utterly chaotic. Again, like the glider-borne troops, their task was to take a bridge and hold until relieved by the Eighth Army. With hindsight the whole thing seems spectacularly optimistic, especially given how badly the glider lift had gone, and indeed the 2nd Parachute Brigade's landings at Augusta were cancelled in the wake of the glider landings. The next operation, FUSTIAN, went ahead anyway.

FUSTIAN's objective, the Primosole Bridge, sat at the confluence of the Simeto River and the Gornalunga Canal. Highway 155 ran towards Catania – taking the bridge would open up the Catania plain for Eighth Army's race to Mount Etna and on to Messina. At least that was the idea. The brigade's three battalions would land on four different drop zones, seize the bridge, the nearby high ground and a gun battery that overlooked the bridge. Even though the fleet had been warned not to fire on Allied aircraft, flak from both sides plagued the paratroopers' approach. Pearson's pilot was in a state of panic, the co-pilot sobbing at the controls. Pearson took off his parachute, squeezed into the cockpit and asked the pilot what the hell he thought he was doing. The pilot said he couldn't go in. 'I'm not committing suicide,' he said. Pearson drew his pistol and threatened to shoot him – 'perhaps it will encourage him' – and claimed that one of his men was an ex-pilot who could fly the plane anyway. The pilot was unsurprisingly convinced to carry on and Pearson and his men jumped into the night, blazing haystacks all around.

Confusion reigned on the battlefield, further complicated by the arrival on the same drop zones of German
Fallschirmjäger. The flak had worked its magic and men
were dispersed for miles: this was meant to be a brigade-
strength drop and, after a scratch force of 50 men had seized
the bridge, only about 120 men made it to there to defend
it. The charges the Germans had laid were disarmed, and
Pearson and his scratch force dug in and waited for the
German counter-attack, which came at six thirty the morning after the drop. Unlike in North Africa, the paras had
artillery at their disposal – by ten, HMS *Mauritius* with her
6-inch guns had destroyed the first counter-attack. German
planes strafed the paras, who had no way to respond. Gradually more men arrived at the bridge, attracted by the
sounds of fighting – just as well, as the Germans and their
Italian reinforcements continued to counter-attack. With
164 men, a couple of mortars and three anti-tank guns
(which had arrived by glider), Pearson told his men to 'fight
the barbarians off as long as possible'.[9] He cajoled, he led by
example, he went to see for himself what was happening
and was seen doing it: 'he fought the battle the way he
thought it ought to be fought rather than by the text book.'[10]
In its own way, that sounds a lot like *Auftragstaktik*.

By the end of the day Pearson and the men from the 1st
and 2nd Battalions had withdrawn to the southern bank of
the river. They were being shelled and the reeds on the
riverbank had caught fire. When night fell, Pearson elected
to withdraw from the river completely, to a crag overlooking it, but he did what he could to make sure that the
Germans couldn't seize it either: an attempt by the Germans to check the charges on the bridge was chased away.
Eighth Army arrived, and the following morning men

from the 151st Brigade of 50th (Tyne Tees) Division tried to take the bridge. The 9th Battalion the Durham Light Infantry put in an attack that, despite being supported by tanks and artillery, was repulsed by the enemy. Pearson and his men watched this attack fail. It was decided that the 151st Brigade should try again; Pearson and Frost, who had made it to the 151st Brigade's HQ, watched in disbelief as the 9th Battalion of the Durham Light Infantry were ordered to have a go at taking the bridge in the same way. Pearson was unable to contain himself: 'Well, if you want to lose another bloody battalion that's the right way to do it.'[11] Rather than chuck Pearson out of his headquarters, the brigadier asked him what he should do. During his withdrawal the night before, Pearson had found a point at which he could ford the river. He offered to guide the Durhams over the river that night, so that they could go around the Germans and outflank them. The brigadier agreed.

That night, Pearson, his batman, Jock Clements (another Jock), and Provost Sergeant Manser with a roll of white tape led the Durhams' company commanders and colonel across the Simeto. The going was tense: one of the Durhams' men was shot through the head by an accidental discharge, but the Germans didn't send out a patrol to investigate. Clements went forward and made sure the coast was clear. Satisfied that he had done what he could to help, Pearson wished them well and returned to what was left of his battalion. As the battalion approached Syracuse, Montgomery appeared, doing his thing of meeting the men. He thanked Pearson for his efforts, and they discussed the battle. Exhausted, and finally in this moment of pause, Alastair Pearson was diagnosed with malaria and hospitalized. His gammy parachutist's knees were also playing up. For all the efforts that had gone into taking the Primosole Bridge, the balance of Montgomery's efforts shifted away from the coast and the bridge lost its importance.

Alastair Pearson had shown incredible verve in command of the 1st Parachute Battalion, not to mention great luck. His style of command suited airborne operations, which, now that the British were eighteen months into running them, had revealed their unique paradoxical nature. Airborne operations required highly detailed planning, robust intelligence, a timetable, wholehearted inter-service cooperation (drawing a pistol and pointing it at the pilot doesn't count), and a very clear aim and objective. Orders were inevitably complex. Slight adjustments to any aspect of the plan could create huge ripples through the rest of the operation. Aircraft allocations, glider manifests, navigation plans, flight plans, allocations for ammunition, food and medical supply drops, the possibilities for rehearsal, would all need to be altered. Any airborne endeavour therefore was inevitably inflexible in its planning, and needed officers and planners who could consider every detail in their work. However, airborne operations, for all the planning, the precise effort and logistical commitment, tended to go wrong because of bad weather, planning oversights – such as the fleet off the Sicilian coast firing on the airlift as it arrived – and the friction of running any complex operation. This meant that the men on the ground, once they had landed, as often as not found their plan in pieces. And this meant officers who could take the initiative were essential, men who understood the aim of what they were trying to achieve and could keep things simple and keep things moving on the ground. This put extra pressure on the officers and

NCOs, plunged into situations that were inherently chaotic and unstable. Major General Roy Urquhart, who commanded the ill-fated Arnhem operation with the 1st Airborne Division, remarked on the dislocation airborne soldiers could experience, suddenly being pitched into battle rather than being brought up to the line like normal soldiers. Urquhart's drops and landings had gone perfectly on the first day, but he still saw his battle descend into complete chaos and eventual defeat.

*

On his return to England, Pearson was recruited by his old boss Richard Gale to raise and command a new battalion for Gale's new division. His brigade commander was to be James Hill, who had recovered from the wounds he had sustained in North Africa. The new battalion, the 8th (Midlands) Parachute Battalion*, had previously been the 15th Warwicks. Second in command was John Marshall, Gale's former adjutant, doubtless there to keep an eye on Pearson. Pearson proceeded to comb through the Warwicks to find out who was up to being a paratrooper, discarding those who weren't. He trained them hard, made sure his subalterns knew their men, were competent with their arms and well-versed in fighting as self-sufficiently as possible. The men were very fit: a battalion was expected to cover 32 miles in 24 hours, a platoon 50

---

* 8th Parachute Battalion was one of the battalions that had been converted from a regular infantry battalion, the 13th Warwickshire Battalion. The reason? Airborne forces had run out of volunteers. The men were put through retraining and those that weren't up to snuff were returned to regular infantry.

miles. Mindful of his early experience of being put on public display, Pearson asked that the battalion not have any official visits for three months so that he could get it into shape, and by May 1944, when the Royal Family paid the 6th Airborne Division a visit, his men were ready for the invasion. As the invasion approached, Gale supposedly allocated a larger parachute to Pearson to make sure his knees survived the landing. Pearson's wedding, planned for 8 June, had to wait.

As the invasion drew closer, Gale, Hill and Pearson found the words needed to prepare their men for the invasion. Addressing the camp, Major General Gale remarked, 'The Hun thinks only a bloody fool will go there: that's why I'm going!'[12] Brigadier James Hill had given Pearson a message to read to the 8th Parachute Battalion as they embarked on the evening of 5 June: 'Gentlemen, in spite of your excellent training and orders, do not be daunted if chaos reigns. It undoubtedly will.'[13] Pearson then added a few comments of his own, stressing the need for the men to focus on the task in hand and not to waste ammunition. He added: 'Men, do you know what your first action will be when you land? You'll all have a pee!'[14]

On the night of D-Day, Pearson's battalion was scattered on its landing, yet fought aggressively and harassed the enemy wherever they found them. Pearson's role on the night was to make sure that the bridges on the rivers Dives and Bures – 5 or so miles to the east of the Caen Canal – were demolished. Bad weather had caused huge disarray on the drop zones, and the sappers who were meant to blow the bridges landed miles from their jeeps and explosives. With push and drive and a dollop of luck, Major Tim Roseveare from 3rd Parachute Squadron Royal Engineers blew up the bridges that night and withdrew safely into the 8th Battalion's area, a most extraordinary story of derring-do. In the weeks that followed, 8th Parachute Battalion set up shop in the Bois de Bavent, a forest to the south of the 6th Airborne divisional area, controlling the road that ran north towards the Caen Canal and the Orne River. Pearson patrolled relentlessly, kept his men going, led from the front until the division was withdrawn after the breakout at Falaise in August and the division's dash to the Seine. The battalion had lost 5 officers and 60 other ranks killed, and 162 officers and men wounded, with another 101 missing, as it shifted roles from shock landing troops to line infantry; hard fighting that demanded everything of its officers and its men.

Pearson fades from view after Normandy; his malaria returned and he couldn't continue fighting in the war. Perhaps he'd not have got further than battalion commander, his natural soldiering environment; perhaps he was simply done, worn out. Hill, despite being wounded by Allied aircraft on D-Day, carried on commanding his brigade until the end of the war. Gale eventually became deputy commander of NATO under Field Marshal Montgomery, where, along with other NATO brains, he could work on the puzzle of what had made the Germans fight so effectively. But all of them knew the value of orders, of initiative, and the cost of being on the front. What other lessons were being applied, and how adaptable was British thinking, in that other arena of relentless military invention and innovation, armoured warfare?

9

Percy Hobart

Funnies

The Second World War was a war of technology, industry and production. A war of factories and steel. A war which saw an unprecedented series of leaps and bounds in technological development, from biplanes in 1939 to jet fighters by the time the war ended, from cavalry to the atom bomb. Equipment and the advances in weapons technology as well as all the other tools of warfare defined the battlefield. As Francis Tuker knew, you could aspire to whatever kind of warfare you liked, but if you didn't have the tools to do it with, your plans were hollow. And soldiers needed to have confidence in their equipment, an understanding that when they were fighting for their lives the kit wouldn't let them down, was the very best that could be provided. Any sense that men were being sent to fight with substandard gear could pull the rug out from under a commander, his men's morale undermined by faulty kit. Tanks were a focus of this kind of technological contest, and that contest generates controversy to this day, of the which-tank-was-the-best type.

It's irresistible. Tanks offer themselves up for comparison, with speed, thickness of armour, firepower all filling the columns of a Top Trumps card with delicious stats. The Tiger, the Panzer VI, with 100mm of frontal armour, its 88mm gun, imposing silhouette and fearsome reputation, is the emblem of this Top Trumps-style debate, and the victories the Germans notched up using Tigers and the equally admired Panthers cast a shadow over the story of the technology and industry of the Second World War. Germany's astonishing victory in France in 1940 sealed the notion that the Germans knew armoured warfare better than anyone else. The British needed answers. And, it seemed, equipment.

The tanks that Britain fielded in 1940 were not that different from what the Germans brought to battle. Light tanks, armed with machine guns, the British vehicles favoured protection for their crews, so weren't as quick as the Panzer Is, Panzer IIs and Czech T-38s the Germans used in the armoured fist that broke through the French lines at the Ardennes. The British, however, had not committed all of their armour to France. Formed in 1937, by the time war broke out the 1st Armoured Division boasted three brigades, two 'light' tank brigades and one 'heavy'. When the Germans attacked on 10 May, the 1st Armoured, the armoured fist of the British Army, was still in England, and was promptly ordered from its base in Dorset to France. Its state reflected the division's torturous and controversial origins: it lacked spare parts, didn't have the radios it needed nor the full complement of tanks it should have come equipped with. Boasting 114 light tanks and 143 cruiser tanks, the 1st Armoured set off for France – the division was rail and sea transportable. The situation was changing fast and the division was separated, some elements landing at Le Havre, others at Cherbourg once it became clear that Le Havre was too dangerous.

On being brought to battle, orders and counter-orders

were issued, some by the BEF, some by the French Army, and it wasn't until a fortnight after the German invasion began that the 1st Armoured went into action, trying to seize and defend bridges on the Somme. Equipped with Mark IV Cruiser tanks, fast tanks that could do 30mph on roads, as well as slow and heavily armoured Matilda Is and IIs, the 1st Armoured's key moment came at the Battle of Arras on 21 May, when a scraped-together counter-attack caught Rommel by surprise. But the consensus was that the German Panzers had the edge. At least, the German way of doing things with tanks seemed far more switched on than the British and French way had been. German Panzer assault benefitted from being taken seriously and, most importantly, being an integrated system.

Tanks had finally fulfilled their potential, or at least so it seemed. Conceived in the First World War by the British as a way to escape the deadlock of the trenches and traverse no man's land in relative safety, tanks had offered tantalizing near-successes, particularly at the First Battle of Cambrai in November and December 1917. Getting through multiple lines of German defence under German artillery fire required good tank and infantry cooperation, and too often in attempted tank-driven breakthroughs infantry couldn't keep up with the tanks or were too exhausted by their efforts to be able to exploit any breakthrough made. British tanks were slow – driving at walking pace – and while they protected their crews from machine-gun and rifle fire, they were not well-armoured enough to withstand an artillery hit fired over open sights or the rounds of a heavy-calibre anti-tank rifle. While the technology looks crude now, it was state of the art at the time and the very best that mechanical engineering and production could come up with while industry was under colossal pressure. New designs, larger and more heavily armed and armoured, were developed in preparation for the war and extending into 1919 – called Plan 1919 – including armoured personnel carriers, which would have solved the problem of infantry being able to keep up. However, the war ended and tanks were no longer needed, except for crowd control in populations filled with revolutionary fever.

Between the wars, there was government investment in new armoured types and trials, as well as private investment in saleable machines. Vickers perfected their carrier designs in the two decades between the wars, developing a vehicle and style that would be ubiquitous in the DUKE inventory for the whole of the Second World War – over 100,000 would be built. The carrier's omnipresence and seeming lack of glamour means that in the breathless reckonings of armoured or tracked vehicles fielded during the war it gets forgotten or overlooked, but its ability to tow a 6-pounder anti-tank gun and be part of an anti-tank screen onto which the enemy might be lured makes it – arguably – as potent as any tank. But it is small, car-sized, open-topped and forever associated with the Bren gun, which doesn't sound like it would stop a Mark IV Panzer, so it falls into the background in the great debates on tanks. In other words, any assessment of tanks has to place them in a broader context of what weapons, machines and systems there are to work with them, as well as those that oppose them. Vickers' carriers led to what were called Tankettes, basically carriers with a machine gun in a turret. Some of these made it to France in 1940 but they were inadequate in the same measure that the carrier itself was ideal.

Spending between the wars was erratic. Vehicle tests for trucks and other machines went ahead in Dorset as well as in Egypt – plans to mechanize the British Army had to take into account the other theatres where DUKE soldiers might be deployed. Valuable experience of running trucks in the desert was gathered, but tanks lagged behind. Armoured cars for imperial policing came to the fore and proved useful; tracked vehicles were harder to build, devising engines that weren't underpowered was problematic, and even though key players like the Chancellor of the Exchequer, Winston Churchill – who as First Sea Lord during the First World War had prominently pushed for 'landships', as tanks were first known – would attend demonstrations, armoured fighting vehicles slid down the British military pecking order. Power and suspension dominated the attempts at designing new tanks, leaving firepower third. Other players were leading the way, innovations were being made. Probably the most influential tank design of the 1930s came in the form of the Christie suspension: the American designer John Walter Christie devised a suspension using large road wheels that eschewed the use of leaf-springs; instead it relied on springs mounted in cranks that allowed the wheels to move much further. This delivered higher cross-country speed. The Soviets had embraced this new technology and used the Christie suspension on their BT-1 tank; it was witnessing these trials that prompted the British to buy one of Christie's machines (the US Army had found working with Christie too frustrating). Having shipped the M1932 over in the guise of agricultural machinery, the War Office tested it and decided it didn't like the tank, but the suspension was taken and incorporated into what was to become the benighted Covenanter tank, and then into further British tank designs, in the form of the Cromwell and Comet. The Soviets stuck with the Christie suspension too, most famously on the T-34.

As a European war came to seem more and more likely, spending suddenly boomed. In 1931, the War Office spent £375,000 on tanks and AFVs; this dipped in the following years, then crept up to £842,000 in 1936, suddenly soaring the next year, with £3,625,000 being spent in 1937. Until 1937, these figures were a tiny fraction of the British Army's budget. Three design types had been settled on: light tanks for reconnaissance, cruiser tanks for exploitation, and infantry tanks to support infantry up close in an assault. Central to this thinking was Percy Hobart, known affectionately, to those who could muster affection, as 'Hobo'.

Hobart is best known, retrospectively, as the commanding officer of the 79th Armoured Division, and his name is, for tank nuts, synonymous with his 'Funnies', specialized tanks that on D-Day in particular were part of the assault force that took the Normandy beaches. Part of a wide range of specialized, almost science-fiction vehicles, Hobart's most famous tank, the Sherman DD – Duplex Drive – which swam ashore onto the landing beaches, remains to this day as mind-boggling and inspired as it was the best part of 80 years ago: what must the German *Landser* defending the beaches have made of that? With a rampaging bull's face for its badge, the 79th Armoured Division was the largest armoured formation of the war, the largest division in the British Army. Yet it never fought as a division, it operated as a decentralized, integrated, cooperative assault force. And it represented the pinnacle of armoured warfare, the perfectly adapted tactical formation that delivered strategic effect. And it was Hobart's baby.

*

Percy Hobart had come to tanks after the First World War. Born in 1885, he had been commissioned into the Royal Engineers in 1904 and went to India. He fought as a sapper in the Mohmand Expedition in 1908, an excursion against rebels on the Afghan border – a huge operation consisting of three brigades – and then, when the war came in France and Mesopotamia, he fought in the attempts to free Kut that Francis Tuker had been involved in. As a sapper, his skills were innovative and in 1916 he was regarded as an expert in aerial reconnaissance, being mentioned in dispatches six times and earning a DSO. After the war, he went to the Staff College at Camberley and returned to India. There he took part in the Waziristan campaign to settle yet another rebellion. In 1923, Hobart saw the light regarding armoured warfare, admiring the work of Basil Liddell Hart, the military opinion writer who believed tanks were the future, and transferred to the Royal Tank Corps. The corps was given its black beret and motto, 'Fear Naught', by the King, which could hardly make up for its lack of equipment, spending, doctrine and manpower, but it was a start. That year, Hobart returned to India to teach at the Staff College at Quetta until 1927. During this time, his sister, Betty, married Bernard Montgomery. Hobart was well-connected, decorated, well-respected as a trainer of men, in first with the form of warfare that would prove to be so important in the Second World War. However, it was at Quetta that he gained a reputation as a ladies' man; as it was, Quetta itself was known for its marital disruption. And it was this that was the fly in Hobart's ointment; while teaching at Quetta, he was named as co-respondent in the divorce of one of his students. Hobart went on to marry Dorothea in 1928, but it meant that he had a reputation beyond his professional competence: he was a rotter. The incident was so notorious the War Office issued a memo that declared any officer who did this ought to resign his commission – Hobart's obstinacy decided otherwise. Divorce was rarer and brought more social opprobrium in the inter-war years, and Hobart was someone who had had an affair with a fellow officer's wife. He was a cad. His marriage would be used against him when arguments erupted, and Hobart's temperament and zeal meant that they often did.

During the 1930s, he worked his way up through the Royal Tank Corps, at the same time the War Office was making up its mind about which machines – all rail trans-portable, which led to some peculiar long, thin, unsteerable prototype vehicles – it might procure. The pressure of advocacy for armoured warfare and Hobart's zeal for the subject burnished his reputation further. He wrote about armoured warfare and was part of the inter-war exchange of ideas about tanks, John the Baptist-style, before spend-ing increased. Liddell Hart and J. F. C. Fuller, who had fought at Cambrai in 1917, were in the vanguard of this thinking, which had attracted a lot of attention in Ger-many. Fuller went on to express his admiration for Hitler, and the porous borders between his enthusiasm for armoured warfare, militarism and envy of totalitarian solutions to perceived inter-war problems ruined his repu-tation in the long run. Panzer pioneer Heinz Guderian kept himself abreast of British writing on armoured warfare; Liddell Hart's post-war reputation survived the association, Fuller's did not. Hobart stayed out of this kind of trouble and was made inspector of the Royal Tank Corps from 1931 to 1933, then promoted to brigadier to found and command the 1st Tank Brigade; by the eve of the war he was the most experienced and switched-on officer in armour. His emphasis was on attacking weakness, using tanks to break open the enemy line and exploit thereon.

During this time he had become part of Churchill's wilderness network of officers whose brains he would pick on matters military. In 1937, Hobart submitted a paper outlining his blueprint for what he called a tank division: a tank brigade, a 'cavalry' brigade of light tanks, mounted infantry, anti-aircraft support, artillery and sappers. The War Office didn't like it and Hobart was told by the Chief of the Imperial General Staff that if he couldn't find a way to fit in he should quit. The scandal around his marriage was held against him – while this seems astonishing by our standards, this was the era of the Abdication Crisis – and few were sympathetic about the death of his sister, Betty Montgomery. Hobart was obstreperous, a bad team player, with a reputation for intolerance, impatience and hot-headedness, and crashed about making enemies with his tactlessness; by 1938, things had got so bad the army needed to find somewhere to send him where he would be less bothersome, even though there was no one else with his single-minded approach to developing tanks. Going through two training positions, he was dispatched to Egypt in October 1938 to form an armoured force in anticipation of fighting the Italians. There was a flap on, fear of an Italian invasion of North Africa, and Hobart was dispatched east in a flying boat post-haste. Two days later Neville Chamberlain flew to Munich.

It was in Egypt that Hobart was, out of sight of London, finally able to bring his methods to bear, and with the assortment of units placed at his disposal he did what he could to form 'Mobile Force'. With a variety of light tanks, trucks, armoured cars and towed anti-aircraft guns, a blend of cavalry that had been mechanized, Royal Tank Regiment tank specialists and Indian Army infantry, Hobart's efforts endeared him to his men and alienated his superiors. He gave 'Mobile Force' – which wags had dubbed 'Mobile Farce' – its new nickname and identity too. Hobart had taken a shine to his intelligence officer Rea Leakey's pet gerbil, or desert rat; Mobile Force went on to become the famous 7th Armoured Division, the Desert Rats. It became clear during training that integrating units and working together was entirely reliant on radio communications: Mobile Force needed to be able to talk to itself. This led to the habit of tank men pushing on; if they couldn't get a reply on artillery support quickly enough, they would try to crack on without it. This habit persisted in the desert in the years that followed, and it was not until 1942 that radio communications equipment and practice caught up with what success on the battlefield demanded. Hobart also perfected the use of supply dumps, which could be topped up by lorries, realizing that the only way to fight with long mechanized columns in the desert was to create vast, corps-sized dumps of food, ammunition and fuel. These 'Field Maintenance Centres' were a crucial factor in the victories of Operation COMPASS in 1940 and became British Army supply doctrine thereafter. Even then, Hobart was making enemies: his immediate superior,

Lieutenant General Sir Robert Gordon-Finlayson, couldn't stand him, annoyed that Hobart would run exercises without his permission (Hobart couldn't bear to be idle). Gordon-Finlayson thought him a nuisance and said he wasn't fit for combat command. Hobart returned to the UK in 1939, but not before he had also made an enemy of his boss Archie Wavell,* Commander-in-Chief, Middle East, whose wife disapproved of Hobart's marital circumstances, and infuriated Jumbo Wilson, General Officer Commanding, Egypt. Wilson had been to visit one of Hobart's exercises and got lost; Hobart had been practising operational security and had not shared radio frequencies. It didn't go down well. Wilson described Hobart as someone whose tactical ideas were

> based on the invincibility and invulnerability of the tank to the exclusion of the employment of other arms in correct proportion [. . .] being self-opinionated and lacking in stability I do not consider General Hobart can be relied on to discard his own ideas and carry out instructions from his superiors in a spirit of loyalty or co-operation.[1]

To top it off, Gordon-Finlayson had also returned to the UK and become Adjutant General, putting paid to any chance Hobart might have had of being given command.

Hobart had enraged everyone everywhere he went just in time for the war, a war that would centre on his speciality. He had no patron and had isolated himself. With the Phoney War in full stasis, his ideas out of favour, at the end

---

* This at the same time that Orde Wingate was gaining Wavell's approval for fighting his low-level counter-insurgency.

of the road career-wise and, at 55, too old to get a second chance, he was forced into retirement, effectively cashiered. By May 1940, he was out of the picture.

*

In the meantime Hobart had joined the Local Defence Volunteers in Chipping Campden in Gloucestershire in preparation for invasion. Needless to say, he quickly became a pain for everyone involved. Nevertheless, he rose swiftly from lance corporal to deputy area organizer, based at Hertford College in Oxford. Interestingly, by July, when the Local Defence Volunteers became the Home Guard, Hobart was trying to involve trade unions with defence organizing. But it was the world-changing German Panzer assault of May 1940 that rescued Hobart from obscurity. Tanks, how to use them, what to do about them suddenly became terribly important, and the army's most experienced armoured warfare expert was guarding his village with a pikestaff and doing admin. Churchill wanted answers, imagining that what he needed was something like German Panzer divisions, as well as a radical thinker who could deliver this for him. General Frederick Pile, who had trained with Hobart, told Churchill about Hobart and how he had just been sacked. This played on Churchill's prejudices about the state of the War Office and the army – neither could be relied on to find the right people for the job now in hand. Hobart wanted his honour and rank restored. While he was waiting to see Churchill, he had written to other tank officers for comments on his proposals. Here Hobart overplayed his hand. He outlined a radical and impractical new direction: an armoured army composed of ten divisions, with 10,000 tanks. Self-contained, working as armoured battle formations, with its own anti-aircraft provision, and all of its ground troops fully motorized, with parachutists as well. It would train closely tactically with the RAF. It resembled Plan 1919 and, more importantly, whatever it was that Blitzkrieg was reckoned to be. The Chief of the Imperial General Staff, Sir John Dill, attached a note pointing out Hobart's flaws: Churchill pushed back saying the army couldn't just rely on people who'd never had a disagreement. Here Churchill's latitude for men whose character might otherwise work against them worked in Hobart's favour. Being a bounder wouldn't count against him, for now.

Aside from the complete shake-up of how the entire army worked, there was one big problem: tanks. Where would 10,000 tanks come from? For, although during the 1930s various car, train and ship manufacturers had had their eye on how tank production was evolving, none had invested heavily enough in delivering vehicles that were reliable. Vickers' success with the Carrier and the reliability that went with it had come after a decade of investment and foreign sales; none of its competitors had gathered that experience during the same time. American industry might be waiting in the wings, and would, eventually, deliver, but would they be light, cruiser or infantry tanks? Or were those categories irrelevant? Had the Germans changed that? And how, actually, would the kind of armoured assault Hobart was proposing be coordinated and commanded? Because the key to the Blitzkrieg had been coordination and command. Radio.

Although some British tanks had been equipped with radios in 1940, British tanks at the Arras counter-attack had gone into battle using hand signals for commands.

The Wireless Set No. 19 had come into service that year, but it wasn't until 1942 that effective radio nets linking infantry, tanks and artillery would become standard practice. The No. 19 set was the tank crew's lifeline and had three functions: the A net, with the regiment; the B net, with the troop; and the IC channel, the internal communications within the tank. The commander would have to filter all three at once, dealing with the overall orders or instructions from the squadron, then what was happening within the troop and his crew. It was important to make sure the IC channel was clear while on the other two nets; internal tank-crew chatter could obscure what was on the troop net. A troop commander had a great deal to juggle communicating with the rest of his troop. Requests for artillery support would go back through the regimental net or be made by a forward observation officer in a spotter tank, which by the time of Normandy in 1944 tended to carry a false gun on its turret so as to accommodate the extra radio equipment. The No. 19 set was made by Pye, and then an improved model, the Mark III, came from Canada. The effectiveness of these radio comms changed the way tanks could be deployed, and once this kind of integration took hold, tanks swanning off on their own and getting picked off by the enemy weren't exactly a thing of the past but became less of a feature. Change became the constant: armoured warfare was changing even as the men were getting to grips with it.

Hobart became intimately involved with the efforts to get to grips with it. After a great deal of to-and-fro and negotiation, Hobart's grand scheme was parked. Alan Brooke deemed it too unwieldy a reform to push through while trying to prepare the army for a possible invasion, but it was clear that Hobart should to be involved in whatever was to come. Unfortunately, Hobart and Brooke had had a run-in in 1938, and Hobart was characteristically unable to compartmentalize professionally; he took disagreement, of whatever kind, personally. He was unable to cultivate Brooke's patronage and remained caught between Churchill and the army. The problem of tanks was still at the forefront of Churchill's enquiries and, in the summer of 1941, he ordered the meeting of what were called 'tank parliaments'. The tank parliaments met four times. At the meetings were the commanding officers of the five armoured divisions, including Hobart, as well as Lord Beaverbrook, Ministry of Supply ministers, the CIGS General John Dill, Brooke and Churchill's science advisor Frederick Lindemann, the soon-to-be Lord Cherwell, amongst others. The idea of these meetings was that the men using the tanks were able to get face to face with the people ordering them; there were arguments about how added armour required a more powerful engine, spare parts supply, air cooperation and so on. Needless to say, there was a great deal of scheming: General Martel, a sapper who had got the job Hobart had been angling for, would call the divisional commanders together and tell them what their talking points were. Hobart would refuse and this upset Martel. Churchill didn't care. He wanted diversity of opinion – and Hobart provided it.

Despite his reputation for being both difficult and a rotter, the army clearly valued Hobart, and in the midst of all this politicking he had been given a new division to raise, the 11th Armoured. He organized it into what became the template for British armoured divisions, with integrated artillery and infantry, and chose the division's logo, a black bull on a yellow field, from his family crest. Hobart quickly became known as a bully and it was said that the only way to deal with him was to stand up to him. He exercised the division ruthlessly, and for all the distaste there was for him and his style, he couldn't be faulted for his progress with the 11th Armoured. Large-scale exercises, made all the more difficult by the division's dispersal across the country, were what gave Hobart the chance to finally gain some influence and protection within the army, rather than riding on Churchill's coat-tails. His brother-in-law, the officer commanding the XII Corps, Lieutenant General Montgomery, whose star as a Brooke protégé was rising, was the umpire on these exercises and was suitably impressed. Brooke followed suit and came to protect Hobart, and this coincided with Brooke's growing authority with Churchill and the War Office as CIGS. When the time came for the 11th Armoured to be sent to North Africa, Hobart was informed he was too old for combat command and wouldn't be going; his value was as a trainer of men, not as a battlefield commander. As bitterly disappointing as this was for Hobart, it probably saved him another ignominious sacking. In October 1942, he was asked to raise a third division, the 79th Armoured Division. The following year, with the invasions of North Africa, Sicily and Italy under their belts, the Allies began planning for the invasion of north-west France. Hobart was asked by Brooke to develop a new, armoured assault force to breach the defences of the Atlantic Wall with 'steel not flesh'. As the last division constituted, the 79th Armoured had been for the chop, but by being given its new role it was saved, and it was to become Hobart's masterpiece. Crucially, Brooke promised him command of the division when it went overseas. With a knighthood, Hobart's rehabilitation was complete. He gave the division its badge, this time a bull's head, full of angry defiance. It doesn't look unlike Percy Hobart, but without the spectacles.

*

In his novel *Flame Thrower*, Andrew Wilson,* a Churchill Crocodile troop commander in 1944 and 1945, describes the Crocodile as a 'terror weapon'. Part of the 79th Armoured's inventory of invention, the Crocodile was mounted on the Churchill Mark VII, a vehicle that was a far cry from the early predecessors which had been rushed out in 1940. A programme of cooperation between Vauxhall and the Royal Armoured Corps had generated a close working relationship between crews and engineers, which had overcome maintenance issues and perfected the Churchill as an infantry tank: slow, reliable, capable of taking on any terrain that it might encounter, with thick armour and port and starboard escape hatches. The Crocodile was the result of a collaboration with the Petroleum Warfare Department. The flamethrowing mechanism as Wilson described it was

> mounted in the front of a Churchill [. . .] four hundred gallons of heavy, viscous flame fuel were carried in a seven-ton trailer connected to the tank by an armoured link connecting the fuel pipe. The liquid was projected from the nozzle of the gun under pressure of nitrogen at 350 lb per square inch. This had been reduced from

* Wilson chose to write about his experiences as fiction to create some distance. At Boulogne in September 1944, he walked through a minefield and returned with the German commander; later in the year he won a Military Cross in the fighting in Mechelen.

5,000 lb per square inch in the five long steel cylinders or 'bottles' in which the nitrogen was stored in the trailer. The rod of fuel was ignited by a jet of burning petrol that had passed over two electrodes. The gun had a range of about 90 yards and, if operated continuously, could flame for about two minutes.[2]

Its effects were appalling. Mythology has sprung up around the Crocodile, stories that crews were dragged from their tanks and killed, that Crocodiles would douse German positions with the fuel and wait for their surrender. It was a truly terrifying and effective weapon, the absolute sharp end of Hobart's spear. There was nothing 'Funny' about it. But what is notable about the Crocodile is that as part of Hobart's arsenal it illustrates two things: that Hobart's thinking about armoured warfare had progressed, and that the view of the 79th Armoured Division that prevails is upside down.

The Crocodile is an assault weapon – Wilson says it was 'intended to be used against German gun emplacements on the Normandy beaches. But after D-Day it became a battlefield terror weapon for use against enemy positions of all kinds.'[3] When Hobart was asked to develop the 79th Armoured Division as a specialized outfit, dedicated to the D-Day assault, breaching the Atlantic Wall, his thinking became truly radical and moved away from what had become the standard tank-thinker's pattern. Rather than concentrate on breakout and exploitation, self-contained tank formations swanning off into the enemy rear, Hobart and the 79th concentrated on something that was both new and true to the tank's original conception. Swanning – exploiting the breakthrough and breaking out – was the exception rather than the rule. There could be no breakout without breakthrough.

Hobart needed to create equipment and doctrine for it in his year long preparation for D-Day. Tank manufacturing, its limitations and priorities shaped his options – the 79th found itself favouring the British built Churchill. While a huge number of M4 Shermans were on order from the US, the British were doing what they could to convert Shermans into a 17-pounder gun platform to deal with the threat of German heavy armour. They had settled on what became known as the Firefly, an ingenious piece of adaptation that arrived in the nick of time for the invasion.* Debate in Montgomery's circles about which tank to use had been influenced by the arrival of the Sherman just in time for his victory at El Alamein; these machines had proved a match for the German Mark IVs – and more than anything else they were reliable. Montgomery wanted to use the Sherman as an all-round tank, rather than the delayed British-built Cromwell – and this freed up Churchill chassis for Hobart's engineers.

They came up with a staggering array of equipment, addressing the problems of how to breach the Atlantic Wall and, most crucially, how to provide support for the infantry from the minute they disembarked. The arsenal at Hobart's disposal, the array of specialized and modified

---

* Though arguably these Fireflies were *almost* surplus to requirements, as there were so few Tiger tanks in Normandy. Furthermore, the ranges at which tanks might encounter each other had reverted from desert distances of North Africa to French close country. And tanks didn't make the lion's share of tank kills anyway. This debate isn't usually found in footnotes!

kit, for this author takes the shine off the German reputation for armoured innovation. German tanks got bigger
and bigger, their weapons more and more powerful, driven
by Hitler's enthusiasm for military hardware and the con-
straints on German industry and its inability to achieve
true mass production of its heavier types. Using old types
and obsolescent chassis, Hobart's engineers became brilliant at coming up with new designs. Completely embracing
his new role with total single-mindedness, Hobart moved
away from cruiser tanks and back to what were essentially
infantry tanks – tanks carrying huge 'fascines', bundles of
logs to breach ditches, bridging tanks, mine-clearing tanks
with 'flails' and 'snakes', 'bobbins'* to lay a coir and scaf-
folding carpet surface onto soft patches of sand, as well as
armoured bulldozers, all of these vehicles were there to
make getting off the beach easier for an integrated infantry assault. Hobart had also moved away from conventional
armoured warfare and all the people he might butt heads
with, shielded by Brooke's patronage. He had taken tanks
back to their First World War siege-breaking role.

The Crocodile epitomized this – it was the Churchill
tank as infantry tank supreme. The AVRE (Armoured
Vehicle Royal Engineers) tanks, manned by sappers of
Hobart's old corps, firing their 'Flying Dustbins', huge spigot
mortar charges† designed to simply knock fortifications

---

* Bobbins were a last-minute addition, a response to a geology report that
suggested ancient blue clay lay under the surface of the Normandy beaches,
which would be too soft to carry traffic of any kind. A similar beach was
found in Norfolk and work went into developing the bobbin tank.
† A close relative of the man-portable Projector Infantry Anti-Tank, the
PIAT, the Flying Dustbin was a 290mm charge that contained 29 lb of
explosive – though with a short range, only 100 yards. The crewman

down, were the purest tank as support weapon system. Without the breakthrough. there could be no breakout, and these vehicles were designed to provide it. Much of Hobart's time was taken up with talking to the navy about how best to deploy his new weapons, as well as conferring with D-Day planners eager to find solutions to every potential problem.

Furthermore, rather than operating as a single self-contained division, the 79th Armoured was devolved, dispersed. This made running and training the division more of a task: Hobart had to travel up and down the country, with Duplex Drive 'DD' tank swimming trials in Scotland, Wales and eventually Gosport, and at the height of preparations he averaged 1,000 miles a week travelling from unit to unit. Hobart decided to turn the division into a think-tank, moving away from the inflexibility of the preceding period. His door was open to ideas, wherever they came from, a method *simpatico* to Churchill's own style:

> Confronting us is the problem of getting ashore on a defended coastline. The success of the operation depends on the element of surprise caused by new equipment. Suggestions from all ranks for improvements in equipment are to be encouraged. To assist secrecy it is preferable for all ranks to have direct access to their CO for putting forward their ideas.[4]

The DD tank was a case in point. Getting tanks to swim had been an avenue of experimentation since their invention in the First World War, but beyond snorkels and

---

would open the hatch below the launcher, attach the bomb, retire inside the tank, and the charge would be fired at its target.

waterproofing the results had been mixed. A Hungarian inventor, Nicholas Straussler, had his own eureka moment and applied Archimedes' principle to armoured fighting vehicles. If enough water could be displaced, then a tank could float: the physics was undeniable. Straussler had devised a canvas shroud on a frame that could be raised and lowered, displacing the water and floating the tank, as well as a gearing system that drove screws at the back of the tank – the Duplex Drive that DD stood for. The DD tank concept was tested thoroughly using obsolete vehicles: Valentines were kitted up with shrouds and propellers; the unofficial history of the division speaks of 30,000 launches 'under all conditions, with only one fatal casualty'.[5] While the tank was unable to fire when approaching the shore, and a rough sea or strong current might overwhelm the canvas or overpower the Duplex Drive, the DD was an astonishing innovation and, when deployed properly, delivered armour where it wasn't expected, fulfilling exactly the element of surprise Hobart had outlined. In preparing the DD tank, the 79th was operating as an experimental establishment; these Shermans were then issued to standard armoured units, the men trained in their use and deployed on D-Day. Three British regiments landed on D-Day with DD tanks, the 4th/7th Royal Dragoon Guards, 13th/18th Royal Hussars, the Sherwood Rangers aka the Nottinghamshire Yeomanry, as well as two Canadians units, the 6th (1 Hussars) and 10th (Fort Garry Horse) Armoured Regiments. Three American battalions, the 70th, 741st and 743rd Tank Battalions, also deployed DDs on D-Day (with notoriously mixed results).

A great deal of effort went into mine clearance, adapting the Sherman with a flail, the 'Crab'. A spinning drum with chains powered by the tank's engine, this would detonate mines, clearing a path. Not everyone rated the Crab – it kicked up a vast cloud of dust that alerted the enemy to its presence, and the chains didn't detonate everything they came into contact with. Hobart told the War Office he wanted the flail tank, and with the zeal of the fanatic said he didn't like the 'rather frigid attitude as regards mechanical matters'.[6] As well as Crabs, mine ploughs were developed, to clear mines by pushing them to one side, creating a clear groove, as well as heavy rollers, pushed by a Churchill, that would, like the flail, detonate the mines they came into contact with. These could only withstand so many hits before they became useless, so results were mixed. Another option for mine clearance was the 'Snake', a 20-foot-long steel pipe packed with explosive that was pushed through an obstacle by a tank and then exploded. The idea was this would detonate mines and cut barbed wire. Another version, which fired a similar explosive cable, the 'Conger', out into a minefield, was tested and deemed too dangerous to use.

Bright ideas were pursued, some of them literally. The Canal Defence Light (CDL) was a tank equipped with a 13 million-candlepower searchlight. This was an idea that had done the rounds, using Matilda II chassis, but by 1944 the CDL was fitted to the M3 Grant tank, where its 75mm gun had been. It was intended to blind defenders at night, but as its obscure name suggests, it was super-top secret, so secret that rumours began to grow up that it was a death-ray. More prosaically, the CDL might well have blinded the defenders it was pointed at, but it also served to light up the battlefield and silhouette advancing infantry. It remained part of the 79th Armoured's kit but a use for it wasn't found until the Rhine crossing in the spring of 1945. Gradually the kit was standardized, the obsolete and unreliable British chassis that had been used for testing prototypes and training were replaced with Shermans, which were in relative abundance, and Churchills, which as infantry tanks were perfectly suited to assault purposes.

These innovations were tried and tested in the face of considerable resistance and irritation in industry. Hobart's single-mindedness and abrasive manner worked its lack of charm on manufacturers, so he would resort to having his Royal Electrical and Mechanical Engineers workshops devise what he wanted, then pass it on to industry to make. Having his eyes down on the one task suited Hobart and his energetic focus.

> There was thus designed a series of techniques; and after the specialist training had been perfected, infantry and other arms of the assaulting divisions went through a number of rehearsals with the Assault Teams. Most of the answers to the assault problems were arrived at by the Trial and Error principle and were modified as new problems arose with fresh intelligence from the continent.[7]

The division was represented at all stages of army planning from January 1944, integrating and devolving itself into the plan, liaising closely with the staffs of corps and divisional headquarters. It was apart from and yet a part of the armoured establishment, and Hobart was getting to do what he'd always wanted: innovate with armour. Staging successful training exercises in January, March and April 1944, the division was confident enough in its progress to accept visitors, including Ike, the King and Churchill. Eisenhower recommended to Bradley that he make use of Hobart's new specialized equipment, by now nicknamed 'Funnies'. He was persuaded by DD tanks but passed on the rest: there were not enough Churchill chassis to deliver AVRE tanks to the Americans, and it was felt that the change in logistics to field different tanks was not, on balance, worth it. On the eve of battle, Hobart's brother-in-law expressed his approval. In his pre-invasion message of 26 May 1944, Montgomery said:

> I would like to say, at this moment of change of duties, how much we owe to you and your team for what you have done since 79th Armoured Division took the job on. The work has been dangerous, and complicated and a continuous struggle to overcome the time factor in production and experiment. Personally, I am more than grateful for the way in which you have carried out your dual responsibilities; I send my very best wishes for the success of your efforts. Good luck to your units: great responsibilities, inasmuch as they are the leaders in this assault, are thrust upon them and I am sure they will justify the skill and trouble you have spent on their training.[8]

As D-Day got closer and deployment in battle loomed, the only thing left for Percy Hobart to do was command. He warned his men of what was to come with a typically back-handed compliment:

> I have heard a lot about how you deal with the obstacles you expect, but what you must be ready for is to get through whatever you encounter. You may be landed anywhere because those in charge of landing craft are even more amateur sailors than you are amateur soldiers[9]

He was to be proved right.

*

On 6 June 1944, Hobart's men were the leaders in the assault. Every order of battle for British and Canadian landings on D-Day of OVERLORD details 'elements' of the 79th Armoured Division, each with their own set of duties and tasks, organized not in a top-down style but trained to get on with it. At Lion-sur-Mer on Sword Beach, the 79th Armoured Division sent an assault force ashore with the 3rd British Division, men from the 22 Dragoons, Westminster Dragoons and the 5 Assault regiment Royal Engineers. A combination of Crabs and Ploughs went in to clear obstacles and mines. These men's exploits are representative of the chaos on the beach and the action that followed. An AVRE went ahead:

> The first *AVRE* was hit repeatedly and drowned. The crew dismounted and made their way into Hermanville on foot, led by the crew commander (Serjeant Kilvert). Reaching a high farm wall they were checked by heavy small arms fire which they answered with Brens; then Serjeant Kilvert burst open the garden door and, covered by his crew, raked the farmhouse with fire, killing 11 Germans. They later routed an enemy patrol on the same road and then handed over to the infantry.[10]

Two more examples tell of the 79th's first day ashore. At Bernières, the AVREs and Crabs gave the infantry the support and firepower they needed before the DD tanks arrived, delayed by the friction of time, tide and enemy action. At Le Hamel, AVREs were decisive in destroying the sanatorium, a large building that overlooked the western end of Gold Beach, the town having held out until the afternoon. Using his Flying Dustbins, Sergeant Scaife RE (Royal Engineers) basically knocked the building down and unlocked the village. Once the main body had gone through, the AVREs got on with filling road craters and tidying up the landing area and, crucially, going forward 'as normal infantry tanks in the attacks on Bayeux and Asnelles'.[11] The men under Hobart's command were adapting to constantly changing circumstances and not letting the chaos get the better of them; his expertise in training had delivered for his men.

Hobart was attached to Montgomery's headquarters as Special Armoured Advisor, but the way the 79th Armoured Division deployed was decentralized; he provided liaison officers to the corps and divisions that might need his assistance, his tanks and equipment were attached as support as and when they were needed, demanding from his crews and command structures greater flexibility than from the dedicated armoured formations. These officers ensured that Hobart knew how his men were faring under the command of other headquarters, allowing him to keep abreast of how things were going, and to ensure that the headquarters asking for help knew what the Funnies were capable of. How distant the 79th Armoured had become from Hobart's conception even only four years earlier, of a gigantic armoured army, is striking: specialization, integration and support for infantry assault, devolved and epitomizing the British technological approach of using 'steel not flesh', deploying technical know-how in battle. It was a far cry from Hobart's Blitzkrieg-inspired notions of not worrying about losses and tanks pushing on regardless.

He had shown great intellectual flexibility in his pursuit of the perfection of this new division, and while his forthright style hadn't diminished, his reputation had been saved. Mutterings about his marriage could no longer derail Hobart's love affair with armour.

After D-Day, the division adapted further. As the bridgehead expanded, and the meat-grinder phase of the Normandy battle evolved, the 79th Armoured continued to be in the thick of things. The more static battle required assault specialists. As the fighting in the high, thick hedge-rows and ultra-close country of the notorious Normandy bocage raged, AVRE tanks were in particular demand.

> *AVRE*s too were fairly prominent in these actions. The 'Bocage' country gave them a new role, that of breach-ing the high 'Bocage' banks. An orthodox action was carried out by 81 Assault Squadron *RE*. on the 1st of August, which consisted of petarding defended houses at Lictot.[12]

These AVRE tanks were the perfected support weapon, though like any tank they needed good cooper-ation with and protection from infantry. Hobart's new methods and focus on assault underlined the importance of the role of the tank as an integrated infantry support and all-arms weapon, in a way that delivered proof of con-cept of the infantry tank. While the Funnies were lacking in the kind of anti-tank punch that is so often the focus of post-war tank-versus-tank comparisons, they were entirely suited to the Normandy battlefield that, it is often argued, the British, Canadians and Americans had simply not pre-pared themselves for. Though the 79th Armoured had been created for the assault on the Normandy beaches, the need for assault went on. Crocodiles were especially well adapted to the new battle.

> One further Crocodile action deserves mention. On the 30th of July 'C' Squadron, 141 *RAC*, routed with flame a machine gun position at Sant-Germain-d'Ectot which had held up three battalion attacks. The Crocodile troop commander dismounted and personally led the infantry, who lacked experience with flame. On the next day, an *AVRE*-cum-Crocodile assault force helped infantry to take a house and orchard in the same area.[13]

The Crocodile was suited to Normandy in deadly style. Those not fighting were directed to the division's training wing to prepare it for whatever fighting in North-West Europe might bring and to keep the division relevant to Allied strategy. To only assess the 79th Armoured as part of D-Day, and note the success of the Funnies as a curio of British strategy, is to misunderstand the division and its role, the same mistake as seeing the D-Day assault in peculiar isolation, disconnected from the titanic battle in Normandy: the months that followed were one long struggle of assault after assault. The Germans had chosen to fight a static defence: to offer line after line for the Allies to break.

*

With the collapse of the German Army at the Falaise Gap from 12 to 21 August and the near-encirclement of the *Heer* in the west, the period of relentless assault finally paid off, the huge struggle ended and the breakout began. The 'Great Swan' followed. Tanks broke out and hared to the

Belgian border, covering greater distances faster than the Panzers that had so shocked the world four summers before. The German defeat in the west was a triumph of Allied industry, technology and firepower, but, more importantly, of how they were applied. Hobart had looked beyond the apparent lessons of the German triumph of 1940, moved his thinking on beyond the vindication that Blitzkrieg offered, and had delivered an essential part of the Allied war-winning infrastructure. Once the Allied lines solidified again, with stiffening German resistance, the failure of MARKET GARDEN and the onset of winter, the 21st Army Group's war reverted to its pattern of assault and gradual exploitation. Hobart's 79th Armoured was integral to this process, with its units again decentralized and distributed to where they were needed.

The division continued to grow and expand its role. Added to Hobart's arsenal were Buffaloes, tracked personnel carriers with scoops on their tracks that could cross water barriers, swim in from the sea, across canals and rivers – another crucial piece of infantry delivery, augmenting the Kangaroos (adapted Priest self-propelled guns, with their guns removed) that had been used as armoured personnel carriers since July. APCs had been part of Plan 1919 had the First World War continued; now, come full circle, the latest tracked technology was being used to solve the same problems of terrain and infantry delivery. Kangaroos featured in the epic winter assaults of Operations VERITABLE and BLACKCOCK, bringing men through the mud and ice up to their start lines, keeping pace with the armour that they there were to fight alongside. As the Germans fell back to the Siegfried Line, with its interlocking defensive sectors, a gruelling process of fighting in atrocious weather began against a still well-motivated enemy. Crocodiles and AVREs were sent to hotspots, as well as bridging tanks and flails, which became ubiquitous. By the time of VERITABLE in February 1945, the 79th Armoured Division's tracked vehicle strength stood at 'over 1,050, about three times the number in a normal armoured division'.[14]

The Americans had come to covet the Crocodile; an order they had made in February 1944 had not been met because production was behind, and their experience in the Pacific told them that flamethrowing armour was well-suited to urban fighting. Come the autumn of 1944, the US 12th Army Group still hadn't been sent their Crocodiles. Montgomery granted a request for B Squadron 141 RAC's Crocodiles to join the US VIII Corps, whose engineers embraced the potential of the flamethrowers at Brest. Hobart's men were able to fit in with the Americans and the assault was a success. Integration of armour, engineers, infantry and artillery, with Crocodiles at the centre, was an irresistible method; Hobart's equipment and training were proving endlessly flexible, as even the ever-opinionated Basil Liddell Hart had to admit, despite his disapproval of British armoured performance throughout the war. He commented: 'Our Army, unfortunately, did not lead the way in armoured warfare during World War II – except at a late stage, and then mainly in the sphere of the 79th Armoured Division.'[15] What Liddell Hart had overlooked was that the methods that had worked so well for the Germans in 1940 were, like the tanks that had executed them, obsolete. Things had moved on, and Percy Hobart was one of the prime movers. He had raised three of Britain's armoured divisions, one of them the famous Desert Rats, the other two wore the bull, his symbol, and one of them reflected his pioneering genius and mastery of armour as a weapon.

The Rhine Crossing, Operation PLUNDER, was the 79th Armoured's last great effort. With Buffaloes crossing the Rhine and DD tanks, as well as AVRE and other assault resources, coming to the fight, the 21st Army Group crossed the last physical frontier into Germany. Like trains that run on time, the contribution of this, the largest armoured formation of the war, has become unremarked, unextraordinary. 'Hobo' ferried the Prime Minister, and his patrons Brooke and Montgomery, across the Rhine in one of his Buffaloes, proof of concept, his tactical mastery having supreme strategic effect – he could perhaps be forgiven for showing off a little. The army that had missed the boat with tanks at the start of the war had turned them into boats – and sailed them across the Rhine. But what was that like for the men on foot, the Poor Bloody Infantry, the men all these tanks had been devised to support, who would have to fight it out to the bitter end?

10

Peter White

To the very end

Landing on Walcheren Island in the autumn of 1944, the bitter joke was that the 52nd Lowland Division, which had trained for mountain warfare, had finally joined the campaign for the liberation of Europe at below sea level. The dazzling successes of the summer were past, the shattering battles in Normandy, the stunning climax at the Falaise Gap, the breakout and the Great Swan to Belgium that followed, the gambles of MARKET GARDEN – the war now entered a phase of grind, of territorial tidying-up in the wake of the summer's victories before the final assault on the Rhine and Germany itself. Walcheren, which dominated the Scheldt estuary and therefore restricted Allied shipping and supply lines – which still stretched back to the Normandy beaches – had to be taken. It was, like so many of the battles in the last few months of the Second World War in Europe, one that had to be won: failure – to embrace the cliché – was not an option.

Second Lieutenant Peter White, of the 4th Battalion The King's Own Scottish Borderers, who had an artist's talent for observation, had not missed the irony of his low-level entry into the war. After years of waiting and training and chop and change, the 52nd Lowland were finally going into action, one of the last British divisions deployed, held back in reserve until the last minute. As the war took White through the Netherlands and into Germany, he keenly noted the changes he and his men underwent as the burden of combat waxed and waned, from the frantic, bleak winter fighting to the spring of tantalizing combat when victory always felt ever so slightly out of reach, and the risks stranger and more tragic, fighting in the puzzle of a country that had been defeated but wouldn't give up. White's account *With the Jocks*, based on the diaries he made at the time, a compulsion he had been ordered to resist, throws light on the fascinating questions of command and responsibility at his level and it is with his experience of commanding his men in the last months of the war, his impressions of what being a soldier and leader was, that we will end this book. He kept the diary up to date and sketched what he saw when he had time – and he had plenty of time: White and his men spent a great deal of time hurrying up and waiting, though never knowing when any pause would suddenly break, and that time afforded him the chance to deliver a memoir that takes the reader to the heart of command.

White may not have been making the big decisions – occasionally, because of casualties among his fellow officers, he would command his company rather than his platoon, but that was as far up the tree as he got – and was divorced from all strategic thinking and considerations, unlike most of the protagonists in this volume. Indeed, he would often admit he had no idea what was going on around him, who was on which flank, even where he was, yet for an infantry platoon commander that was plenty enough to be getting on with. The immediacy of infantry command is where this history of the war ends, a world of patrolling day and night, of stand-tos and stags, of looking for boobytraps in every house they entered, of slugging it out in up-close combat, the sheer randomness of who held on to life and whom death took, of stolen sleep and purloined chickens, haughty captives, sullen civilians, men sticking together in a world with a permanently uncertain future. An unremittingly hard life devoid of comfort, yet, for a subaltern, overlaid with unending personal responsibility. It was men like White who would have to command to the bitter end, on the front line, and whose lives were in daily mortal peril.

With its garrison in Berwick-upon-Tweed, the King's Own Scottish Borderers (KOSB), like so many of the infantry regiments in the British Army, had battalions deployed in every theatre, from France to Burma. In 1940, men from the KOSB had fought in both BEFs: the 1st battalion was evacuated at Dunkirk with the original BEF, while the 4th and 5th Battalions* as part of 52nd Lowland Division landed at Saint-Malo in the stillborn attempt by the second BEF to disrupt the German victory in France – that wild goose chase ending swiftly in retreat via Cherbourg as part of Operation AERIAL. After the fall of France, the 52nd Lowland Division, like all of the formations that remained in the UK, trained in preparation to defend against a German invasion. By 1942, the 52nd had been repurposed as a mountain division, with an invasion of Norway in mind. Keeping the Germans fixated upon the idea that the Allies might invade Norway – as improbable as it might seem – was a central plank of pre-D-Day strategy, and it was very successful and effective: believing this deception, the

---

* These were the KOSB's Territorial battalions; the 4th was drawn from the Borders and east, the 5th from the west of the region.

Germans kept 300,000 men waiting in Norway for nothing to happen who could have been deployed elsewhere.

Of course, this invasion-that-never-was-to-be didn't happen, so after D-Day the division was released from its role as a non-invasion invasion force and retrained – at least to the extent of learning how to get in and out of aircraft – as an air-portable unit. Leaving their mountain training aside, the 52nd Lowland, under Major General Hakewill Smith, worked on becoming a self-contained unit in the airborne mould, and the officers got to grips with how to load their men into aircraft in precisely weighed amounts for air portability. But essentially the change meant they went into the Supreme Headquarters Allied Expeditionary Force (SHAEF) strategic reserve – a spare division standing by, waiting for something to do, as part of the First Allied Airborne Army, said to be burning a hole in SHAEF's pocket. Several operations that weren't to be came and went. and then for the airborne operation that did happen, MARKET GARDEN, the 52nd Lowland were earmarked to be landed by transport plane at Deelen airfield once the Arnhem area had been captured and cleared. Hakewill Smith had offered his men as glider-borne reinforcements for Arnhem – perhaps fortunately for them it came to nothing. The 4th KOSB war diary tells of two and a quarter hours on 22 September 1944 when it looked like they might be going to the Netherlands:

1400: *CO* held further briefing Conf for Coy Cmd and equivalents: op to be known in Bn as *YANK*. Outline plan: 4 *KOSB* with similar force from 5 *KOSB* and skeleton Bde *HQ*, sp by modified Bty, Fd Arty, to land in gliders West of main *NIJMEGEN–ARNHEM* axis, and move up to southern bank of river near Arnhem to protect rear of 1st Airborne Div posns.

1615: Op cancelled.[1]

Sister battalion the 5th's diary is even more laconic: 'op planned, op cancelled'.[2] Another addition to the Arnhem 'what if?' pile.

With the failure of MARKET GARDEN, the 52nd Lowland were released from First Allied Airborne Army and sent into the line. The British and Canadian armies were both feeling the pinch in terms of manpower as the year drew to a close, particularly with infantry. Well-trained infantry would be needed as the autumn turned to winter, to plug the gaps in the Allied armies. The DUKE effort was beginning to reach the buffers, and had fallen behind the number of Americans in the theatre in August. Manpower was running low to the point where the Canadian government was trying to send conscripts overseas – breaking its promise not to and prompting a mutiny. It was the fate of the 52nd Lowland to enter the battle as the days got shorter and the weather far, far worse, at a time of year when the armies of the past had done what they could to avoid campaigning. Campaigning season was over, but modern warfare was no respecter of tradition. It was the Poor Bloody Infantry who would have to deal with the squalor of a winter campaign, in a winter that was typically bitter for the 1940s.*

*

* James Holland, ad nauseam.

Peter White, born in South Africa but transposed to Surrey when his parents wanted to make sure their sons had a British education, religious to the point of pacifism and arty too, might seem an unlikely officer for a regiment that despite its border title nevertheless recruited men from all over Scotland. White had joined the Royal Artillery, but then, as the army began to anticipate shortages in infantry, he was reassigned, choosing the Kings Own Scottish Borderers because his father had grown up in the Borders. By 1944, the army had long lost touch with the localities of regiments, and men were sent where they were needed; among the men White commanded there were English and, inevitably, Irish soldiers, too. Training together helped the men fit together – White's ear became attuned to the accents he had grown up ignorant of, and his men – and fellow officers, who at first had thought him too reserved to lead – got used to him in return. As White's brigade, 155 Brigade – seconded to the Canadians for Operation INFATUATE, the invasion of Walcheren Island to secure the Schedlt and approaches to Antwerp – were assembled in preparation for going forward, White pondered on what was to come. His training had been excellent, he thought; battle school had done what it could to get him used to the idea of combat, and he had been subjected to exhaustion beyond all of his previous experience, but in the end he didn't know if he was ready.

> The biggest unknown factor was the mental reaction of the individual, especially of those in responsibility. What part would fear play? How well could it be overcome, or hidden? The tense realization dawned ever larger that the lives of one's friends and one's own life

would depend on split-second decisions in an unknown world of utter chaos.[3]

This is a long way from Montgomery dealing with stuff about VD coming across his desk, from Tuker organizing his division in his style, from Patton or Bradley navigating the US Army and the press – it could hardly be further away. It is closer to Alastair Pearson's war, though unencumbered by brigade-level Orders (O) Group and the bigger picture a lieutenant colonel would have to contend with. And yet, all of White's superiors had, to varying degrees, experienced his level of command, split-second decisions that meant the difference between life and death. The future was now immediately unknowable:

I glanced round at all the rugged friendly faces and felt reassured. We were all in the same boat, but it was difficult not to wonder a bit, to think of the families of each at home. Where would each be in a couple of days, a week hence?[4]

The 4th KOSB were to land on Walcheren Island, on Uncle Beach. White at the time was with the carrier platoon; its duties included towing anti-tank guns, bringing up supplies and evacuating casualties, but because the beach was only 85 yards wide, the guns and universal carriers would be held back for the time being. The beach being so narrow, the worry was that any decent German gunnery would make landing extremely difficult. White was detailed with ensuring that the supplies that came ashore for the battalion were adequately managed, with ammunition prioritized. Once the beach had been seized, the worry was that British artillery might fall short and hit the gigantic ammunition dump White and his men had been building. Tons of ammunition at risk, shells ripping down through the air onto German positions, German rifle fire from houses that No. 4 Commando, who had gone in first, had not yet been able to clear . . . as a baptism in battle, a first day on the job, there was plenty to make White anxious. As the morning came, stalking snipers supplanted loading ammunition. This first action, using the 52nd Lowland as shock troops to crack open the German defences at Walcheren, was the last whiff of special-forces-style operations the division would get – then they went into the line and the grind began.

Peter White's war was characterized by the cold and the wet of winter and the dreaded words 'prepare to move'. Whatever White and his men were doing would have to be abandoned, tea thrown away, meals scoffed or ditched, freshly dug positions forgotten, either to embus in trucks or Kangaroos if they were lucky or to march forward to the site of new positions and to start digging all over again. Tiredness dominated everything, especially the business of steeling yourself for going forward to a start line: 'It required a major mental adjustment and a complete overhaul of values to feel in any way used to them. I found a similar process of thought necessary later each time we went into action, one which came no more easily through repetition, perhaps largely because of constant lack of sleep.' White also understood clearly how, in the end, despite all the equipment and materiel that might be brought to bear on a battlefield, 'the farther one got towards the enemy, the thinner the evidence of accompaniment might become until finally in sight of the enemy there one was – rifle in hand, the enemy ahead, perhaps ten or less Jocks actually in sight at any one time, and almost as often as not one was the recipient of the artillery fire of both sides'.[5] The entire Allied war machine might be behind you, but in the end, in the infantry, it was just you and the men around you, if you could see them.

Even when doing nothing more than holding the line, rather than engaging in offensive operations, life was extremely dangerous. Snipers, or at least Germans taking pot shots with rifles, were a daily nuisance. There was a steady attrition of men that made, for the individual, the idea of overwhelming Allied might pretty irrelevant. And warfare involves plenty of friction in the day-to-day, beyond encounters with the enemy. The front line carried on chewing men up. Almost insatiably. While holding the Tripsrath Woods, the battalion suffered a shocking accident. At ten to four on 7 January 1945, a gigantic explosion rang out, disturbing everyone on the line: 'No gun or shell we had yet heard had made a fraction of such an explosion and we fervently hoped Jerry had not brought up some new weapon. The colossal blast must have shaken him even as much as it did us.'[6] Thirty-two sappers were killed, along with seventeen KOSBs (of whom only fourteen could be identified) when 2,400 anti-tank grenades blew up. The men were carrying a sack of anti-tank mines each, and the man at the front of the line's grenades went up – cause unknown. 'Sympathetic' explosions rippled all the way down the line and back to the dump, which detonated last. Rumour had it one man in the line had survived. The 4th KOSB's CO, Lieutenant Colonel Chris Melville, escaped unhurt, but five HQ batmen were killed – the explosion had been only a hundred yards from the battalion HQ. Melville's first thought was to call for stretcher-bearers. But there was no one left alive. The only thing to do, he reasoned, was to order up more grenades from the rear and carry on as if it hadn't happened, so some of White's platoon was volunteered for this uneasy task. The day returned to sniping and the occasional mortar landing on the lines, and three days later the battalion held a memorial service for the men killed in the accident.

A couple of weeks later, at Klosterhof Farm on the north-west outskirts of Heinsberg during Operation BLACKCOCK, cut off on a hillside in full view of German troops holding a farmhouse, White and his platoon had to make the best use of the exposed ground around them to protect themselves from machine-gun fire – always described as 'Spandaus', MG 42s. They were ground down by well-organized mortar fire, as well as the occasional 'stonk' from British 25-pounders firing short – White and his men had quickly acquired the ability to distinguish different artillery by its signature sound. Despite the colossal Allied preponderance of ordnance and equipment, German artillery, even at its most threadbare, was entirely deadly, and mortar fire was particularly hard to hide from when the ground was frozen hard and difficult to dig into properly.

A call went up for White to go back to the company HQ. As bullets zipped around him from well-concealed German positions, he prepared to leave – exchanging looks with Sergeant Dickinson: they both knew that White might be killed any second – and then, his heavier equipment removed, ran hell for leather. He tumbled to the ground in an icy rut, shots pinging around him, and realized his small pack must be showing above ground level. As White 'played possum', Dickinson thought he was dead: 'The whole business had an odd quality of almost farcical unreality despite its grimness,' he noted.[7] Summoning his courage and his strength, and uttering a prayer, White dashed on to Company HQ to find that mortars had been exploding in the trees above the HQ position, with deadly effect. White realized that lying in the open hadn't been as short a straw as he had thought it to be. The company commander was badly injured, the company sergeant major and the company HQ signaller, too, the 2i/c, Captain John Elliott, had been killed. The signaller was calling for smoke from the artillery, though it was clear the company knew it had not been prioritized for artillery support. Their precarious position, in the grand scheme of things, was not so important. Major Colin Hogg, the company commander, had been hit in the chest and lungs:

> Very faintly Colin croaked with agony: '. . . John . . . dead . . . poor . . .' but he could not manage any more and choked, coughing weakly as his voice tailed off. 'Pete . . . y'll . . . have . . . take over . . .' Colin managed to gasp and then crumpled up again after the effort 'Sorry . . . leave . . . you . . .', he croaked in a whisper I would have missed if our heads had not been so close as we lay side by side.[8]

The 4th KOSB battalion war diary put it like this:

Coy, W of orchards 847751, caught in shallow trenches by observed shell & mor fire – enemy located *KLOS-TERHOF* 844749. Maj *HOGG* C.F. wounded, *CSM* wounded and Capt J. *ELLIOTT* Killed. L/Cpl *LEITCH*, Coy signaller, severely wounded in leg and buttocks, remained at Coy *HQ* and directed Arty smoke shoot to cover withdrawal of Coy to houses.[9]

White was now in command of the company, such as there was one, spread across a hillside, cut off: he took stock as he waited for the artillery to deliver the smoke shells that the signaller Leitch had requested. He didn't dare broadcast on the air in the open to battalion how bad things were, nor did he want to send a runner, who would surely be killed. Probably the only benefit of fighting in the winter then came into play: the short day. Knowing it wouldn't be long until it got dark again, White was able to regroup the men, evacuate casualties and shore up his positions: other attacks by the Royal Scots, who were at a different angle to the German lines, and by the battalion's carrier platoon helped relieve the strain on the company position. White felt as night fell that he had done everything he could, and set about organizing his men, checking on the wounded and putting the dead to one side. One of his men, Middleton, had been lying at the bottom of a wet crater for nine hours with a back wound and needed to be rescued. White made sure that he was recovered and sent on to the regimental aid post. It's worth noting here that White only appears once in the battalion diary: in March 1944, when he is posted to the KOSB from the Royal Artillery. Despite his daily deadly exertions and tribulations, he doesn't get a look in.

*

By 1945, the British Army, decentralized at best, globally overcommitted at worst, had essentially gone through three iterations – the army it had been at the start of the war, which suffered its calamitous debut as the BEF, the one it raised as soon as the war began in earnest and then the army that came together in anticipation of its return to France. The last of those armies was recruited and trained during the period when the army as a whole was experiencing its worst reverses, which created challenges for the men being recruited and for the institution into which they were being initiated. As the war progressed, the armies that were raised cross-fertilized, sharing techniques – and the men at the top who were no good were weeded out. Territorial or non-career war-only civilian soldiers were ingested and exploited, though never quite allowed to reach giddy heights – one exemplary exception being Bill Williams, Montgomery's intelligence officer, an Oxford don of brilliant mind yet no experience, whom Monty regarded as an essential sounding board, one that the army simply couldn't provide (and someone in Monty's debt). Though he too made his fair share of howlers. But at the other end, the business end, officer recruitment had to change, to update in much the same way it had been forced to in the previous war. In a society so bound by class, and in an army strapped for cash, pre-war recruitment had devolved to the officer classes, plans for Sandhurst to become more university-like, in the mould of West Point, abandoned. The army had tried to quietly drop some of the radical officer selection methods it had adopted during the Great War, and although it paid lip service to leaving officer recruitment more socially open, it reverted to the norm. Inevitably, public schools dominated officer recruitment.

Once the war began, the army faced several problems with recruiting and training officers. In terms of general recruitment, before conscription, the army was at the back of the queue, behind the Royal Navy and the Royal Air Force. The navy had its reputation as the Senior Service to coax the ambitious in its direction, while the RAF was the modern, high-tech, cutting-edge branch of the services. The army offered none of this glamour. And the army had fresh public memories of the Great War to contend with, the squalor and slaughter of the trenches. Patterns of volunteering meant the army had to make do with whoever was left. Once the war got going – and panned out unexpectedly – the army had to address a shortage of officer manpower that was pressurized by both huge expansion and the dull inevitable fact of the rates of attrition for junior officers. Even this pressure didn't stop the army from selecting from the usual suspects for the first few years of the war. If you had been in a public-school Officer Training Corps (OTC) and joined up, you would be barracked together and treated with the expectation that you'd serve as an officer. Similarly, university OTC time put you at the front of the queue for immediate commission. This is perhaps why it is a trope in a great deal of Second World War literature to find the posh chap in the ranks, who didn't want to serve as his peers might, because it was such a striking decision to make. Class dominated. You had to have gone to the right school, or at least give the appearance of having done, to get into and then through the Officer Cadet Training Unit (OCTU). For example:

> Leslie Philips sailed through his pre-*OCTU* interview, even though he was a Tottenham factory worker's son, because stage school elocution lessons had equipped him with a pitch-perfect simulacrum of a patrician

accent. 'Nobody would have guessed that I had never been at Radley, Harrow, or Wellington.'[10]

Ding-dong.

In 1942, Adjutant General Ronald Adam, who was 100 per cent a product of the public-school old guard, made two radical changes that shook up officer recruitment, creating the General Service Corps (GSC) and the War Office Selection Board (WOSB). The shift was dramatic. The GSC's role was to process new soldiers and assess everyone who came into the army, judging which roles they might be best suited to as well as passing on people it regarded as having leadership potential to the WOSB. The WOSB then did what it could to weed out the duds, with tests and psychological evaluations, and it would pick out those it thought suitable and send them on to the OCTU – and it became clear quickly that plenty of men who had not been to public school were suited to officer roles. This democratized the officer classes, at least where it was most dangerous, broadening the opportunities for people from all classes to be killed leading from the front.

By the time Peter White had joined up Adam's reforms had gone through, and despite some resistance from established officers – Adam understood well that citizen soldiers weren't much interested in the peacetime army activities characterized as 'bullshit' – other external forces were at work that drove the army into more democratized practices. The Beveridge Report (1942) had defined the country's post-war challenge: 'The five giants on the road to reconstruction were Want, Disease, Ignorance, Squalor and Idleness', and had electrified the debate about what men were fighting for – particularly in

Europe. The army that had been saying it was fighting for democracy now had to face the social contract its men thought they were subject to being publicly stated. There was a marked contrast between the Beveridge Report, the way it looked at society and the state's obligations to its citizens, and a good portion of the army brass's opinions of its citizen soldiers: there was a widespread belief within the army that the generation of recruits it was having to rely on were soft compared with their fathers' generation. Some of these fell into the basic broad and old-as-time 'kids these days don't know they're born' genre: they had been spoon-fed entertainment, baled out by the dole. This is perhaps an unusual conclusion to have drawn given the privations of the Great Depression, but institutionalized officer classes have rarely had the best grip on what is going on in the society they seek to serve. Such reactionary views had to go, even though they ran to the very top – grumblings about manliness and 'pansydom' went as high up as the secretary of state for war, a British echo of Patton's hard-blowing about manhood. Churchill, too, couldn't understand why the modern soldier didn't hang on in the same way he felt they had in the First World War, even as he did what he could to wriggle out of domestic commitments for post-war reconstruction. Beveridge had changed that: what men were fighting for had become clearer, and who would lead the people doing the fighting was refined alongside it.

*

The intimacy of command and White's responsibilities, the agony of making decisions that could get men killed, hung over every moment. Outside Bremen, near Groß

Eilstorf, White's platoon was asked to patrol through the woods outside the village and clear them of the enemy. Although the weather was beginning to improve, the nights were bitterly cold, and White felt that no fire could warm him through. His orders were plain, making it clear that the platoon would have to manage by itself:

'You take your Platoon ahead, Peter, spread out to provide a screen. Pip, your Platoon on the right to the rear. Sgt Cowie on the left rear. Company HQ, centre. We'll work right through this block of wood first, swinging up to cover the hill on the right before swinging over to this part of the wood on the left. Fix bayonets, check all magazines are loaded, put one up the spout, safety catches off. Keep well spread out, and see your chaps keep in line. Any questions?'

'Any supporting arms, sir?'

'No. Tanks would be no use in the wood. Artillery can't be used. We don't know just where the enemy are and there are some of our own chaps to the right. Watch your flanks, the light'll not last long. Right?'[11]

This was an infantry encounter, the enemy were fighting on their own territory, knew the ground – and seeing clearly through the dense woods and what might be hidden in the trees would strain all of his men's nerves. Since they had entered Germany itself, the 4th KOSB had cleared plenty of woods, but usually with armoured support, the tanks slithering up the causeways through the mud or rolling along the edge of the wood on the flank, ready to deliver supporting fire on any opposition. They were dangerous to any infantry around them, attracting fire and hard to communicate with, but they offered reassurance at least. But

tanks weren't on offer: these Germans needed to be win-
kled out by infantrymen.

When would the enemy open fire and from where? As
the men spread out across the woods, White hoped they
would hold their fire and when – not if: some German
civilians, from their woodland cottages, had watched the
KOSBs go on into the trees – they were ambushed things
wouldn't descend into complete chaos. As they edged forward, White reminded himself of what a pleasant walk it
would have been under any other circumstances – it
reminded him of a wood he sued to walk through in Surrey. It was dark under the pines, darker than he had
thought it would be. The section commanders' voices
clipped out across the woods, telling their men to keep up
and not bunch together. The platoon was below strength.
White wondered if his men had realized that they wouldn't
know where the Germans were until they were fired on at
point-blank range. He found the weight of his rifle in his
hand to be a comfort: to be without a weapon would be
like 'walking naked through a blizzard'.[12] He also thanked
himself for having chosen to carry a rifle and not a Sten
gun – the ordinary rifleman's weapon made him less likely
a target. He wished a passing squirrel would tell him where
the enemy was.

The ground rose and fell, and finally as twilight came
the platoon had to crest a small ridge, something you
wouldn't think twice about in peacetime. 'Cresting' meant
breaking the skyline, being totally exposed as they moved
forward, in silhouette. It was the most likely place for them
to be ambushed, terrain he would have used himself to his
own advantage – White knew precisely what the danger
was. As White and four others crested the ridge, Corporal

Parry was shot through the head; tall, bespectacled Corporal Parry, nervy, gangly, killed instantly. Time slowed down. Private Byles was shot in the stomach and fell down the crest, towards the invisible enemy. Another volley followed – a third man was hit and fell, writhing in the dirt, his fellows angrily hushing him as he moaned in pain, as astonished as anyone else that he was still alive. White – in the splits of the second that followed – knew he didn't know where the enemy were, but he had enough of an idea where they must be, and he needed them to get their heads down. Quickly, he ordered a couple of mortar bombs to be lobbed into the other side of what appeared be a quarry, where the enemy must be, only 25 yards away. White thought of Corporal Parry's family in Glasgow. Parry had shown White photos of them: 'only a child himself' – he regretted that the last encounter he had had with Parry was putting him on a charge; Parry, he felt, was reaching the end of his tether with the war. Byles was wounded, that much White knew, but he knew he couldn't look over the skyline and check on him without being shot. The Germans knew where they were, and at that range they couldn't miss. Byles's shovel, sticking up, didn't seem to be moving, so White couldn't tell if he was still breathing. The light was failing, and with another mile of woods to go, moving forward was no longer an option. White would have to leave Byles. The third man was helped away by a stretcher-bearer, being told to shut up all the way back. And at the same time White worried that the enemy might have infiltrated around behind his platoon, ready to ambush his men again as they withdrew.

And so it was in the gloom of evening that Peter White wrestled with his appalling responsibility. He knew that

Parry was dead; even so, he didn't want to leave Parry's body where he had fallen. He didn't know if Byles could be saved, whether stretcher-bearers would be able to get him back to the regimental aid post and safely home. Byles hadn't been the same since one of his friends, Jones, a larger-than-life figure in the platoon, had been killed. To go back for these men, one alive, one dead, would be certain death – shot at a range where the bullets' crack of being fired and thump of striking their targets was one sound. Having pulled back, he conferred with the other platoon commanders.

> As our eyes met, there each of us read what was in our hearts: a dilemma which was one of the most awful moments of my life. The consciousness of what might have hung on it still haunts me. Each of us felt impelled to reach the body to be sure, yet we each as certainly knew that to attempt it would be fatal. In that moment of silence together we each must have realized that none of us could muster the madness or courage, whichever it should be called, to make this fatal gesture in cold blood and from a standing start. Smyg's voice in sudden decision cut the awful silence. 'Pull back. We'll have to put in a proper attack to clean Jerry out when we can see what we are doing in the morning.'[13]

This was to be perhaps White's lowest moment. He had done everything he could to make sure his men weren't exposed to danger, and yet here he was having to abandon his wounded to their fate, to the possibility they would bleed out or freeze to death in the icy night.

The next morning, tanks and artillery were available.

The wood wasn't worth any more infantrymen. White's platoon was to go first as it knew the ground. The company commander held an Orders (O) Group. An O Group would take on the form available to it, the officers might sit around a map, crouched in a hollow or a slit trench, lying down in the dirt or mud, in a tent or in a house around a candle on a table, and trade map references, take in any intelligence they knew they had or had been granted, and orders would be issued, passed down from the battalion and delivered to the platoons. Often, the presence of a radio aerial – the Type 38 Wireless Set was 12 feet in height for its full-range configuration or 4 feet in its 'battle' mode – could draw the attention of enemy spotters. Sniping or mortar fire would be drawn to the aerial, adding to the probability of officers being killed or injured. Orders could be brief and improvised, as simple as 'get your men to that ridgeline', or they could be formal and more prescriptive. White's company commander would pool opinions to an extent, but only because he trusted his platoon commanders' judgement and expected them to get things right. An O Group could happen at a moment's notice, overrule what had happened at the last O Group, contradict and confuse. But it was the time and place where the business of deciding how to fight took place – the tactical point of the strategic picture.

This new sweep through the woods required more coordination: three Cromwell tanks were to roll along the edge of the wood, blasting anything that looked suspicious as well as providing a rolling barrage as the infantry moved forward on foot, while an artillery barrage would go in at H-hour (the appointed time), to move on or at least suppress the enemy. If they were still there. There were stretcher-bearers on hand to pick up Byles's and Parry's bodies on the way through. Unlike the previous day, the Jocks advanced firing, the tanks' Besa machine guns laying down fire all the way through the wood, plastering where the enemy might be hiding, the racket an ear-shattering contrast to the day before's silent and deadly pussyfooting. The civilians had seen them set off again, and this time the wood crackled and thudded to machine-gun fire and the tanks' 75mm shells whamming into the sandy soil, trees crashing down, shattering, splinters flying. Grease oozed from White's rifle as it got hot from being fired. As they reached the crest, he saw his men's bodies, mercifully untouched by the artillery barrage that had rained down around them. Ten Germans who had broken cover were lying dead in the sand, near where White had imagined their positions to be – they had fled at the last minute but were cut down by the onslaught of fire from the British tanks and infantry. One German had survived, and although the Jocks had gone into the woods determined to avenge the deaths of two of their number he was spared. As he was marched back to the rear, a cigarette someone had given him dangled from his lips, his eyes at once brimful with tears and clearer again as he realized he wouldn't be killed.

And Byles: Byles had lived some while after he had been hit, he had vomited as a result of his stomach wound, but he can't have lived much longer. White reproached himself ('and have done ever since') for not having gone back, but then he, too, would most likely be dead:

> Yet common sense told me that I would certainly have been killed too and perhaps have caused a chain of more casualties in attempted rescues for we knew now

that the enemy slit trenches overlooked the bodies from slightly higher ground less than 20 yards away, and the bodies were silhouetted against the light-coloured sand which would have shown up the least movement, even in the half-light.[14]

As Parry and Byles were buried alongside one another in the sandy soil, White thought of other mornings in the woods, the fresh air, the hubbub of chat, music played on a mouth organ drifting through the trees, and how few of the faces around him now were that familiar – the losses they had sustained had replaced so many of the old hands he had trained and then started with in Walcheren. Since then, he had often mused about what the difference between someone alive and dead was: simple blind chance. It could be you. It could be him. You had no way of knowing, the future was blank, uncertain. Word came to 'prepare to move'. On went the war.

*

So what was Peter White fighting for, as the war drew to an end? Survival, chiefly, if anything; after all:

> Life seemed to have so completely departed from familiar values, I found my mind just refused to react more deeply than to try to follow the best human course available from minute to minute.[15]

Through his faith, and by what comes across in his memoir as a heavy dose of good sense, Peter White hung on to his familiar values. He notes expressions of dismay and disbelief from his men as they find dead Germans who seem to be school age, who shouldn't be anywhere near a battlefield, but it doesn't deter them from fighting any further. That life and death were so randomly differentiated – one minute you could be sharing a brew with a pal, the next they, or you, could be dead, blown apart, crushed, sliced, shattered – preoccupied White. Every minute in action could be your last, and sometimes not even when you were in action. White recalls getting out of a lorry in which he had been riding up front in the passenger seat; minutes later, a shell struck exactly where he had been sitting. The driver – nicknamed Walrus Whiskers – was unscathed but never seen again; he'd had his fill. And with the high turnover in men, White's platoon before the battle in Bremen is down to a handful of men. So fighting for each other, or as a 'band of brothers', won't quite do to explain what kept the 4th KOSB going – new faces came in the entire time, old faces would suddenly be gone, some would return having recovered from their wounds, others never. If they were fighting for anything, they were fighting to get the thing done.

It was from this aspect that Peter White led his men. Every night his men were in the line, having made sure they had eaten, he would organize the stag (the watch) for the evening, and then spend his night going from position to position to make sure his men were okay, and awake. He learned to be lenient – or at least understanding. Living in a state of permanent exhaustion, his men needed encouragement, he knew, rather than bollockings to get them to do what he wanted; the bollockings he gives in the course of the eight months he is leading platoons are few and far between. The one man he had put on a charge was Corporal Parry, shortly before Parry had been killed, something he bitterly regretted. More importantly, he makes sure his men get the rest they need but also that they take due care in the field; on occasion they inherit positions from other outfits who have drawn attention to their presence by moving around their slit trenches or making too much noise, giving rise to bitter and justified resentment, so he makes sure his men don't do the same. Discipline is a means to an end, the end being everyone getting home safely.

White also found that when one of his soldiers, the platoon radio operator, Private Cutter, became unreliable, windy, however he might express it, it was better to let the man desert temporarily, wander off, make himself absent, than to have him in a role where he was relied on. That way everyone would be in less danger. Cutter would be given roles that removed him from the fighting. That White exercised his own judgement in this matter and didn't resort to putting the man on a charge is indicative of his understanding of the torment he was going through as well as the nuance required to keep a platoon going. Every moment living in the shadow of death or disfigurement could be agony, and not everyone could bear it. Even so, White believed that to show much sympathy would compound Cutter's misery, and he walked this line the whole time Cutter was in his platoon: '[I] felt a wealth of sympathy for Pte Cutter, but dared not show it for I felt he would just collapse the more.'[16]

The end finally came, after a series of attacks on Bremen – the 4th KOSB had a ringside seat as the city was bombed when the authorities refused to surrender. The last month of war had been a mixture of 'swanning' – going around looking for encounters with the enemy – and bitter fighting against Germans holding out, recruits, die-hard Nazis, at one point fighting a training school at

Ibbenburen. Word of the atrocities that had been discovered throughout the Reich had got round to every man in the British Army, and White's experience of the chaos of the camp at Falingbostel, which contained not only British POWs but men from all over Europe, desperate to get home or, more immediately, to get revenge, had hardened him to get the job done. The camp was full of plundered possessions, too: Germany was running on stolen goods, enslaved people. But when the end did come, the news trickled through – the BBC reported that the Germans had surrendered to Montgomery on Lüneburg Heath. White's diary on the evening of 6 May 1945 simply read: 'P.M. RUMOUR of peace & at 1900 hrs THE NEWS.' The following day, the KOSB held a church service for the fallen. The next day it was official. The war was over.

Muted reactions followed. Danger had been dissipated, but there was no normal to return to. Lives had been permanently changed, friends killed, mutilated. White was in his billet, a farmhouse, like many other farmhouses he had stayed in over the last few months, often consigning the farmer and his family to sleep with the livestock while his Jocks slept in huge snoring piles on the beds in the house. White had had to deal with families simmering with resentment at the presence of the enemy, dead livestock and destruction, slave farm labourers plotting a reckoning, and, again and again, Germans who were desperate to make it clear that they had had no time for Hitler and the Nazis. White broke the news: '"Der Krieg ist kaput, be-ended," I said in my pidgin German.' For them all, the war was over.

'Zo . . . allus kaput, allus kaput. Keine zieg, Hitler! Verdamt schwein!' The farmer muttered, or something to that phonetic effect, as he drew a deep breath in between pursed leathery lips, nodding his head in ponderous slow weariness. 'Zo . . . Engelandt keine zieg, Deutchland keine zieg . . . der verdamt Nazis.' He turned to put his arms round the shoulders of his wife and of his children, sighing thinly through straggly, decaying teeth. There were tears in the eyes of his wife and then in the eyes of the daughter. The frizzy-haired son, looking puzzled, pulled his shirt on again. Behind him I caught a glimpse of the two smaller children, who, sensing something amiss, looked out from over the coverlet in which they were curled on some straw in a corner of the room. Their eyes shone brightly and wide in query like a couple of mice in torchlight. The farmer had moved slowly back with his wife to a table in the lamplight. She, bent and sobbing, had picked up something from the chimney-piece which I could not make out as she crouched over it at the table. Her distress was upsetting the others. The husband, himself looking strained and tired, tried to comfort her. I felt very uncomfortable and puzzled that my news should have occasioned such a distressing scene. The tightly clenched bony hands of the woman jerked, trembling in their grasp of whatever it was she held, so that her knuckles showed white. A short strip of what looked like black velvet showed between her fists as she pressed the object in her hands to her breast, then, sobbing anew, dropped the thing onto the table and buried her head in her arms as it clattered. It was a black-banded photograph in quite a small frame of a young man in a Luftwaffe uniform. One of the woman's hands still fingered an iron cross which had become detached and its movements seemed the focus of the tear-staining eyes of the rest of the family whom I don't think were even aware of my presence any more as I gently closed the door.

Nothing could have so eloquently summed up the utter waste and stupidity of the war, and the futile tragedy it had brought to so many homes right round the world than this family at that moment. There were no real winners. Each country taking part had lost. Perhaps, though, there was a credit side; if matter and material forces had done all the losing, then the unseen credit balance must be on the side of materiality's opposite, a gain for the things of the spirit.[17]

The war might be over, but it would never end.

Acknowledgments

This book is a by-product of the Great Covid-19 Pandemic of 2020–? With time stretching out before me in new and daunting ways, I filled much of it by podcasting with the indefatigable James Holland about the Second World War on *We Have Ways of Making You Talk*. A community of like-minded souls, or 'The Afflicted' as we dubbed them, grew up around the podcast, and so it was that Iain MacGregor found us in the depths of lockdown and persuaded me to turn my pen to something more serious than usual.

I have been immensely fortunate in the last two years to have had my understanding and imagination about this subject stretched and stimulated through conversations with James, with the incredibly generous historians who have joined us on the podcast, and with the listeners, whose curiosity and perspectives have egged us on. That stimulus is what has made this book possible.

This book comes with the caveats and qualifications of a comedian trying to do something serious: we are all supposed to want to play Hamlet; maybe this is my version. I hope that 'Though this be madness, yet there is method in 't'.

There are many generous people to thank, so, in no particular order:

Everyone at the Tank Museum for being truly wonderful,

kind people, generous with their time and their peerless collection. Thanks to Richard, Roz and Tom, and everyone who works there.

Andy Aitcheson, who brought to my attention Peter White and the mighty 52nd Lowland Division, easily the greatest fighting division in the British forces apart from the 6th Airborne. Andy's passion for the subject prompted me to read *With the Jocks* – I am forever in his debt for directing me to Peter White's writing.

The sartorially impeccable Peter Caddick Adams for knowing not just when to sport a cravat but everything else as well, and for not minding my glaring errors when I'm holding forth. His contribution has always made me realize how little I know and how much more there is to learn.

Robert Lyman for showing the way in Burma. This theatre, though no longer 'forgotten', is by no means as exhaustively written about as Western Europe and the desert, and Rob has been a huge help and he has done it in excellent humour.

Tony Pastor and the Goalhanger team for making *We Have Ways* work so well and be such fun. Jon Gill, Harry Lineker, Vasco Andrade, Joey McCarthy and Izzy Reid. Our contributors, who have helped me in what feels like an informal master's degree in the subject in the last two years. They are legion! A *Who's Who* of interesting people: Julia Jones, John Tregoning, Philip Mould, Helen Fry, Tami Davis Biddle, Caroline Shenton, Mark Zuehlke, Marc Milner, Grace Taylor, Autumn Hendrickson, Mike Neiberg, Ian Toll, John Concagh, Victoria Taylor, John C. McManus, Bernhard Kast, David Willey, Lucy Betteridge Dyson, Calum Douglas, Hans Oderwater, Richard Grace, Paul Woodadge, Jill Lepore, Ronny Scott, Viky Unwin, David

Baddiel, Guy Martin, Dermot O'Leary, Steve Ballinger, Matthew Ford, Dan Ellin, Selma Van De Perre, Frank McDonough, Paul McGann, Oliver Moody, Dave Roberts, Inge Auerbacher, Sarah Kovner, Patrick Marnham, Colin Bell, Waitman Beorn, John Buckley, Luke Daly-Groves, Jonathan Fennell, Niklas Frank, Katja Hoyer, Ben Kite, Alex Richie, Hal Sosabowski, Guy Walters, Paul Beaver, Andy Chatterton, Christoph Bergs, Maurice Blick, Jonathan Boff, Joe Coles, Des Curtis, Saul David, Max Hastings, Katrin Himmler, Will Iredale, Rana Mitter, Phillips Payson O'Brien, Stephen Prince, Séan Scullion, Gajendra Singh, Jens Wehner, Bastiaan Willem, Taylor Downing, Joe Ricci, Nicholas Moran, Michel Paradis, Paul Dickson, Marty Morgan, Roland White, Glyn Prysor, Jeremy Black, Robert Harris, Brian Johnson, Tom Holland, John Orloff, Andrew Ziminski, Gary Sheffield, Tim Bouverie, Nora Krug, Michael Wood, Pierre-Samuel Natanson, Seb Cox, Philippe Sands, R. G. Poulussen, Dan Snow.

James Holland for his encouragement, being a sounding board and for the last two years' adventures in history; every time we talk there's more to discover and discuss. His key attribute? 'Imperturbability' as Wanklyn used to say.

My manager, Richard Allen Turner, for 30 years and more of zigs and zags. He has always encouraged my love of the subject, though back in September 2004 he did tell me I didn't have to parachute into Arnhem if I was worried about breaking my neck. I was, but we wouldn't have had a programme if I'd not done it.

My parents, Juliet and Ingram Murray, aka the Colonel, for inspiring this whole thing. I've written before about Dad and his love of the subject, and how it became an interest I have been unable to shake off. His involvement in *We Have*

Acknowledgments

Ways has been an extremely satisfying part of the project. Mum has endured and, I hope, been entertained by our pursuit of this passion.

And finally, my wife, Eleanor, and our family, our daughters and the whole gang of Murrays and Relfs.

Bibliography

While there are books that I have quoted from in the text, in reading around and trying to pull together ideas and personal histories for *Command* there are books that would assist the curious reader well; these smaller pictures of individuals have to sit in their broader context. I've categorized them by chapter and offered some general reading that I have too found indispensable.

GENERAL

Alan Allport *Browned Off and Bloody Minded: The British Soldier Goes to War* (London: Yale University Press, reprint edition, 2017)

Alex Danchev & Dan Todman (eds) *Alan Brooke War Diaries* (London: Weidenfeld & Nicolson, new edition, 2015)

John Ellis *The Sharp End* (London: Pimlico, new edition, 1993)

Jonathan Fennell *Fighting the People's War* (Cambridge: Cambridge University Press, 2019)

David French *Raising Churchill's Army* (Oxford: Oxford University Press, 2001)

John Keegan (ed.) *Churchill's Generals* (London: Weidenfeld & Nicolson, new edition, 2012)

Spike Milligan *Monty: His Part in My Victory* (London: Penguin, 1976)

Daniel Todman *Britain's War* Volumes 1&2 (London: Penguin, 2016 & 2020 respectively)

MONTGOMERY

Richard Marshall *The British Army's Fight against Venereal Disease in the 'Heroic Age of Prostitution'*, ww1centenary. oucs.ox.ac.uk/body-and-mind/the-british-army% E2%80%99s-fight-against-venereal-disease-in- the-%E2%80%98heroic-age-of-prostitution% E2%80%99/

Brian Montgomery *A Field Marshal in the Family* (Barnsley: Pen & Sword Books, illustrated edition, 2010)

Viscount Montgomery of Alamein *Memoirs of Field Marshal Montgomery* (Barnsley: Pen & Sword Books, 2006)

Ian Palmer 'Sexuality and Soldiery Combat & Condoms, Continence & Cornflakes' (*Journal of the Royal Army Medical Corps* 149, April 2003)

FREYBERG

John Ferris *Behind the Enigma: The Authorised Biography of GCHQ* (London: Bloomsbury Publishing, 2020)

There are lots of excellent and differing(!) accounts of the Battle of Crete. The *Fallshirmjäger Commandments* appear in most of those accounts. I used the version in Alan Clark's *The Fall of Crete* (London: Morrow, 1962)

TUKER

Lieutenant General Francis Tuker *Approach to Battle* (London: Cassell and Co. Ltd, 1963)

Lieutenant General Francis Tuker *The Pattern of War* (London: Cassell and Co. Ltd, 1948) – good luck finding a copy!

Lieutenant Col GR Stevens *Fourth Indian Division* (Uckfield: Naval and Military Press, 2014)

SLIM/WINGATE

Mike Calvert *Fighting Mad: One Man's Guerilla War* (Barnsley: Pen & Sword Books, revised edition, 2004)

Mike Calvert *Prisoners of Hope* (Barnsley: Pen & Sword Books, revised edition, 2004)

Robert Lyman *A War of Empires* (Oxford: Osprey Publishing, 2021)

Robert Lyman *Slim Master of War Burma 1942-45* (London: Constable, 2016)

Allan Jeffreys (ed.) *The Jungle Survival Manual* (Pennsylvania: Casemate Publishers, 2016)

Richard Rhodes James *Chindit* (London: Penguin, 2022)

David Rooney *Wingate and the Chindits: Redressing the Balance* (London: Sharpe Books, 2019)

Trevor Royle *Orde Wingate: A Man of Genius* (Barnsley: Pen & Sword Books, 2014)

Field Marshal Sir William Slim *Defeat into Victory* (London: Pan Books, 2012)

Field Marshal Sir William Slim *Unofficial History* (Barnsley: Pen & Sword Books, illustrated edition, 2008)

Slim's short stories – hard to find – come (via Rob Lyman) from *Fifty Enthralling Stories of the Mysterious East* (London: Odhams Press, 1937)

BRADLEY/PATTON

Omar Bradley *On Leadership* US Army War College Quarterly Parameters (Speech delivered at the US Army College in Carlisle on 8 October 1971)

Omar Bradley and Clay Blair *A General's Life* (Massachusetts: Plunkett Lake Press, 2019)

Martin Blumenson *The Patton Papers* (Massachusetts: Da Capo Press, 2009)

Paul Dickson *The Rise of the G. I. Army, 1940-1941* (New York: Atlantic Monthly Press, illustrated edition, 2020)

Richard A Gabriel *No More Heroes: Madness and Psychiatry in War* (New York: Hill and Wang, reissue, 1988)

Neil M Maher *Nature's New Deal* (Oxford: Oxford University Press, illustrated edition, 2009)

Ernie Pyle *Here Is Your War, Brave Men* (Winnipeg: Bison Books, 2004)

Ben Shephard *A War of Nerves* (London: Pimlico, 2002)

PEARSON/6th AIRBORNE DIVISION

Major Mark H. Ayers *Azimuth Check: Where Are We with Commander's Intent: A Monograph* (Infantry School of Advanced Military Studies United States Army Command and General Staff College Fort Leavenworth, Kansas First Term AY 96-97)

William F. Buckingham *Paras: The Birth of British Airborne Forces from Churchill's Raiders to 1st Parachute*

Brigade (Cheltenham: The History Press Ltd, 2005)

Napier Crookenden *Dropzone Normandy* (London: Macmillan Publishers, book club edition, 1976)

Julian Jones *A Fierce Quality: The Fighting Life of Alistair Pearson, Para Extraordinaire, DSO and 3 Bars MC* (Barnsley: Pen & Sword Books, 1989)

Lieutenant Colonel TB Otway *Airborne Forces of the Second World War 1939-1945: Official History of the Second World War* (Uckfield: Naval & Military Press, 2019)

HOBART

Anon. *The Story of the 79th Armoured Division October 1942-June 1945* (Uckfield: Naval & Military Press, 2013)

John Buckley *British Armour in the Normandy Campaign* (Abingdon: Routledge, 2007)

Major Michael J. Daniels *Innovation in the Face of Adversity: Major-General Sir Percy Hobart and the 79th Armoured Division (British)* (Auckland: Pickle Partners Publishing, 2015)

Richard Doherty *Hobart's 79th Armoured Division at War* (Barnsley: Pen & Sword Books, 2012)

Kenneth Macksey *Armoured Crusader: The Biography of Major-General Sir Percy 'Hobo' Hobart, One of the Most Influential Military Commanders of the Second World War* (London: Grub Street Publishing, 2004)

William Suttie *The Tank Factory: British Military Vehicle Development and the Chobham Establishment* (Cheltenham: The History Press, illustrated edition, 2015)

Andrew Wilson *Flame Thrower* (London: William Kimber
      & Co., 1956)

WHITE
Peter White *With the Jocks: A Soldier's Struggle for Europe
      1944-45* (Cheltenham: The History Press, 2002)
The King's Own Scottish Borderers War Diaries can be
      found here: www.royalscotskosbwardiaries.co.uk/
      war-diaries-kosb

Notes

Chapter 1: Montgomery

1 Field Marshal Bernard Montgomery, *The Memoirs of Field Marshal Montgomery* (Barnsley: Pen & Sword Books, eBook, 2006), location 646.
2 Ibid., location 652.
3 Field Marshal Lord Alan Brooke, *War Diaries, 1939–1945* (London: Orion Books, eBook, 2015), location 1489.
4 Montgomery, *Memoirs*, location 728.
5 Ian Palmer, 'Sexuality And Soldiery Combat & Condoms, Continence & Cornflakes' (*Journal of the Royal Army Medical Corps* 149, April 2003) p. 39.
6 Richard Marshall, *The British Army's Fight against Venereal Disease in the 'Heroic Age of Prostitution'*,* World War I Centenary (ox.ac.uk): http://ww1centenary.oucs.ox.ac.uk/body-and-mind/the-british-army%E2%80%99s-fight-against-venereal-disease-in-the-%E2%80%98heroic-age-of-prostitution%E2%80%99/.
7 Ibid.
8 Ibid.
9 http://ww2poster.co.uk/phd-research/phd-ww2poster-2004/chapter-7-the-%E2%80%98problem%E2%80%99-of-venereal-disease-in-wartime0/.
10 Brian Montgomery, *A Field Marshal in the Family* (Barnsley: Pen & Sword Books, eBook, 2010), location 4079.
11 Ibid., location 4121.
12 Montgomery, *Memoirs*, location 885.
13 Brooke, *War Diaries*, location 1456.
14 Brian Montgomery, *A Field Marshal in the Family*, location 3918.

Notes

Chapter 2: Freyberg

1 'Parachutists (German)' from *Intelligence Bulletin* September 1942, on LoneSentry.com. The *Fallshirmjäger Commandments* appear in most of those accounts – I used the version in Alan Clark's *The Fall of Crete* (London: Morrow, 1962)
2 John Ferris, *Behind the Enigma* (London: Bloomsbury Publishing, eBook, 2021), p. 251.
3 Ibid., pp. 251–2.
4 Ibid., p. 245, quoting COS to SACSEA, Ultra 196, 'Security of Ultra Intelligence', 9.6.44, WO 203/5157. Ferris's book is an invaluable, dispassionate and illuminating guide to the far-from-straight-line story of how the British dominated in the intelligence war in the Western theatre.
5 Jonathan Fennell, *Fighting the People's War: The British and Commonwealth Armies and the Second World War* (Cambridge: Cambridge University Press, eBook, 2019), p. 5.
6 Ibid., p. 135.
7 Ibid., pp. 135–6.

Chapter 3: Tuker

1 Tuker, *Approach to Battle, a Commentary: Eighth Army, November 1941 to May 1943* (London: Cassell, 1963), p. i.
2 Ibid., p. i.
3 Tuker, *The Pattern of War* (London: Cassell, 1948), p. 49.
4 Ibid., p. 28.
5 Ibid., p. 20.
6 Ibid., p. 48.
7 Ibid., p. 49.
8 Tuker, *Approach to Battle*, p. 11.
9 Ibid., p. 19.
10 Ibid., pp. 112–13.
11 Ibid., p. 126.
12 Ibid., pp. 377–9.

Chapter 4: Wingate

1 Trevor Royle, *Orde Wingate: A Man of Genius* (Barnsley: Pen & Sword Books, 2014), location 976.
2 Michael Calvert, *Fighting Mad: One Man's Guerilla War* (Barnsley: Pen & Sword Books, eBook, 2007), p. 76.

3 Royle, *Orde Wingate*, location 4564.
4 Ibid., location 4877.
5 Royle referencing Major B. E. Ferguson, 77 Indian Infantry Bde, Preliminary Outline Report, 1 May 1943.
6 Richard Rhodes James, *Chindit* (London: Penguin, 2022), p. 94.

Chapter 5: Slim

1 William Slim, *Defeat into Victory: Battling Japan in Burma and India* (London: Pan Macmillan, eBook, 2012), location 197.
2 Ibid., location 2005.
3 Anthony Mills, 'I See Death' in *Fifty Enthralling Stories of the Mysterious East* (London: Odhams Press, 1937).
4 Slim, *Defeat into Victory*, location 95.
5 Ibid., location 3015.
6 Ibid., location 2314.
7 Robert Lyman, *Slim, Master of War: Burma, 1942–5* (London: Little, Brown Book Group, eBook, 2016), location 2805.
8 Slim, *Defeat Into Victory*, location 2303.
9 Ibid., location 2889.
10 Ibid., location 2956.

Chapter 6: Bradley

1 Omar Bradley & Clay Blair, *A General's Life: An Autobiography by General of the Army Omar N. Bradley and Clay Blair* (Lexington, Mass.: Plunkett Lake Press, eBook, 2019), p. 35.
2 Ibid., p. 39.
3 Ibid., p. 84.
4 Ibid., p. 84.
5 Ibid., p. 78.
6 Ibid., p. 117.
7 Ibid., p. 117.
8 Ibid., p. 118.
9 Ibid., p. 184.
10 Ernie Pyle, *Brave Men* (Lincoln, Neb.: Bison Books, 2001), p. 325.
11 Ibid., p. 325.
12 Ibid., p. 327.
13 Ibid., p. 326.
14 Ibid.
15 Ibid., p. 327.

16 Paul Dickson, *The Rise of the G. I. Army, 1940–1941* (New York: Atlantic Monthly Press, Illustrated edition, 2020), p. 42.

17 Pyle, *Brave Men*, p. 456.

Chapter 7: Patton

1 Martin Blumenson, *The Patton Papers: 1940–1945* (Boston, Mass.: Da Capo Press, eBook, 2009), p. 734.

2 Ibid., p. 766.

3 Ibid., p. 816 – chapter IX covering Patton's death is entitled 'Death and Transfiguration'.

4 Omar Bradley & Clay Blair, *A General's Life: An Autobiography by General of the Army Omar N. Bradley and Clay Blair* (Lexington, Mass.: Plunkett Lake Press, eBook, 2019), p. 111.

5 Blumenson, *Patton Papers*, p. 329.

6 Ibid., p. 328.

7 Ibid., p. 330.

8 Ibid., p. 332.

9 Richard A. Gabriel, *No More Heroes: Madness and Psychiatry in War* (New York: Hill & Wang, eBook, 1988), p. 91.

10 Ibid., p. 91.

11 Blumenson, *Patton Papers*, p. 457.

12 Terry Brighton, *Masters of Battle: Monty, Patton and Rommel at War* (London: Penguin Books, eBook, 2009) p. 263. Brighton states: 'This reconstruction is derived from the written recollections of Gilbert R. Cook (Cook Papers, Dwight D. Eisenhower Library, Abilene, Kansas), Hobart R. Gay (Hobart R. Gay Papers, United States Military Academy Library, West Point), Lynn A. Hoppe (Patton Papers), Colonel Theodore J. Krokus (Patton Papers), Lieutenant Joshua Miner (Oral History Research Office, Columbia University Library, New York City), and Neil H. Shreve (XII Corps Third Army unit history).'

13 Ibid., p. 263.

14 Ibid., p. 264.

15 Ibid., p. 265.

16 Ibid.

17 Ibid.

18 Ibid.

19 Ibid.

20 Ibid.

21 Ibid.
22 Ibid., p. 266.
23 Ibid.
24 Ibid.

Chapter 8: Pearson

1 Major Mark H. Ayers, *Azimuth Check: Where Are We with Commander's Intent A Monograph* (Ayers Infantry School of Advanced Military Studies United States Army Command and General Staff College Fort Leavenworth, Kansas First Term AY 96-97), p. 15.
2 Ibid., p. 15.
3 Letter to General Ismay, 22 June 1940.
4 Lieutenant General RN Gale, CB DSO OBE MC, *With the 6th Airborne Division in Normandy* (London: Sampson Low, Marston & Co., 1948), p. 60.
5 Julian James, *A Fierce Quality: The Fighting Life of Alastair Pearson* (Barnsley: Pen & Sword Books, eBook, 2014), location 1733.
6 Ibid., location 1750.
7 Lieutenant Colonel T. B. H. Otway, *Airborne Forces of the Second World War 1939–45* (Uckfield: Navel & Military Press, 2019), p. 77.
8 Ibid., p. 77.
9 James, *A Fierce Quality*, location 1188.
10 Ibid., location 1212.
11 Ibid., location 1246.
12 Napier Crockenden, *Dropzone Normandy* (New York: Charles Scribner's Sons, 1976), p. 183.
13 James, *A Fierce Quality*, location 1390.
14 Ibid., location 1398.

Chapter 9: Hobart

1 Macksey, *Armoured Crusader: Wilson to Wavell*, p. 171.
2 Andrew Wilson, *Flame Thrower* (New York: Bantam Books, 1984), p. xii.
3 Ibid.
4 Major Michael J. Daniels, *Innovation in the Face of Adversity: Major-General Sir Percy Hobart and the 79th Armoured Division (British)*, (New Zealand: Pickle Partners Publishing, eBook, 2015), p. 21.
5 Anon., *Story of the 79th Armoured Division, October 1942–June 1945* (Uckfield: Naval & Military Press, eBook, 2013), p. 20.

6 Daniels, *Innovation in the Face of Adversity*, p. 25.

7 Anon., *Story of the 79th Armoured Division*, p. 20.

8 Ibid., p. 30.

9 Daniels, *Innovation in the Face of Adversity*, p. 45.

10 Anon., *Story of the 79th Armoured Division*, p. 57.

11 Ibid., p. 44.

12 Ibid., p. 92.

13 Ibid.

14 Ibid., p. 278.

15 Doherty, p. 277.

Chapter 10: White

1 War Diaries – KOSB | royalscotskosb (royalscotskosbwardiaries. co.uk).

2 Ibid.

3 Peter White, *With the Jocks: A Soldier's Struggle for Europe 1944–45* (Cheltenham: The History Press, eBook, 2002), p. 22.

4 Ibid.

5 Ibid., p. 126.

6 Ibid., p. 66.

7 Ibid., p. 146.

8 Ibid. p. 148.

9 War Diaries – KOSB | royalscotskosb (royalscotskosbwardiaries. co.uk).

10 Alan Allport, *Browned Off and Bloody-Minded: The British Soldier Goes to War, 1939–1945* (New Haven, Conn.: Yale University Press, eBook, 2015), location 2635.

11 White, *With the Jocks*, p. 386.

12 Ibid., p. 389.

13 Ibid., p. 392.

14 Ibid., p. 400.

15 Ibid., pp. 68–9.

16 Ibid., p. 194.

17 Ibid., pp. 539–40.

Index

Index